31751

KU-258-640

THE
PAUL HAMLYN
LIBRARY

TRANSFERRED FROM

THE
CENTRAL LIBRARY
OF THE
BRITISH MUSEUM

2010

WITHDRAWN

Coll. of Ripon & York St John

3 8025 00225232 1

The Golden Road to Samarkand

Wilfrid Blunt   The

Golden Road to Samarkand

Hamish Hamilton · London

This book was designed and produced by
George Rainbird Ltd
Marble Arch House
44 Edgware Road
London W2

© Wilfrid Blunt 1973

All rights reserved. No part of this
publication may be reproduced, stored
in a retrieval system, or transmitted,
in any form or by any means, electronic,
mechanical, photocopying, recording or
otherwise, without the prior permission
of Hamish Hamilton Ltd

Published in Great Britain in 1973 by
Hamish Hamilton Ltd
90 Great Russell Street
London WC1

House editor: Yorke Crompton
Picture research and indexing: Ellen Crampton
Design: Margaret Thomas
Cartography: T. Stalker Miller

Filmset, printed, and bound in Great Britain.
The text was set by BAS Printers Ltd,
Over Wallop, Hampshire, and the book printed
by Westerham Press Ltd, Westerham, Kent,
and bound by Dorstel Press Ltd, Harlow, Essex

SBN 241 02298 3

To the memory of

GEORGE FREDERIC WATTS, O.M., R.A.

and MARY SETON WATTS

in deep gratitude

7279

CENTRAL LIBRARY · THE BRITISH MUSEUM

WITHDRAWN

BM8 (BLU)

'Emperors and kings, dukes and marquises,
counts, knights, and townsfolk, and all
people who wish to know the various races
of men and the peculiarities of the various
regions of the world, take this book and
have it read to you....

The opening words of the Prologue to Marco Polo's
Description of the World – lifted, in fact, *verbatim* by
Rustichello of Pisa, Marco Polo's amanuensis, from one of
his own romances.

Acknowledgments

I have, as always, to acknowledge with gratitude the help of many friends. That distinguished orientalist, Mr Basil Gray, read my typescript with great care and made many helpful suggestions; but he is in no way responsible for any errors that remain. The staffs of the Museum of the History of Science and the Bodleian at Oxford, of the British Museum, the Victoria and Albert Museum, and the London Library, gave me much assistance. I would also take the opportunity to thank the following for help and advice: Professor Sir Harold Bailey, Sir Fitzroy Maclean, Bt, Dr E. W. Maddison, Mr Andrew Gow, Mr Antony Hutt, Mr Derek Hill, Mr John Semple, Mr John Stuart, Mr Christopher Sinclair-Stevenson (for suggesting a book with this title), Mrs Arthur Harrison and Miss Sandra Raphael; Mr Yorke Crompton, Mrs Ellen Crampton and Miss Margaret Thomas of Messrs George Rainbird; and my invaluable typist Miss Charmian Young.

Special mention must be made of the truly royal treatment that I received at the hands of Professor Hamid Suleyman, Director of the Alisher Navoi Institute in Tashkent, who, together with his wife and assembled staff, greeted me on the steps of his delightful museum with an enormous bunch of red roses, continued to shower me with valuable gifts of books and medals, and finally arranged certain facilities for me in Samarkand (directors of Western European Museums please copy); I only regret that communication with Professor Suleyman, through a mildly French-speaking Uzbek interpretress, was somewhat restricted.

W.J.W.B.

Contents

Colour Plates

Foreword

There are few things more irritating to an author than to find himself accused, by a reviewer or a reader, of failing to write the kind of book he had no intention of writing; it is therefore perhaps expedient for me – indeed, since the advent of the Trade Descriptions Act perhaps even necessary for me – to explain to what extent the title and sub-title of this book describe its contents.

A book is none the worse for having a golden title; but *The Golden Road to Samarkand* is not simply about Samarkand and the ways thither, whether from north, south, east or west. Nor does it attempt to be a history of Central Asia, a subject of unbelievable complexity which, in my opinion, cannot be written for general consumption. Open almost any such history – Skrine and Ross's classic *The Heart of Asia*, for example – and sooner or later (probably sooner) you will be confronted by something such as the following:

> About the year A.H. 870 (1465) a number of these Uzbegs, discontented with their Khān, Abū-l-Khayr, migrated into Moghūlistan, with the Sultans Girāy and Jānibeg, of the line of Jūjī. Isan Bughā, the then Khān of Moghūlistan, or Jatah, received them hospitably, and allotted them some territories on the River Chū, to the west of his own domains. These emigrants were subsequently known as the Uzbeg-Kazāks, or simply Kazāks. . . .

This, in any quantity, is indigestible pabulum for all but the specialist. Yet there must be many people who would like to be given some account of this romantic part of the world, provided that it comes to them in palatable form. But the attempt to prepare such a meal has shown me how difficult it is, and I fear that in places the meat may turn out to be tough.

What I have done is as follows. I have chosen a number of men associated with that rather ill-defined territory that we call Central Asia – conquerors, travellers, merchants, patrons, priests, pilgrims and archaeologists – and written essays about them in which I have sometimes also dealt with parts of their careers not strictly relevant; but more than once I have felt obliged, reluctantly, to leave my hero to continue alone on his journey when he strays too far or for too long outside the heart of the Continent. Or if you prefer it, the book may be considered as a series of tableaux, selected to suit a personal taste yet in the hope that they may chance to suit the taste of others also. I have, as it were, gone to a heavily-laden apple tree and picked a handful of easily accessible ripe fruit which took my fancy. This will explain many otherwise inexplicable omissions: for example, any discussion of the Samanids or the Seljuqs, or the jump of two centuries from Jenkinson to Wolff which leapfrogs Nadir Shah.

Like every writer on an Oriental theme I have been faced with spelling problems. I can only plead that I have done my best. Most scholars now write 'Chingiz' Khan, but there are perfectly reputable authors who prefer 'Genghis', 'Genghiz', 'Jenghiz', etc., etc., while Voltaire wrote 'Gengis' and Gibbon 'Zingis'. I have opted for 'Jenghiz'. I spell the Prophet's name 'Mahomet', following the advice of Fowler (see his amusing article on the subject under 'Mahomet' in his *Modern English Usage*); but elsewhere I write 'Muhammad'. However, I agree with Lawrence of Arabia in thinking that the matter is of no importance.

For me one thing alone is important. If my book serves to persuade even a handful of its readers to visit Samarkand and Bukhara (which is now perfectly easy) or to turn to the delightful pages of Babur's Memoirs or the Travels of Friar Rubruck – then I shall be fully rewarded for my pains.

W.J.W.B.
The Watts Gallery
Compton
near Guildford
Surrey

Dancing in a Central Asian market place: boys 'of special kinds', extolled by Flecker in the deleted stanza, BELOW LEFT, *of his poem* The Golden Journey to Samarcand

Prologue: Samarkand

Samarkand is a magical, evocative work; like Mesopotamia it is a blessed word, like Chimborazo and Cotopaxi it 'steals the soul away'.

Many poets have been charmed by the cadence of it. Hafiz wrote that he was ready to barter Bukhara and Samarkand for the black mole on the cheek of his 'sweet Turkish maid'; and Hatem, in Goethe's *West-Östlicher Divan,* was even more lavish, adding Balkh to Bukhara and Samarkand as an offering to Suleika. Marlowe, in his *Tamburlaine the Great*, has much to say of Samarcanda, and Milton speaks of 'Samarchand by Oxus, Temir's throne'. For Keats, who recalled the caravans that passed that way from China, Samarkand was 'silken', while Oscar Wilde, throwing botany to the winds, wrote of

> The almond-groves of Samarcand,
>   Bokhara, where red lilies blow,
> And Oxus, by whose yellow sand
>   The grave white-turbaned merchants go.

But to the English-speaking world there is one line of poetry which above all others comes to mind when Samarkand is mentioned: it is, of course, that from which the title of this book is taken – a line written by a man who fell in love with the fabulous East he read of in the *Arabian Nights* but who hated the East he found in Beirut, which was as far as he himself ever got along his Golden Road. Perhaps it would have been better if, like Edward Fitzgerald, he had never left Europe.

Tradition ascribes the foundation of Samarkand to Afrasiyab, a semi-mythical hero of Firdausi's *Book of Kings*; but recently the Russians have proposed the year 530 B.C. for the city's origin, thus conveniently providing the excuse to celebrate in 1970 its two thousand five hundredth birthday. Whether or not the armies of the Achaemenid rulers of Persia actually reached Maracanda (as Samarkand was at first called) is uncertain; but Alexander the Great 'paused there in his mad career' in the year 328 B.C., and from that moment the city emerges from legend into history. For a time Samarkand became Sa-mo-kien, the westernmost province of the Celestial Empire; but towards the end of the seventh century the irresistible armies of Islam conquered and soon after annexed Transoxiana, establishing a religion which survived and for the most part flourished there until the advent of Communism in the present century. That romantic but much over-praised Caliph of Baghdad, Harun al-Rashid, who owes his reputation to his legendary exploits in the *Arabian Nights* rather than to his actual achievements, died near Meshed in 809 on his way to quell a rebellion in Samarkand.

Under the Persian Samanids Samarkand and Bukhara became in the tenth century great centres of learning. They were succeeded by the Seljuq Turks, whose empire under Malik Shah (1055–92) was so far-flung that prayers for the King's health 'were every day offered up in the cities of Jerusalem, Mecca, Medina, Bagdad, Isfahan, Rhe, Bokhara, Samarcund, Ourgunje, and Kashgar' (Malcolm).

Then in 1221 came the great Mongol cataclysm which resulted in the capture and sacking and eventually to the abandonment of Samarkand. But under Tamerlane in the closing decades of the fourteenth century the city rose again, on a new site a mile or two to the south-west, to become in his lifetime the finest in Central Asia and the capital of an empire which extended over a third of the known world. In 1512 the successors of Tamerlane were ejected by the Uzbek Turks, compelling Babur, his great-great-great-grandson, to seek his fortune in Afghanistan, and finally in India where he became the first of the Moghul Emperors.

By the middle of the eighteenth century Samarkand, after two hundred years of changing fortunes, had become almost uninhabited. Then for a time it came again under Chinese rule, and was subsequently a dependency of Bukhara. In 1868 it fell to the Russians, who twenty years later built a railway there from the shores of the Caspian. After the Bolshevik Revolution it was made the capital of the Uzbek S.S.R., now Uzbekistan, and is today a flourishing modern metropolis.

Such, in brief, is the history of the city which has been called the 'Mirror of the World', the 'Garden of Souls', the 'Fourth Paradise' and by Tamerlane the 'eye and star' of his empire; a city which, for better or for worse, is at long last open to the vulgar gaze of tourists who, year by year in ever-growing numbers, 'take the Golden Road to Samarkand'.

OPPOSITE *The Shah-Zinda, Samarkand*

OVERLEAF *Lion attacking a bull: a detail from one of the staircases in the Apadana Palace at Persepolis, which was partly destroyed by Alexander in 330* B.C.

CHAPTER ONE

Alexander the Great
An Invader from the West

Sikander (Alexander) and the dying Dara, a detail from a Persian miniature dated 1486

The story of Samarkand opens with a tragedy: the shameful murder there by Alexander the Great of one of his oldest friends and most loyal generals, 'Black' Cleitus.

Alexander has been called the most famous man who ever lived. His empire, greater even than that of the Persians two centuries earlier, stretched at the time of his death – and he was not yet thirty-three when he died – from Macedonia and Libya to the Indus and the Jaxartes (Syr-Darya), and his legendary exploits were told and retold throughout the length and breadth of the medieval world. Even today, wrote Sir Percy Sykes, 'throughout Asia as far as the confines of China his name is one by which to conjure'.

Born in Macedonia in 356 B.C., Alexander succeeded to the throne at the age of twenty after the murder, probably by an assassin in Persian pay, of his father, Philip of Macedon, and having ruthlessly eliminated potential rivals set about the subjugation of Greece. In the spring of 334 he crossed the Dardanelles with a small but efficient army which was to conquer the vastness of the Persian empire. His first victory, over the Persians and Asiatic Greeks, was at Granicus, just across the water, during which his life was saved by this same Cleitus whom he was later to murder. At Issus (November 333) the Persian King, Darius III, who not long previously had sent his youthful adversary the gift of a bat and a ball[1], fled, leaving his wife and family in Alexander's hands and the way to Egypt and Mesopotamia open; and in October 331 the victory of Arbela put an end to serious Persian resistance, brought vast wealth to the conqueror and a clear road to Persia and Central Asia.

A splendid (though damaged) Roman mosaic and a remarkable German Renaissance painting record respectively these two memorable battles. The mosaic, found in 1831 in the House of the Faun at Pompeii and now in the Naples Museum, shows Alexander, who has lost his helmet in the heat of the fray, charging Darius at the battle of Issus; it is a brilliant design in which lances play much the same part that they do in Velazquez's *Surrender of Breda* and Uccello's *Rout of San Romano*. Altdorfer's *Battle of Arbela* – a battle which was in fact fought at Gaugamela, thirty-five miles away and near the site of ancient Nineveh – cannot

[1] It may be necessary, in this sports-mad age, to remind readers that such a gift was intended to be insulting. See also Shakespeare's *King Henry V*, Act 1, SC. 2.

claim to attempt a historic representation of the scene, and was no doubt inspired by one of the many medieval romantic poems about Alexander; yet for all its anachronisms and absurdities it succeeds in giving a vivid picture of the clamour and the turmoil of cavalry and infantry warfare. And just as Arbela was one of the decisive battles of the world, so is this painting, which was made in 1529, one of the world's greatest artistic treasures.

After Arbela, Susa and Babylon fell; Persepolis surrendered, and Xerxes's palace was deliberately fired to show all Asia that Alexander had revenged the destruction by Xerxes of the temple at Babylon. 'The well-known story of Alexander's feast,' wrote that great champion of Alexander, Sir William Tarn, 'with Thais inciting him to the burning, is legend, invented for the dramatic effect: it had needed Xerxes and his myriads to burn Athens, but now an Athenian girl could burn Persepolis.' Not all authorities, however, are agreed that it was fiction, and excavation has proved that the palace was destroyed by fire. The story

LEFT *Alexander and* OPPOSITE *Darius in battle at Issus: details of a 2nd–1st century* B.C. *mosaic found in the House of the Faun at Pompeii*

of Thais's part in the destruction, whether true or not, has at least given the world Massenet's opera *Thais* and Dryden's *Alexander's Feast*:

> The lovely Thais, by his side,
> Sate like a blooming Eastern bride,
> In flower of youth and beauty's pride.
> Happy, happy, happy pair!
> None but the brave,
> None but the brave,
> None but the brave deserves the fair.

At the beginning of 330 Alexander advanced through Media into Parthia in pursuit of Darius; he arrived at a point near the modern Shahrud, south-east of the Elburz mountains, to find that his enemy had been treacherously taken prisoner by Bessus, the Satrap of Bactria, and mortally wounded. A fifteenth-century miniature illustrating Firdausi's *Book of Kings* shows Sikander (Alexander) holding on his knee the head of the dying Dara (Darius) though in fact he was already dead by the time Alexander arrived:

> Dismounting quickly, he in sorrow placed
> The head of Dara on his lap, and wept
> In bitterness of soul, to see that form
> Mangled with ghastly wounds . . .

Alexander ordered Darius's body to be embalmed and taken to Persepolis for fitting burial. Abandoning for the moment the pursuit of Bessus, he now drove, first eastwards and then south, quelling uprisings and pausing to found the city of Alexandria in Aria (the modern Herat). Then swinging south-eastwards he founded yet another Alexandria (the modern Ghazni) and continued on his victorious way till he reached the foothills of the Hindu Kush. Within the space of five years he had humiliated a great nation and put paid to an ancient empire; vast wealth was his, and nothing, it seemed, could prevent the rest of Central Asia from falling into his hands.

But during these past months trouble had been brewing. After long years of fighting, Alexander's men had begun to murmur. Even victories eventually pall, and they longed above all else to get back to their homes and their families. A rumour swept the army that he was about to halt his advance, and there was huge rejoicing round the camp fires; but it proved to be false. Bessus, now styling himself 'King Artaxerxes' and assuming the stiff upright *tiara* of the Persian monarchs, was still at large and mobilizing an army in Bactria, north of the Hindu Kush. Past victories, said Alexander, had been great, but they were as yet unconsolidated. The war must go on.

There was a further cause of discontent: Alexander's character seemed to have changed – and for the worse. Wooed by the soft and luxurious way of life of the Persians he had begun to 'go native'. The dry climate of Turkestan and the tainted water had led the Macedonians to indulge freely in the strong local wines; and though Tarn maintains that it was only the malice of a gossip-writer, a man who was not even present during the campaign, that started the rumour that the

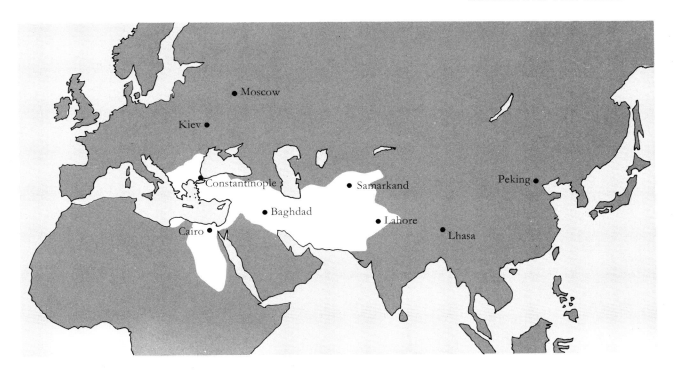

The Empire of Alexander
the Great

formerly abstemious Alexander now took to the bottle, there seems little doubt that he began drinking heavily. He had also come to adopt the sensible and comfortable native dress. This was probably in part to ingratiate himself with his newly-won subjects, for dwindling manpower and lines of communication stretched almost to breaking-point made it vital for him to win their cooperation, or at all events their esteem. Indeed he later tried to insist upon those who approached him making the deep Persian prostration or 'kow-tow' – an act which aroused much resentment among the Macedonians, who considered it appropriate only to a god.

Persian ostentation and effeminacy were having an even worse effect on Alexander's generals, whose extravagance and self-indulgence went so far that, though it might seem that it was hardly for him to cast the first stone, he felt himself obliged to reprimand them. Plutarch gives some examples: one of these generals wore silver nails in his shoes; another sent camels to Egypt to fetch his favourite 'powder' for use when wrestling[1]; yet another had hunting nets more than twelve miles long. For the common oil used as an unguent after the bath, many officers now substituted precious ointments and 'took their batmen with them everywhere to massage them'. 'Have you still to learn', asked Alexander, 'that to make our victories perfect we must avoid the vices and follies of those we have conquered?' Such moralizings fell strangely from his lips.

Then something even more sinister occurred: there was a plot – and it was not to be the last – to kill Alexander. The details need not concern us; it is enough to say that the secret leaked out and that a number of heads fell, including that of old

[1] Burn suggests that it may have been soft sand for his gymnasium.

Parmenion, one of Alexander's most loyal marshals but also the father of a young man closely involved in the conspiracy. It was an ancient and barbarous Macedonian practice thus to take revenge, in cases of high treason, on the relations of the condemned man; but the murder of Parmenion, for being both cold-blooded and ungenerous, is perhaps the worst crime that can be laid to Alexander's charge. It was also a rash act because it further antagonized his men, and it was probably with the intention of keeping them from fresh mischief that, contrary to his usual custom, he continued to campaign far into the winter. It may well have been the very end of the year (329) before he finally reached the skirts of the Hindu Kush – which, incidentally, he believed to be a continuation of the Caucasus.

Even now there was to be no more than brief respite for the troops. While snows still lay deep on the passes, Alexander marched his men northwards to

Alexander wearing the horns of Ammon as a token of his divine ancestry: a silver coin of King Lysimachus, struck about 300 B.C.

subdue the truculent Bessus, who was laying waste the northern valleys of the Hindu Kush to obstruct his advance. It was a terrible journey which those who survived it were never to forget. Half starving, existing only on a scanty and improbable diet of wild silphium and terebinth enlivened by an occasional scrap of raw mule, they struggled onwards, in spite of snow-blindness and frostbite, through snow that came up to their thighs, over the 11,600-foot Khawak Pass and down into the Bactria which Bessus had devastated.

At Bactra (Balkh), where a halt was made, Alexander learned that Bessus had fled across the Oxus (Amu-Darya) into Sogdia, burning his boats behind him. Advancing now to the Oxus the Macedonians, in spite of strong opposition from a band of Scythians, crossed the great river – and it took them five days – on rafts made of skins stuffed with rushes. Then Bessus, betrayed in his turn, was taken near Bukhara by a flying column and brought into Alexander's presence. He was stripped naked but for the wooden collar that was the mark of the slave, and displayed before the whole army, flogged and dispatched to Balkh to await trial. Later his nose and ears were cut off and he was sent to Ecbatana (Hamadan) for execution. Then Alexander marched to Maracanda (Samarkand), the summer royal residence of Sogdia.

It was a Macedonian custom to hold, on a particular day each year, a festival in honour of Dionysus – a festival which combined sacrifice to the god and, as was appropriate, a great deal of drinking. This year (328) it was held at Maracanda and for some unknown reason Alexander offered his sacrifice not to Dionysus but to the twin gods Castor and Polydeuces (Pollux).

Various authors give differing accounts of what exactly took place on that tragic evening when Cleitus was killed, but the main facts are not in dispute; we chiefly follow Arrian (in Aubrey de Selincourt's elegant translation). It seems that at the feast there was talk of Castor and Pollux, who claimed descent from Zeus as now did Alexander also. The usual sycophants who cling hopefully to the skirts of the great lost no time in telling Alexander that his exploits far exceeded those of the twin gods; and as they drained their cups yet deeper they began to compare him with Heracles himself. For some time past Cleitus had been among those who particularly deplored the change that had come over Alexander, and he further deprecated the gross flattery that was increasingly lavished upon him by those who sought to curry favour; drunk, he staggered to his feet and (wrote Arrian) angrily intervened:

It was intolerable, he declared, to offer such an insult to divine beings, and he would allow no one to pay Alexander a compliment at the expense of the mighty ones of long ago – such a compliment was not for his honour but for his shame. In any case, he continued, they grossly exaggerated the marvellous nature of Alexander's achievements, none of which were mere personal triumphs; on the contrary, most of them were the work of the Macedonians as a whole.

Alexander, drunk also, was deeply offended. But worse was to come, for someone began to attack Alexander's father, Philip of Macedon, absurdly suggesting that by comparison with Alexander's his achievements were negligible. At this, Cleitus lost all control of himself and started to laud Philip and to denigrate Alexander. 'And this,' he said, stretching out his hand towards Alexander – 'this is the hand that saved your life at Granicus!'

Alexander could take no more. Springing to his feet he was about to strike him, but the others held him back. Cleitus, however, continued to taunt Alexander, who, goaded beyond endurance, shouted for the guards. No one came.

'What,' he cried, 'have I nothing left of royalty but its name?'

Now no one could restrain him any longer, and, snatching a pike from one of the attendants, he broke loose and pierced Cleitus through the heart.

Arrian, like the good biographer he is, gives his own carefully considered opinion of this regrettable affair. 'Personally,' he wrote, 'I strongly deprecate Cleitus's unseemly behaviour to his sovereign. . . . I feel that his words were ill-judged. In view of the fact that most of the party were drunk, he could, in my opinion, have quite well avoided the grossness of joining in the general flattery simply by keeping his thoughts to himself.' He continues:

> For Alexander I feel pity, in that he showed himself on this occasion the slave of anger and drunkenness, two vices to neither of which a self-respecting man should ever yield. But when the deed was done, Alexander immediately felt its horror; and for that I admire him. Some have said that he fixed the butt of the pike against the wall, meaning to fall upon it himself, because a man who murdered his friend when his wits were fuddled with wine was not fit to live. Most writers, however, say nothing of this; they tell us that Alexander lay on his bed in tears, calling the name of Cleitus and of his sister, Lanice, who had been his nurse. 'Ah,' he cried, 'a good return I have made you for your care, now I am a man! You have lived to see your sons die fighting for me, and now with my own hand I have killed your brother.' Again and again he called himself the murderer of his friends, and for three days lay without food or drink, careless of all personal comfort.

Soothsayers lost no time in proclaiming that this tragedy was the result of Dionysus's anger at being deprived of his sacrifice. This afforded Alexander some consolation, for it shifted the blame from his own wickedness to the peevishness of a god. The philosopher Anaxarchus, summoned to comfort him, went still further, assuring him that a great king, like the gods themselves, could not commit a crime. 'But in my opinion [wrote Arrian] he did Alexander a wrong more grievous than his grief, if he seriously, as a philosopher, put forward the view that a king need not act justly, or labour to the best of his ability to distinguish between right and wrong – if he really meant that whatever a king does, by whatever means, should be considered right.' It was, however, generous of Arrian to add that though many kings had done wrong he had never heard of another who had shown remorse.

It was the spring of 327, and after wintering at Nautaca (Bukhara?) the army was once more on the move. There had been serious revolts and much guerilla warfare during the previous summer, and the Macedonians had suffered more than one reverse. A new leader, Spitamenes, had besieged Maracanda while Alexander was up country; but Alexander had returned by forced marches, covering one hundred and seventy miles in three days and nights, to find that Spitamenes had fled. Later Spitamenes was beheaded by the Scythians, and his head sent to Alexander.

Only a single Sogdian stronghold now remained in enemy hands: the famous 'Sogdian Rock' – probably a peak in the Hissar range. It was considered impregnable, and among those who had been sent there for safety were the wife and daughters of an important Bactrian chieftain named Oxyartes. Alexander marched his troops there and found that, as he had been told, the rock rose sheer on every side. The natives had provisioned it against a long siege, and the snow that lay deep upon it was doubly disadvantageous to the attackers in that it made an ascent more difficult and at the same time guaranteed the defenders an unlimited supply of water. To Alexander it was a challenge.

But he began by making an offer to the defenders: if they surrendered they would be allowed to return unmolested to their homes. The proposal was greeted with shouts of derision. 'Unless you have men who can fly,' they said, 'we have nothing to fear.' So Alexander decided to attack. His soldiers were eager enough to make the attempt; they were even more eager when he offered a prize of twelve talents to the first man up, eleven to the second, and so on to the twelfth, who was to receive three hundred gold darics. This was big money.

Among the troops were some three hundred men who had had previous experience of rock-climbing, and these were now assembled:

> They had provided themselves with small iron tent-pegs, which they proposed to drive into the snow where it was frozen hard or into any bare bit of earth they might come across, and they had attached strong flaxen lines to the pegs.
>
> The party set off under cover of darkness to the steepest part of the rock-face, knowing that it was the least likely to be guarded; then using their pegs . . . they hauled themselves up, wherever each could find a way. About thirty men lost their lives during the ascent (and falling in various places in the snow, their bodies were never recovered), but the rest reached the top as dawn was breaking, and the summit of the Rock was theirs.
>
> Then, in accordance with Alexander's orders, they signalled their success to the troops below by waving bits of linen, and Alexander sent a crier to shout the news to the enemy's advanced posts that they might now surrender without further delay, for the men with wings had been found and were already in possession of the summit. And as the crier gave them this information, Alexander pointed to his men, where they stood on the top of the Rock.

The defenders were caught completely off their guard, and, imagining that the soldiers they saw were the spearhead of a much bigger force, immediately surrendered. Among the prisoners taken were a large number of women and children, including the wife and daughters of Oxyartes:

> One of these daughters was named Roxana. She was a girl of marriageable age, and men who took part in the campaign used to say that she was the loveliest woman they had seen in Asia, with the one exception of Darius's wife. Alexander fell in love with her at sight; but, captive though she was, he refused, for all his passion, to force her to his will, and condescended to marry her.

That this was really 'love at first sight', as Arrian alleges, or indeed 'love' at all, is improbable. Alexander was much praised by his early biographers for 'offering no violence' to Darius's wife, but there is no reason to suppose that he was in the least tempted to do so; there is nowhere any suggestion that he ever kept a mistress. Tarn, who loyally dismisses as fiction Curtius's story that Alexander took over Darius's catamite, the beautiful young eunuch Bagaos, attributes Alexander's apparent lack of interest in sex to 'self-conquest'; but it would seem that his will-power was not strong enough to keep him from heavy drinking. Alexander's attitude to women can only be explained by his being a homosexual – Justin and Aelian, among other writers, allege that his favourite, Hephaestion, was his minion – or by his having virtually no sexual urge of any kind; Theophrastus called him 'semi-impotent'. Alexander's marriage to Roxana, which was celebrated at Balkh, was a political match, and it was not until the last year of his life that she became pregnant by him, bearing him a posthumous son who was to become the ill-fated Alexander IV. The alliance did not please the Macedonian nobility; it proved, however, a shrewd move, and thereafter Alexander could count upon the allegiance of Oxyartes.

In the early summer of 327 Alexander set out from Balkh, recrossing the Hindu Kush to conquer India. What he understood by India was little more than the Indus valley (the Punjab), which had been a part of the empire of Darius I, and its conquest was to be the appropriate finishing touch to his eastern campaigns; he had no idea of the vast lands which lay to the south. Four years later, at Babylon as he was making preparations to march into Arabia, he was struck down by a fever. He was carried into Nebuchadrezzar's palace, where at sunset on 13 June he died; he was not yet thirty-three years old.

   That Alexander died 'weeping because there were no more worlds to conquer' is a legend nowhere mentioned in ancient literature, and by the end of the forty years of bitter civil wars which followed upon his death the Macedonians had abandoned for ever their hopes of ruling the whole world.

*   *   *

Hardly less miraculous than the true exploits of the great conqueror is the wide dissemination, in the Dark and Middle Ages, of his legendary exploits. As Chaucer wrote in the *Monk's Tale*:

> The storie of Alisaundre is so comune,
> That every wight that hath discrecioun
> Hath herd somewhat or al of his fortune.

   Manuscripts of the Romance of Alexander are to be found in almost all European languages including Czech (*c.* 1265), Bulgarian (twelfth century or earlier), Polish, Flemish, Russian, Magyar and Swedish (fourteenth century); an Icelandic version was made in the middle of the thirteenth century. The substance of many of these was derived, directly or indirectly, from a Greek manuscript falsely attributed to Alexander's historian Callisthenes and embroidered, as each scribe's fancy took him, with fantastic mythical adventures. There were Syriac and Armenian versions as early as the fifth century, and Ethiopian versions with a strongly Christian slant in which the Greek gods appear as Old Testament prophets and Philip of Macedon as a Christian martyr. The Persian poet Firdausi (*c.* 1000) wrote of him in his *Shah-nama* (Book of Kings), and another famous Persian poet, Nizami, composed a *Book of Alexander* in the twelfth century. The best of the English Alexander-books is *Kyng Alisaunder*, a Middle English metrical romance of the first half of the fourteenth century, and the most successful prose version is the French *Alixandre le Grant*. Sixteen manuscripts of this survive, and it was printed no fewer than eleven times between 1506 and 1630, with the title *L'Histoire du noble et vaillant roy Alixandre le Grant*.

   The tale, in this French version, opens with an account of the ancient history of

The flying machine of Alexander, propelled by griffins: a miniature from an English manuscript, C. A.D. *1400*

Macedonia and of the birth of Alexander, whose true father was said to be the magician Nectanebus in the guise of a dragon. On the death of Philip, Alexander conquers Rome and receives homage and tribute from all the nations of Europe. He then invades Persia and India, where the story becomes ever more fantastic:

> The conqueror visits a cannibal kingdom and finds many marvels in the palace of Porus, among them a vine with golden branches, emerald leaves and fruit of other precious stones. In one country he meets with women who, after the burial in the winter, become alive again in the spring full of youth and beauty. Having reached the ends of the earth and conquered all nations, he aspires to the dominion of the air. He obtains a magic glass cage, yoked with eight griffins, flies through the clouds, and, thanks to enchanters who know the language of birds, gets information as to their manners and customs, and ultimately receives their submission. The excessive heat of the upper regions compels him to descend, . . .[1]

A woodcut in the 1506 *editio princeps* of *Alixandre le Grant* shows only four griffins, lack of space no doubt preventing the inclusion of more, and the King is seated in an iron cage. The bait which entices the hungry creatures ever upwards (for they had been kept for three days without food) is a leg of mutton spitted on a spear just out of their reach, while the two spherical objects are sponges soaked in cold water *'por rafrescir lor alaines'* – to refresh their breaths. Below, diminished to the size of a tiny islet, lies the world. This episode is frequently represented on the façades and misericords of churches, and there is a famous twelfth-century mosaic, on the floor of Otranto Cathedral, which includes it.

Even more prophetic than the account of this flying-machine is that which

[1] Margaret Bryant in the *Encyclopaedia Britannica*, 11th edn.

follows of Alexander's bathysphere – a glass diving-bell in which he descends to the ocean bed, where the fish crowd round him and pay him homage. Finally Alexander returns to Babylon, where, soon after his coronation, he died by poison.

Such are but a few of the innumerable adventures related in the French version of the Alexander Romance. In *Kyng Alisaunder* we find the King encamped by the shores of a poisonous lake, where many of his men die, but are restored to life by a magical herb to which he is directed by an angel. His armies are assaulted by dragons, monstrous crabs, lions, tigers and fabulous beasts called *deutigrans*. He comes, 'somewhere between Egypt and India', upon a marvellous people who live in the sea and possess a building material which hardens under water; he descends with

BELOW LEFT *Alexander in his diving-bell admiring the ocean depths*

them under the sea, lives with them for six months and returns to the surface with enough of this 'concrete' to block the port of Taracounte 'in the sea of Calpias' – perhaps the Caspian. He encounters the *catathleba* and other mythical animals, and finds a curious volcano in Abyssinia. Needless to say, he engages in single combat with various kings and is always victorious. Nor is romance lacking, for he allows himself to be seduced by the lovely and artful Candace.

The medieval world seemed never to tire of these tales of wonder. And the modern world is no less insatiable for serious biographies of Alexander, for, after more than two thousand years, scholars are still trying to explain how a young man of thirty succeeded in building the greatest empire the world had ever seen.

Found at Sidon: the sarcophagus of Alexander, showing a lion-hunt arranged by him for his Persian guests

CHAPTER TWO

Hsuan-tsang
A Pilgrim from the East

Buddhism, which may possibly have reached China as early as the year 217 B.C., had been the State religion there since the middle of the fifth century A.D., and during the following two hundred years many Chinese Buddhist monks journeyed to India, as did Christians to the Holy Land, on pious pilgrimages to the sacred sites connected with the life and work of the founder of their religion. Among these was Hsuan-tsang, who in the year 629 set out for India by one of the trans-Asian trade-routes – there were some who preferred to go by sea – which took him briefly to Samarkand; his is the first recorded visit to the city from the East and important as such, though the information he gives us about it is sadly scant.

Another of these itinerant monks was Fa-hien, who more than two hundred years earlier had travelled across Central Asia to India, even reaching Ceylon, leaving a valuable account of his experiences. But Hsuan-tsang's journey, which lasted sixteen years, is the most important and the best documented, there surviving, besides his own 'Record of Western Countries', a biography, compiled by two of his pupils, which is tantamount to an autobiography. In them we find an interesting report on the state of Buddhism in Turkestan and Afghanistan just before the tidal wave of Islam burst into Central Asia from the west and the Chinese armies from the east.

Hsuan-tsang, usually known as the 'Master of the Law', was launched into the troublous whirl of birth and death (as his biographers put it) in the province of Honan in the year 602. He was the youngest of four sons of a scholar without worldly ambitions, a man who preferred the life of a recluse in a small country town to the limelight of a public career. As an infant Hsuan-tsang was 'rosy as the evening mists and round as the rising moon', in boyhood 'sweet as the odour of cinnamon or the vanilla tree, of prepossessing appearance and solemn as a prince'. He was exceptionally able, precocious indeed, and already by the age of eight steeped in the Chinese classics; he would not even glance at an improper book or associate with any but the virtuous. He refused to mix with children of his own age or to dally in the market-place, and when the sound of cymbals, drums and singing drew the other boys and girls of the town to dance in the streets, he preferred to remain at home, studying with his father or helping his mother with household chores. To his contemporaries he no doubt seemed something of a prig.

Hsuan-tsang equipped as a traveller

One of his brothers, Chang-tsi, also intelligent and serious-minded, was a postulant at the Pure Land Buddhist monastery at Lo-yang (Honan), the eastern capital. Here Hsuan-tsang joined him, and such was the impression that he made on a commissioner who soon afterwards visited the monastery to choose from among three hundred applicants fourteen exemplary youths for free training for the priesthood, that the thirteen-year-old-boy, although really too young to stand, was invited to do so and was one of those selected. The Masters of the Law and the priests watched his progress with amazement. He understood every book the first time he read it, and after a second reading had it by heart. They invited him to preach, and were even more astonished by the lucidity and precision of his exposition. He was a wonder-child.

It was unfortunate for Hsuan-tsang that at this moment – it was the year 618 – the short-lived Sui dynasty collapsed, plunging the whole country into confusion. Bands of brigands roamed Lo-yang. 'The magistrates were murdered and so were those priests who failed to make their escape. The streets were filled with bleached bones and the charred ruins of buildings.' Hsuan-tsang and his brother, who were lucky enough to be among those who got away, decided to make for the capital, Ch'ang-an (Si-an) in the north-west, where the Prince of the house of T'ang who had overthrown the Sui had established himself, and which was soon to become the greatest city in the world of its day. This Prince was the founder of China's most brilliant dynasty, and his son, who ruled as the Emperor T'ai-tsung from 627 to 649, the greatest of all Chinese Emperors.

But even in Ch'ang-an religious life had come to a standstill, and nobody talked of anything but the war. So the two brothers moved on to Ch'eng-tu, in the province of Szechuan, where they found many other monks who had taken advantage of the peace and plenty that prevailed there. At Ch'eng-tu they passed several years in one of the monasteries, charming everyone by their good manners and ability. The elder brother was, it seems, hardly less of a paragon than the younger; moreover he was so spectacularly handsome that, when he passed through the streets, people would stop their carriages merely to look at him.

In 623 Hsuan-tsang received full ordination, and in the years that followed, he visited many of the principal Buddhist monasteries in the country, finding always that his fame had preceded him and being fêted everywhere. But he was worried. There were passages in the holy books which seemed to him to be irreconcilable; in particular, was he to accept – as he felt inclined to – the *Mahayana* (the Greater Vehicle of Salvation), or the more old-fashioned *Hinayana*[1] (the lesser Vehicle of Salvation)? He saw that only by going to India, the fountain-head of Buddhism, could he secure copies of certain books which had not yet reached China, and so find the answer. Several of his colleagues agreed to accompany him; but living as they did apart from the world, they were all at first unaware of an imperial rescript forbidding travel abroad – though in fact there is some doubt as to whether monks were included in the restriction. However, it gave his companions an excuse to cry off; but Hsuan-tsang, quite undaunted, determined to slip past the frontier guards and go alone.

It was the year 629, and he now had a complicated dream about mountains,

[1] Its characteristics are 'the preponderance of active moral asceticism and the absence of speculative mysticism and quietism'.

rough seas and whirlwinds, and a lotus of stone which burst as it were exultingly from the deep but which retreated each time he tried to put his foot on it. He woke in a state of the wildest excitement, for the interpretation of the dream was obvious to him: it meant that he was to go to India.

The news of his intention spread rapidly and soon reached the ears of the provincial Governor, who summoned him to his presence, heard what he had to say, and then ordered him not to leave the country. Hsuan-tsang decided to lie low for the present, and to devote his time to making himself physically fit for the rigours of such a journey by subjecting himself to 'every hardship known to man'. He also took a crash course in foreign languages which might prove useful, among them probably Tocharian, which was spoken to the west of the Gobi Desert. Then some Buddhist friends rallied round and produced two novices who were said to be prepared to accompany him on this risky enterprise; in the event, however, one backed down and the other was found to lack the necessary stamina.

After several false starts Hsuan-tsang was finally about to set out on one of the two principal trade routes from Ch'ang-an to the west – that which skirts the north of the Takla Makan Desert. A fortune-teller had told him that he could accomplish the journey if he chose for his mount a scraggy old roan horse, and he had managed to buy just such an unpromising beast – one, moreover, which was said to have crossed the Gobi Desert fifteen times and, as it were, knew the way blindfold. The old man who had sold it him warned him of the dangers that lay ahead. 'The western roads', he said, 'are difficult and bad. Oceans of sand stretch far and wide; evil spirits and burning winds, when they come, cannot be avoided; even large caravans lose their way and perish. How can you hope to accomplish this journey alone? Think it over carefully and don't trifle with your life.'

But Hsuan-tsang was not to be put off. Further, he was no longer intending to go alone, for at the last moment a young guide had offered to accompany him. On the very first night, however, this ruffian attempted to assassinate him, and the next morning made off. 'And now, alone and deserted, he crossed the sandy waste with nothing but horse-droppings and heaps of bones to guide him. As he slowly went forward he suddenly saw a troop of several hundred horsemen. They were wearing furs and felt clothes, and sometimes they advanced, sometimes halted. Then came camels and horses and the glitter of standards and lances. . . .' He took them for robbers. But even as he watched them their forms changed – now growing larger, now smaller – till finally they dissolved into thin air. He had been seeing, even before he had come to the frontier, his first mirage or, as he called it, 'demonic hallucination'.

The border between China and Eastern Turkestan[1] was guarded by five forts, near the very first of which Hsuan-tsang was struck in the knee by an arrow as he was filling his water-bottle from a small stream. He was brought before the captain, who being himself a Buddhist proved sympathetic, but who felt that the long journey was pointless; 'You can get all the information you want at Tun-huang,' he said, 'and it is only a day's journey from here.' When Hsuan-tsang denied that the monks of Tun-huang could have anything new to teach him, the captain sent him forward with a hamper of provisions and an introduction to the captain of the

[1] Also called Chinese Turkestan, Serindia (the name given it by Sir Aurel Stein), the Tarim Basin and (more vaguely) Central Asia. It is now the Chinese province of Sinkiang.

next fort. The remaining forts were in due course safely negotiated, and at last Hsuan-tsang reached his first major obstacle, the River of Sand – the western extremity of the Gobi Desert where, changing its name but not its total desolation, it becomes the Desert of Lop and eventually the Takla Makan. He must have been near An-hsi, a place dreaded by travellers for the fierce winds which blow there for three hundred and sixty days of the year.

The terrible Gobi: the greatest desert in the world! Mildred Cable and Francesca French, those two courageous missionaries who spent many years in Eastern Turkestan, open their delightful book, *The Gobi Desert,* with a quotation translated from the *Géographie Universelle:*

> The Gobi Desert measures nearly one thousand two hundred miles from north to south near the 104° meridian, and two thousand miles following the length of the 44° parallel. To the east it reaches nearly five hundred miles beyond the central Khingan; to the west its extent is limited only by the use of the word Gobi. Actually it lies in an uninterrupted stretch over the Dzungarian wilderness and the wastes of Eastern Turkestan, separated from each other by the hilly and fertile belt of the Tienshan. Thus from the Pamirs to the confines of Manchuria it covers a distance of three thousand six hundred miles.

Actually the Gobi is not quite so big as that, for the authors of the *Géographie Universelle* wrote kilometres where the Cables have translated miles. But it is large enough, and some idea of the scale of it may be gathered from the fact that the Takla Makan – the oval-shaped sandy desert which lies due north of the Tibetan plateau – is just five times the size of England.

Admittedly Hsuan-tsang had only to cross a narrow neck of the desert; but the journey over these nearly three hundred desolate miles of sand, stones and crumbling rock to Hami, on the southern slopes of the T'ien Shan (or Celestial) Mountains, took Sir Aurel Stein's well organized expedition eleven long marches in the early years of the present century; no doubt Hsuan-tsang, on his ancient steed, was at least several weeks on the way. 'There are no birds in the sky,' he wrote, 'no beasts on the ground, no water and no vegetation anywhere'; this was not quite true, for he later mentions the existence of a well that he failed to locate. One day his water-bottle fell from his hands as he was about to drink, and for four days and five nights he battled on without a drop of water for man or beast. 'By night demons and goblins burned torches as many in numbers as the stars; by day the winds whipped up terrible sandstorms. . . . His stomach was wracked with a burning heat and he was almost at his last gasp. Unable to go any further he dropped down on the sand, invoking Kwan Yin ceaselessly although exhausted by his sufferings.'

The German archaeologist, Albert von Le Coq, gives a terrifying description of these sandstorms, or *burans,* which he more than once experienced:

> Quite suddenly the sky grows dark, the sun becomes a dark-red ball of fire seen through the fast-thickening veil of dust, a muffled howl is followed by a piercing whistle, and a moment after, the storm bursts with appalling violence upon the caravan. Enormous masses of sand, mixed with pebbles, are forcibly lifted up, whirled

round and dashed down on man and beast; the darkness increases and strange, clashing noises mingle with the roar and howl of the storm, caused by the violent contact of great stones as they are whirled up through the air. The whole happening is like hell let loose, and the Chinese tell of the scream of the spirit eagle so confusing men, that they rush madly into the desert wilds and there meet a terrible death far from frequented paths.

Any traveller overwhelmed by such a storm must, in spite of the heat, entirely envelop himself in felts to escape injury from the stones dashing round him with such mad force; man and horse must lie down and endure the rage of the hurricane, which often lasts for hours together. And woe to the rider who does not keep a firm hold on his horse's bridle, for the beasts, too, lose their reason from terror of the sand-storm, and rush off to a lingering death in the desert solitudes. . . .[1]

Hsuan-tsang's prayers to Kwan Yin were answered, for the goddess, protectress of travellers, immediately responded with a cooling wind which lulled him to sleep – a sleep in which he saw a vision of a gigantic celestial being who urged him to take courage and proceed on his way. He rose and remounted, and before long his horse, now divinely guided, brought him to 'acres of lush meadows . . . and a shining pool of crystal-clear water'. The Bactrian camel had a reputation for being able to sniff out subterranean springs and also to predict the approach of a sand-storm; Hsuan-tsang's horse seems to have possessed at least the art of locating water.

Two days later Hsuan-tsang arrived safely at Hami, where he was welcomed with tears of joy by three Chinese monks in one of the monasteries there. Hami is the easternmost of a string of oases, skirting the southern slopes of the T'ien Shan Mountains, which had been overrun by the White Huns in the first half of the fifth century; their fruit – and in particular their melons – are famous throughout Asia. The elder Polos passed through Turfan about 1265 on their outward journey, and that intrepid Portuguese Jesuit Benedict de Goes ('who sought Cathay and found heaven') 'staid a whole moneth in that fortified Citie' in 1604. The next European at Turfan after Goes was the German-Russian botanist, Dr E. A. Regel, in 1878.

The excavations carried out in these oases by Le Coq and his team, shortly before the First World War, brought to light a large number of manuscripts, sculptures and splendid mural paintings dating principally from the sixth to the tenth centuries. The subjects illustrated in the paintings are both religious and secular, the influences Hellenistic, Indian, Chinese, Iranian, and even Byzantine; the most remarkable, from an artistic point of view, belong to the later period, after the Chinese who had gained control of the country in the middle of the seventh century had relinquished it to the Uighur Turks. Le Coq's finds were taken to the Berlin Ethnological Museum, which had sponsored the expeditions; unhappily many of them were destroyed in the Second World War.

News of Hsuan-tsang's arrival at Hami was soon brought to the King of Turfan, ruler of a dynasty that had come under Chinese influence, whose capital lay some two hundred miles further to the west in a depression which is in places five hundred feet below sea level and among the hottest spots on earth. It seems that the king had long known, from merchants whose caravans passed through his

[1] Albert von Le Coq, *Buried Treasures of Chinese Turkestan*, p. 36.

country, of the reputation of Hsuan-tsang, and was already his ardent admirer; he immediately sent a squadron of cavalry and his principal ministers to conduct the Master on the ten days' journey to his capital. Though it was midnight when Hsuan-tsang arrived outside the walls of Turfan, the King, who had been unable to sleep for excitement, came to the city gates with a torch-lit procession to welcome his guest in person.

Hsuan-tsang was led to a splendid pavilion, where he eventually managed to convey to the King that he was worn out and only wanted to sleep. But next morning, even before he was awake, the entire royal family appeared at his bedside. 'From the very first day I heard your name,' said the King, 'I have been in a state of ecstasy; I couldn't keep my hands or my feet still for excitement. I feel the deepest affection for you.' And, bursting into tears, he implored Hsuan-tsang to remain with him always and give instruction to the two or three thousand monks in the monasteries of Turfan.

Hsuan-tsang begged to be excused the honour. His programme was already fixed: he was bound for India. But the King, unaccustomed to opposition, lost his temper: 'Growing red in the face with anger, and stretching out his hand beyond his sleeve, he bellowed menacingly, "I know how to deal with people like you. . . . I will stop you by force and then send you back home. Think over what I have said. You had better obey me." ' Hsuan-tsang replied to these threats by going on hunger-strike, 'sitting for three days in a grave posture and refusing both food and

Two men, a horse, and a Bactrian camel: a drawing found in the Caves of the Thousand Buddhas

drink'. But on the fourth day the King, seeing him grow steadily weaker, was overcome with remorse and relented. 'You have my permission to continue your westward journey,' he said. 'And now you must try to eat something.'

Hsuan-tsang had won. But he agreed to remain at Turfan for a month, to preside over a hastily summoned religious 'sit-in' and to allow time for the preparation of thirty made-to-measure priest's vestments and a wardrobe of warm clothes – including 'face-coverings, gloves, leather boots, and so on' – which he would need when crossing the high passes of the Celestial Mountains. The King now began to shower his hero with gifts: 'a hundred ounces of gold, thirty thousand silver pieces and five hundred rolls of satin and taffeta – enough for the outward and homeward journey of the Master even if it took him twenty years'. He also gave him thirty horses, twenty-five servants and four attendant monks. To these he added innumerable letters of introduction to various princes, and finally two waggon-loads of satin, taffeta and luscious fruits as a present for the powerful Great Khan of the Western Turks, who ruled from the Altai Mountains to Bactria.

Hsuan-tsang was deeply grateful. In an almost interminable oration he thanked his benefactor for gifts which made the Celestial Mountains seem tiny by comparison, and promised to spend three years at Turfan on his way home; but this was not to be, for by then the King had died and his country had been absorbed into the Chinese Empire. At last it was time for Hsuan-tsang to go. Then 'the

A ravine at Kyzil,
Eastern Turkestan, with
monks' cells carved high
in the face of the cliff

King and the people embraced him tearfully, and their cries and groans resounded on every side' as the Master set out for the next oasis, Kharashahr.

Hsuan-tsang's caravan left Turfan in the company of a caravan of merchants. One night some of these men, eager to beat their companions to the Kharashahr markets, slipped away under cover of darkness; they were surprised by a band of robbers and killed to a man. Hsuan-tsang came upon their corpses the following day and shed a tear at the sight. At Kharashahr the Master remained for only one night; though he himself was cordially received by its King, this monarch was not on good terms with his neighbour the King of Turfan, and therefore felt disinclined to show much hospitality to Hsuan-tsang's Turfanese escort.

At Kucha, his next port of call, the whole town turned out to welcome the travellers. The King and his ministers were there, together with a great assembly of priests, one of whom greeted the Master with a posy of wild flowers. After a round of visits to the various monasteries, where flowers and wine were given him to place before the images of the Buddha, the Master accepted the offer of a bed from some priests who came from his own country.

The most revered priest in Kucha was a man named Mokshagupta, who had spent twenty years in India and who was looked upon locally as a paragon of learning. The Master went to pay his respects, and was somewhat patronizingly informed that it was pointless for him to visit India: 'We have', he said, 'all the necessary literature here.' Mokshagupta was an adherent of the Lesser Vehicle of Salvation, and an acrimonious religious discussion ensued, in the course of which Mokshagupta's ignorance was exposed. The old man, much abashed, blamed his failing memory.

It was the early spring of the year 639, and the Master was obliged to wait two months at Kucha until the passes of the Celestial Mountains were open. But at last it was considered safe for the caravan to leave, though events would seem to show that they left too soon. On the second day they came upon a large band of Turkish robbers; but the men were so busy fighting like vultures over the division of recently captured spoil that the caravan was able to slip past unmolested. Now they began to climb in earnest into the T'ien Shan, at this point about forty miles wide.

'These mountains', wrote the Master, 'are steep and treacherous. They reach to the skies, and ever since the beginning of the world snow has been accumulating on them – snow that has been converted into ice which never melts either in spring or in summer and whose glare is blinding. Even heavy fur-lined clothes cannot prevent the wind and the driving snow from freezing the body. There is nowhere dry where one can stop to eat or sleep; in order to cook one has to suspend the cooking-pot, and for a bed there is nothing but a mat spread on the ice.' He mentions without comment that during the passage, which took them a week, thirteen or fourteen men and an even larger number of animals lost their lives. For the guidance of future travellers he adds that it is inadvisable to wear red or to carry calabashes; presumably the former irritated the demons, while the latter, when the water in them froze, might burst and release an avalanche. It may well have been an avalanche that caused the death of so many of his party.

Passing now along the southern shores of Lake Issik-kul – the 'warm lake', so called because its waters never froze – they reached Tokmak, where they found the Khan of the Western Turks and his army engaged in a hunting expedition. This man, whose name was Tung, was a real monarch, not just one of the innumerable semi-dependent princelings who styled themselves kings; his capital was Tashkent. 'He was dressed in a robe of green satin and his hair was uncovered; but bound round his forehead was a silken band, ten feet long, whose ends hung down behind. He was surrounded by about two hundred of his officers, all dressed in brocades and with their hair plaited. The remaining troops, who were mounted on camels or horses, wore furs and costly fabrics; they carried long lances, standards and bows, and there were so many of them that they were lost in the distance.'

Hsuan-tsang was conducted to the Khan's quarters – 'a large pavilion adorned with golden flowers whose glitter dazzled the eyes. Officials, dressed in shining garments of embroidered silk, had spread two rows of mats on which they were sitting, while the Khan's bodyguard stood behind him. Although the Khan was a barbarian Prince who lived in a tent of felt, one could not look at him without a certain feeling of admiration and respect.' Thus patronizingly did the civilized Chinese admit that these half-savages were not quite so beyond the pale as he had imagined.

Some of these Turks were Zoroastrians. 'They worship fire, and do not use wooden seats because wood contains fire . . . but for the Master's sake they brought in an iron warming-pan covered with thick padding and invited him to sit on it.' Then the presents were fetched and duly admired, after which came music and feasting and a good deal of heavy drinking; 'and although the music was of a rather barbaric kind, yet it charmed the ear and warmed the heart'. The thoughtful host had provided his guest with a non-alcoholic drink, and instead of mutton and veal he was offered a fattening meal of sweetmeats such as 'rice-cakes, cream, sugar-candy, honey-sticks, raisins, etc.'

The Master was made to earn his supper by delivering a postprandial sermon. He chose for his theme the Ten Precepts of Buddhism, which roughly correspond to the Ten Commandments of Christianity. The Khan, we are told, was quite overwhelmed, 'prostrating himself humbly to the ground and joyously accepting the teaching of the Master'. Indeed he too begged Hsuan-tsang to remain permanently at his court. 'There is no point in your going to India,' he said. 'It is very hot there – their tenth month is like our fifth here. To judge from your appearance I would imagine that you would simply melt away. The Indians are naked Blacks and have no sense of decency; they are not worth a visit.' When Hsuan-tsang refused to take his advice, the Khan, unlike the King of Turfan, made no attempt to detain him by force, but provided him with a guide-interpreter and, loading him with gifts and letters of introduction, sent him on his way.

The Master probably passed through Tashkent to reach 'Sa-mo-kien' (Samarkand). Here the King and his subjects were also Zoroastrians, and though there were two

Buddhist monasteries they had long stood empty. 'If visiting priests seek shelter in them, the barbarians pursue them with fire and drive them out.' The King, too, was at first pointedly unfriendly; but on the second day he allowed Hsuan-tsang to preach to him, and to such effect that he immediately asked to receive the Vows of Abstinence. Thus overnight he became the Master's staunch ally; indeed, when two of the young monks who were travelling with Hsuan-tsang were set upon by some of his subjects as they were praying in one of the deserted monasteries, he ordered the latter to be arrested and their hands cut off. Hsuan-tsang humanely interceded on their behalf, and the sentence was reduced to one of flogging and expulsion from Samarkand.

Turning south, the Master passed through Shahr-i-Sabz (where Tamerlane was one day to build a great palace) and once more entered the mountains, where in places the track was hardly wide enough for two men to pass. This was the regular trade-route from Samarkand to the Oxus and so to India, the narrowest gorge being the famous Iron Gates, shut in on both sides by high vertical walls of rock. 'At its entrance double gates have been erected, over which hang innumerable little iron bells.' Then, crossing the Oxus, Hsuan-tsang reached what today is northern Afghanistan and arrived at Kunduz.

The ruler of Kunduz, a man named Tardu, was the eldest son of the Khan of the Western Turks, and his wife a sister of the King of Turfan; the Master was therefore well provided with letters of introduction to him. But Hsuan-tsang had arrived at a bad moment, for the Queen had just died and the King was ill. Worse, however, was to follow. The King, as soon as he had recovered, married his late wife's younger sister, a vicious woman who immediately poisoned her husband and married his successor, her stepson. Etiquette obliged the Master to remain at Kunduz while the long-protracted funeral and marriage ceremonies took place.

One might have expected Hsuan-tsang to have avoided all dealings with the new King, who had undoubtedly been involved in his father's murder; in fact he seems to have consulted him and to have accepted his advice to visit Balkh, the second capital of the kingdom and an important Buddhist centre. Hsuan-tsang travelled the hundred miles to Balkh in the company of a body of priests who had come to Kunduz with the curious but no doubt politic intention of offering sympathy to the patricide on the death of his father.

Balkh, the 'Mother of Cities', is one of the oldest inhabited towns in the world; and it was here, it may be remembered, that Alexander the Great had married Roxana nearly a thousand years earlier. Those who know Balkh today will read with surprise the Master's glowing account of 'this truly privileged country' with its extremely fertile plains and valleys, its hundred monasteries and their three thousand monks. At the New Monastery – one of the finest in the whole Buddhist world – he was shown various relics of the Buddha: his water-pot (holding about four gallons) and sweeping-brush, and the inevitable tooth – 'nearly an inch in length, rather less in breadth, and of a whitish-yellow colour' – which glowed miraculously for all to see; the light emitted by the other relics was too dim to be visible to any but the exceptionally devout. Here too the Master was at last to meet a monk – a man named Prajnakara – who, though a follower of the Lesser Vehicle,

OPPOSITE *Hsuan-tsang, from a painting found in the Caves of the Thousand Buddhas*

OVERLEAF *A Uighur prince and two princesses: details of wall paintings c. A.D. 900 at Bezeklik in Eastern Turkestan*

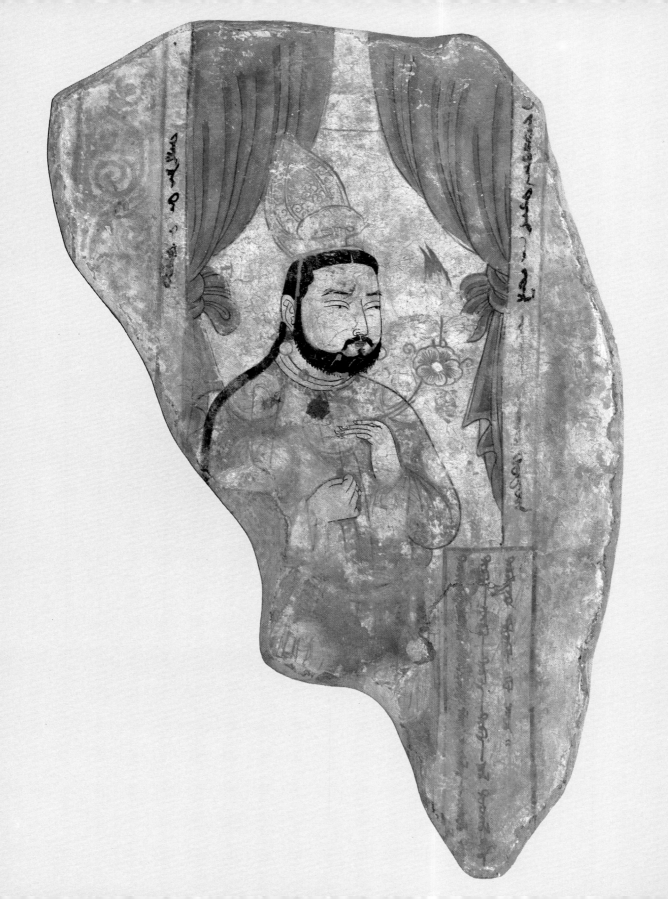

A god and a celestial musician in a 7th century A.D. *wall-painting from the Cave of the Painted Floor at Kyzil*

really understood the Buddhist scriptures; indeed Hsuan-tsang was so impressed that he remained with him for a month and then set out in his company across the 'great Snowy Mountains' (the Hindu Kush) to Bamiyan.

Like the soldiers of Alexander the Great, the two monks found the journey terrible. It was winter, with incessant blizzards and hailstorms, and snowdrifts that in places were twenty or thirty feet deep; more than once the Master, had his mission not still been unfulfilled, would have wished for death. But at last and indeed more dead than alive, they reached Bamiyan.

The general appearance of Bamiyan today, in spite of the destruction that was to be wrought by Jenghiz Khan, is still much as the Master described it. 'It clings to the mountain side and extends across the valley,' he wrote. 'Winter corn is grown there, but there are few flowers and little fruit. The country is suitable for the rearing of cattle, and there are great quantities of sheep and horses. The climate is very cold and the customs of the people crude. The clothes most commonly worn are furs and coarse woollen garments, which are locally produced.' He goes on to speak of the two giant standing figures of the Buddha which are cut in the rock-face, giving their heights as 150 feet and 100 feet; here, unlike most travellers, he underestimates, the actual heights being 174 feet and 115 feet. In these circumstances one is reluctant to doubt him when he mentions, in one of Bamiyan's ten monasteries, a no longer extant recumbent Buddha a thousand feet long. He describes the smaller standing figure as being made of bronze; no doubt both were once gilded.

These remarkable but grotesque pieces of sculpture, which stand like giant sentries in giant sentry-boxes, probably date from the fourth or fifth century A.D.; with the frescoes (not mentioned by Hsuan-tsang) that decorate the niches in which they stand and some of the innumerable cells that honeycomb the cliff-face, they testify to the cosmopolitan character of this so-called Gandharan art, in which Hellenistic, Indian and Iranian cultures came together in the early centuries of the Christian era. Buddhist art probably originated in Gandhara, to the east of Kabul, and much Graeco-Buddhist sculpture is very impressive; but of the standing Buddhas Robert Byron wrote: 'Neither has any artistic value. But one could bear that; it is their negation of sense, the lack of any pride in their monstrous flaccid bulk, that sickens. Even the material is unbeautiful, for the cliff is made, not of stone, but of compressed gravel. A host of monastic navvies were given picks and told to copy some frightful semi-Hellenistic image from India or China. The result has not even the dignity of labour'. Admittedly the statues have suffered much from time and the hand of man. Stucco and gilding, and such parts of the draperies as were formed of rope and cement, are victims of the weather; Moslems used the figures as targets for shooting practice across the valley, and in the eighteenth century Nadir Shah broke the legs of the larger one. But even allowing for all this, no one can deny the justness of Byron's verdict. Unlike, for example, the giant recumbent Buddha at Polonnaruwa (Ceylon), they impress only by their size.

The two monks now continued on their way eastwards across the ten-thousand-foot Shibar pass. Here there is a famous watershed: on one side of the pass the

River Kunduz begins its long journey to the Oxus and so to the Sea of Aral; on the other a tributary of the Indus sets out towards the distant Indian Ocean. Caught in a blizzard, the travellers were completely lost; but by good chance some hunters came upon them and put them on their way to Kapisi: the capital of a kingdom north of Kabul and an important city in Hellenistic days.

The monasteries at Kapisi were in part Mahayana and in part Hinayana; the King, who came out of the town with a long procession of monks to greet the travellers, followed the Greater Vehicle. Everyone wanted to have the honour of providing lodging for the two distinguished visitors, and this led to an unseemly monastic squabble. Prajnakara's refusal to stay at a Mahayana monastery – the Master showed himself more broadminded in the matter – limited their choice, and it was finally decided that they should accept the invitation of the monks of a Hinayana monastery said to have been founded by a 'Chinese' (or more probably Serindian) prince who had once been held a hostage in Kapisi.

ABOVE *From Gandhara, NW. India: a head of the Buddha carved in the 4th or 5th century* A.D.

OPPOSITE *The larger of the two giant Buddhas at Bamiyan, in Afghanistan, visited by Hsuan-tsang*

This prince had left behind him a buried treasure which was only to be dug up at a time of acute financial embarrassment – an act of generosity commemorated in several portraits of the benefactor, 'looking very Chinese', on the monastery walls. A 'wicked King' had once attempted to snatch the treasure, but an earthquake and other sinister happenings had frightened him away. The coincidence of the simultaneous arrival of a Chinese monk and the collapse of the outer walls of the monastery's pagoda seemed clear indication that the time had come to exhume the treasure, which had been buried at the feet of an image guarding the entrance to the Buddha-hall. The operation, supervised by Hsuan-tsang, disclosed at a depth of seven or eight feet a large copper vessel containing several hundred pounds of gold and a number of pearls.

The King, a great lover of religious debates, now organized a five-days' religious conference. The Master presided and, needless to add, carried all before him, revealing, to the general astonishment, that he had mastered the doctrines of all the different schools, whereas his opponents understood only those of their own. After the conference was over, Prajnakara returned to Balkh while Hsuan-tsang went on to Nagarahara, near the modern town of Jalalabad. He was now on holy ground and, like all pilgrims to sacred places, about to discover what an expensive affair religious sightseeing can be.

Just outside Nagarahara was a *stupa* (mound enclosing sacred relics) marking the spot where many hundreds of thousands of years ago Sakyamuni Buddha, in a former existence, had met Dipamkara, the former Buddha. Like Sir Walter Raleigh, Sakyamuni had spread his deerskin cloak on the ground so that Dipamkara might pass dryshod across a puddle; indeed he went one better than Raleigh in that he laid his long hair upon the cloak to convert it into the equivalent of a pile carpet.

Hsuan-tsang, wrote Arthur Waley, 'was the sort of sightseer who is a trial to vergers':

When the old monk in charge of the sacred site told him this story, [Hsuan-tsang] at once asked how the place where this event happened could still be in existence. Several cosmic cycles had passed since then, and it is well known that at the end of every cycle the whole universe is destroyed by fire. Even Mount Sumeru is completely burnt out. The verger was equal to the occasion. 'No doubt,' he said, 'when the Universe was destroyed this holy site was also destroyed. But when the Universe came into being again, the site reappeared in its old place. We all know that Mount Sumeru is still there; so why should this holy site not also be in its old place? Bear that in mind, and you won't be bothered with any further doubts.'

A few miles to the south-east of the town stood a pagoda containing various relics of the Buddha, including his walking-stick and robe, and an eyeball which irradiated so strong a light that it penetrated the box which enclosed it. But most revered of all was the top of the Buddha's skull. Pilgrims paid one piece of gold to see this, and for five pieces were allowed to take an impression of it in clay, which was then used for divination. The Master paid the larger sum and was rewarded by an image on the clay of the sacred Bodhi-tree (*Ficus religiosa*) – the tree under which Gautama became the Buddha, the Enlightened One. The monk-guide was much struck by this uncommon occurrence, which signified that Hsuan-tsang had 'a portion of the true wisdom'.

Having seen and adored every possible relic, the Master paused to take stock of what his piety had cost him. He found that in all he was the poorer by fifty pieces of gold, a thousand small pieces of silver, four silk banners, two pieces of brocade and two cassocks. 'Then having scattered flowers and once more prostrated himself in worship, he left the building.'

The Master now learned – and it would seem that it was almost by chance – that there was in the neighbourhood another essential pilgrimage spot: the cave in which the Buddha had 'left his shadow' after fighting the dragon Gopala. His official escort had kept silent about this, for the way there was infested by robbers, the climb exhausting, and of recent years the shadow reluctant to show itself. But the Master was not to be put off. 'In a million cosmic periods,' he said, 'I might never get such a chance again.' In the end he set out alone.

It was difficult finding the way, and nobody seemed anxious to help him. But at last he came upon a small boy who led him to a farm at the foot of the cliff below the cave. Here an old man agreed to act as his guide. But hardly had they left the farm when there appeared five robbers with drawn swords. Hsuan-tsang, quite undismayed, removed his hat to show his tonsure and explained the purpose of his journey. He knew, he said in answer to their questions, that he might expect to meet robbers. 'But even robbers are human beings. On such an errand I wouldn't even be afraid of meeting a pack of wild beasts.' The robbers were so astonished by this display of fearlessness that they sheathed their swords and asked whether they might join the expedition.

The shadow, as predicted, proved coy and had to be wooed by innumerable prayers and prostrations. But at last, after various encouraging signs, Hsuan-tsang's patience was rewarded; for the whole cave was suddenly flooded with light, and there on the wall was the gleaming shadow of the Buddha, the body and clothes orange-coloured and sharply defined, the lotus upon which he sat remaining indistinct. For good measure were added the shadows of various Bodhi-

The Buddha: a sculpture from Gandhara

sattvas and attendant priests. The old man and the robbers, who had waited at the entrance of the cave, were hastily summoned to burn incense and share the vision; but the light of their torches put it to flight. Five of the six members of the party were, however, just able to catch a glimpse of it after their torches had been extinguished. 'The entire story of the "Shadow",' comments Dr Beal in a rather acid footnote in his edition of the Master's travels, 'seems to indicate the use of a lantern and slide as a pious fraud.'

*   *   *

The Master now crossed the Khyber Pass into India and so, for the next twelve or thirteen years, passes out of our story. He travelled extensively through the sub-continent, reaching the south but being prevented by the disturbed state of the country from visiting Ceylon. In 643 or 644 we find him again on the banks of the Indus – a man in his forties now and eager to set out on his homeward journey through Central Asia.

Hsuan-tsang returning from India on his elephant: from an early 8th-century fresco

His particular friend and admirer, King Harsha, who ruled over most of northern India, had provided him with an elephant to carry the innumerable books and relics he had collected in India. This beast was a veritable Rolls Royce among elephants – so steady that it could carry a full basin of water on its back without a drop being spilt, so large that its howdah could accommodate eight persons as well as the baggage, and with so voracious an appetite that it consumed forty bundles of hay and over twenty pounds of buns a day. It was a princely gift, and one apparently without precedent where the recipient was a monk.

The Indus was at this point about a mile wide, but relatively shallow. For some unknown reason the baggage was unloaded and ferried across the river, while the Master rode in style on his elephant. When the ferry-boat was in mid-stream a sudden and violent storm arose. 'The man who had been put in charge of the baggage was seized with terror and fell overboard, but was eventually rescued by the passengers. About fifty manuscripts and a collection of flower-seeds of various kinds were, however, lost. Everything else was saved.' These seeds were of rare plants which the Master had hoped to introduce into China.

The King of Kapisi had come from his winter capital (near Attock) to the far bank of the river to welcome the Master, and his first question was, 'Did you happen to have any seeds of Indian plants with you?' 'I did indeed,' replied the Master. 'Then that explains everything,' said the King. 'Accidents like this always happen to people who try to export flower-seeds from India.'

The death of the King of Turfan and the overthrow of his kingdom released the Master from his promise to spend three years with him on his way home; he therefore decided to travel by the southern Takla Makan caravan-route which passed through Khargalik and Khotan to reach the Chinese frontier near Tun-huang, the great Buddhist centre, shrine, library and gallery of religious art, which will be discussed in a later chapter. After leaving the Indus valley he spent about two months with the King of Kapisi at his winter capital, waiting while copies of some of the more important of the lost texts were made for him at Uddiyana; then he set out for the Hindu Kush. The King provided a team of porters and fodder for the elephant, and himself accompanied the Master as far as the foothills.

The trials experienced in the crossing of the Snowy Mountains are again described in detail. After many weeks the Master finally reached the upper Oxus, where he stumbled upon the camp of his old friend the Khan of the Western Turks and spent a month as his guest. With an escort provided by the Khan, and in the company of some merchants, he then travelled up the higher reaches of the Oxus. Here he came upon a settlement of White Huns who had been driven to seek refuge in the mountains. He mentions the curious three-foot-tall horned head-dresses worn by the married women. 'The upper branch of the horn represents a woman's father-in-law, the lower her mother-in-law. When one of these dies she removes the relevant branch, and when both are dead the whole horn is discarded.' Advancing still further he was held up for more than a month by blizzards – and this was midsummer! Continuing in due course across mountainous country he reached a tribe of tough, ugly and uncivil people – presumably of Aryan origin, for he mentions their grey-green eyes – and a small monastery with a miracle-working statue of the Buddha.

Now came the Pamirs (which, so far as is known, he was the first to explore and describe). Here, at a height of over fifteen thousand feet, he reached the banks of the 'Great Dragon Lake', rediscovered in 1838 by Lieutenant Wood and less romantically named Lake Victoria in modern maps. The local fauna was rich, varied, and vociferous, the noise of their 'ten thousand cries' being 'like the din of a hundred workshops'. There were also 'birds ten feet tall, with eggs as large as pitchers', which he thought must be ostriches. Arthur Waley points out that this conjecture 'is not so fanciful as it sounds. The *Encyclopaedia Britannica* (1911) mentions the possibility that ostriches still exist on the lower Oxus', and it is known that ostrich-egg cups were sent in T'ang times from Samarkand and Bukhara to China.

It was stoon after this that the Master lost his elephant which, during an attack by robbers, stampeded and plunged into a river where it was drowned. One must suppose that the precious manuscripts and relics were at this time being carried by the mules, for nothing of Hsuan-tsang's appears to have been missing when the

ABOVE *A cowherd listening to a sermon, in a fresco of about* A.D. *500 found at Kyzil*

OPPOSITE *Musicians carried on a wheeled platform: from a tapestry found at Tun-huang in the Kansu province of China*

bandits finally made off, satisfied perhaps with the more easily disposable wares of the merchants.

The Master thought well of the oasis of Khotan. 'The soil, though stony and sandy in places, is elsewhere very fertile and all kinds of cereals are cultivated. The inhabitants make woollen rugs, fine felt and taffetas, and out of the ground they get large quantities of both light and dark jade. The climate is temperate and the people law-abiding; they value learning and are fond of music. They are upright and honest – in this respect very different from other Tartars. There are a hundred monasteries and about five thousand monks, mostly followers of the Greater Vehicle. The King is good, wise and valiant, and treats well all who deserve it. He claims descent from Vaisravana [the god of wealth].'

Khotan jade was famous throughout Asia, and especially prized in China. Chinese records mention the gift in 632 from the King of Khotan to the Emperor T'ai-tsung of a belt made of twenty-four green jade discs in the forms of full and crescent moons. It was at Khotan that silk was first produced outside China, silk-worms and seeds of the mulberry tree having been smuggled across the border in the fifth century by a Chinese princess who married a King of Khotan.

The King received Hsuan-tsang very cordially and arranged for him to stay in one of the monasteries. The Master remained there for nearly eight months, partly because he was hoping to replace other of his lost books and had sent messengers to Kucha and Kashgar in search of them, partly because he felt it wise to inform the Chinese Emperor of his imminent return; he had – or at all events he believed he had – broken the law by leaving China without permission, and he was not sure of the reception that awaited him. A Turfan merchant who was on his way to Ch'ang-an agreed to take a letter for him in which he gave the Emperor a brief account of his adventures, adding that owing to the loss of his elephant he was in difficulties over the transport of his books.

Hsuan-tsang was not idle during his months of waiting, his time being spent in lecturing and expounding the sacred texts to the monks and the King himself. At last the Emperor's reply came: 'I was delighted to hear that you are on your way home after studying Buddhism abroad. Come here as soon as you can and report to me personally. Bring with you from where you are now any monks who understand Sanskrit and the meaning of the Scriptures. I have already instructed Khotan and the other districts through which you will pass to supply you with an escort, and you will find that you have all the porters and packhorses that you need. The officials at Tun-huang have been told to go out into the desert to meet you, and a party from Shan-shan will await you at Cherchen.'[1]

From Khotan the Master continued eastwards to Niya, where one day Sir Aurel Stein was to unearth a remarkable collection of Greco-Buddhist objects, and then plunged into the southern Takla Makan desert:

> On leaving Niya he came to an enormous desert of shifting sands that accumulate or disperse at the caprice of the whirlwinds. This desert stretches in all directions as far as the eye can see, and none know how to find their way. For only guide there are the bones of men and of animals left behind by other caravans. Nowhere is there water

[1] *The Real Tripitaka* by Arthur Waley, who quotes from Chinese sources not available elsewhere.

or pasturage. Often the desert winds burn like fire, and then men and animals fall swooning on the ground. Sometimes come sounds like singing and whistling, sometimes like cries of anguish; and those who hear them grow dizzy and incapable of deciding which way to go. Travellers often lose their lives there.

From now onwards the Master provides scarcely any further information about his journey; this is disappointing, because one would much have liked his impressions of Tun-huang. He reached Ch'ang-an in the spring of 645, to receive – though he arrived ahead of schedule – a spontaneous welcome from the whole city, people trampling on one another in their eagerness to catch a glimpse of him. So great, indeed, were the crowds in the street that he was unable, on the first night, to get to the lodging prepared for him.

Next day the various objects which he had brought back were carried in stately procession to the Hung-fa Monastery. These included a number of statues of the Buddha in gold, silver and sandalwood and – still more precious – a hundred and fifty pellets of his flesh. There were no fewer than six hundred and fifty-seven books, and twenty horses were needed to carry them; in one portrait of Hsuan-tsang here reproduced, in which he looks rather like a modern hiker, he is presumably shown with only the choicest of his manuscripts. When he had rested he set out to report to the Emperor, who was at Lo-yang. He was warmly received and immediately forgiven for having left the country without permission: 'If you had been a layman,' said the Emperor, 'it would have been a different matter.' The Master was cross-examined in detail about his journey and then offered a government post; but this honour he begged to be excused, preferring to devote the years that remained to him to a monastic life and the translation of his manuscripts.

Hsuan-tsang lived on for another nineteen years, working tirelessly with a team of assistant translators; and the magnitude of his task may be imagined when we read that the corpus of Prajna literature, which was translated during the last five years of his life, is said to be eighty-four times the length of the Bible. Royal favours were constantly showered upon him, both by T'ai-tsung and, after his death in 649, by his successor.

It is clear, wrote Waley, that we cannot accept as history all that is told us of Hsuan-tsang. 'It may be that in reality his opponents did sometimes think of answers to his arguments and that his hearers did not always give up the convictions of a lifetime so readily as his biographers make out.' Like Alexander the Great, Hsuan-tsang too became posthumously the theme for a whole cycle of fantastic legends which were used in plays and novels. Wu Ch'eng-en's famous *Monkey,* written in the sixteenth century and 'unique in its combination of beauty with absurdity, of profundity with nonsense', is well known in the West through Waley's felicitous translation. In the main, however, Hsuan-tsang's biography is entirely credible, and a great deal of the information he gives has been checked on the spot by Aurel Stein and proved accurate. As Lord Curzon once wrote of the author of a prolix and pompous but valuable seventeenth-century tale of travels, much may be forgiven of a man 'who lifts for our gaze the dim curtains of the past'.

CHAPTER THREE

Mahomet and Kutayba, the Sword of Islam

Everyone knows that Islam is, and has long been, the dominant religion in Western and most of Central Asia, but it may come as a surprise to many to learn how widely Christianity, in its unorthodox forms, was disseminated throughout the East in the early centuries of the Christian era. Asia became, in fact, the asylum for the adherents of all those heretical Christian sects – Washington Irving mentions more than twenty of them and admits that his list is far from complete – who had been driven out of Europe by Greek Orthodoxy or the hostility of Rome. There were the Nestorians, the Sabellians, the Arians, the Monophysites, the Eutychians, the Marianites, the Collyridians, the Ebionites, and many more. Each sect clung obstinately to its own little heresy: the Marianites, for example, regarded the Trinity as composed of God the Father, God the Son and God the Virgin Mary.

By far the most far-flung and influential of these sects in Asia was the Nestorian. Nestorius, Bishop of Constantinople in the early part of the fifth century, believed that the Virgin Mary should not be called the Mother of God since she was the mother only of the human, not of the divine, nature of Jesus. He was violently attacked by Cyril, Bishop of Alexandria (described as 'one of the most unpleasant saints who ever lived'), and after the Council of Ephesus in 431 banished to Antioch and subsequently hounded still further afield. But the Nestorians positively thrived on persecution, and their missionary zeal was astonishing.

A Nestorian mission reached China in 631. On the orders of that wise and liberal-minded Emperor, T'ai-tsung, whose tolerance Chairman Mao might do well to remember and imitate, the creed of the Nestorians – known in China as the Luminous Doctrine – was examined and warmly approved, after which a convent of twenty-one monks was established at Ch'ang-an. There were metropolitan sees of Nestorians in Herat and Samarkand by the early years of the eighth century, and these had undoubtedly been preceded by bishoprics. In China all religions received a sharp set-back in the middle of the ninth century under the iconoclastic Emperor Wu-tsung.

Miraculous incidents at the birth of Mahomet: a Moghul painting, 1570

The part played by Buddhism in Central Asia has been touched upon in the previous chapter; the role of Islam is of such paramount importance as to provide excuse for the inclusion of a brief biography of its founder, and perhaps the necessary brevity may in its turn excuse a little levity of treatment. What follows is based briefly upon the now outmoded but perennially entertaining fiftieth chapter of Gibbon's *Decline and Fall* and Washington Irving's *Life of Mahomet* (1849–50), in which stress is laid on the legends of Mahomet's life. Anyone who wishes for something more earnest and more up-to-date will have no difficulty in obtaining access to it.

The ascent of Mahomet to paradise, riding Burak and preceded by the angel Gabriel

In or about the year 570 there was born in Mecca a child whose activities were in due course to render the lot of the Christians in Western Asia very unenviable: his name – to use the long-familiar though inaccurate spelling of it – was Mahomet. Abdullah, the infant's father, was a member of the Koreish tribe and guardian of the Ka'ba ('cube') – a shrine enclosing a tribal fetish in the form of a black stone, probably a meteorite; and so dazzling (according to Moslem tradition) were his good looks that on the night of his marriage to Amina, Mahomet's mother, two hundred inconsolable Koreish virgins committed suicide. 'The base and plebeian origin of Mahomet', wrote Gibbon, 'is an unskilful calumny of the Christians, who exalt instead of degrading the merit of their adversary.'

Mahomet, the only fruit of this union, gave early sign that he was no ordinary child. At the moment of his birth (during which Amina experienced no pain) the surrounding country was miraculously flood-lit, and the infant, to put the matter beyond any possible doubt, modestly announced to all present, 'God is great! There is no God but God, and *I* am his Prophet' – the eternal truth and necessary fiction (as Gibbon put it) which was to be the foundation-stone of Islam.

Some authorities state that Mahomet was a posthumous child, others that Abdullah died when his son was two months old, but the loss of a father does not seem to have affected the infant's sensational precocity. At three months he could stand unaided, at seven months run, at nine months engage in rational conversation and at ten months handle a bow and arrow; in view of all this it seems strange that he never learned to read or write. There were continuing signs that he was one apart: sheep bowed down to him as he passed by, and one day a mule which was carrying him suddenly acquired the gift of speech to announce that he bore on his back the greatest prophet of them all. At the age of three the boy was visited by two angels who painlessly opened his breast, removed his heart, washed it clean of original sin and then replaced it – a cardiac operation of a complexity not again attempted until the present century, and one which left behind no visible mark beyond a mole the size of a pigeon's egg.

When Mahomet was six his mother also died, and the orphan, after a brief stay at his grandfather's house, was adopted by an uncle – his father's eldest brother, Abu Taleb. This excellent man, a well-to-do merchant who traded with Syria and the Yemen, soon afterwards succeeded his brother as guardian of the Ka'ba, so that the boy grew up (as every potential religious leader should) with some knowledge of both business matters and religious ritual. At the age of twelve he went for the first time with one of his uncle's caravans to Syria, where they were hospitably entertained at a convent of Nestorian monks, with one of whom the boy struck up a friendship and had long conversations which made a lasting impression on him.

*At Medina: the mosque
designed by Mahomet*

The visits were repeated on subsequent journeys, and it is believed that the Prophet's hatred of any form of idolatry was the result of his contact with the Nestorians, who went so far in this as to reject the use of the crucifix. Another visit or two to the convent, a little more indoctrination on the part of the proselytizing monk, and – who knows? – the eager, intelligent boy might have become a Christian and the whole course of world history have been changed.

Indeed, Islam, with its monotheistic creed, its emphasis on prayer and fasting, its promise of a future life of bliss for the righteous, its advocacy of charity, its acceptance of the Old Testament and above all, of course, of Jesus as a great prophet, was hardly more remote from orthodox Christianity than were some of the heretical Christian sects. Father Ronald Knox, in his famous ecumenical satire *Reunion All Round,* jokingly suggested that with a little give and take on both sides unity might yet be reached: let, for example, the *muezzin* call at dawn from the church tower, but with an announcement 'both less provocative, and more appropriate', such as 'the early bird catches the worm'.

In due course Mahomet was engaged over a number of years by various Meccans to accompany caravan journeys to Syria and elsewhere, and among his employers was a wealthy middle-aged woman named Khadija who had recently buried her second husband. Khadija was much impressed by the young man's business acumen, but still more by his good looks. 'He was distinguished [wrote Gibbon] by the beauty of his person, an outward gift which is seldom despised, except by those to whom it is refused'; it is therefore a pity that Moslem artists so often portray the Prophet veiled or featureless. It was Khadija's idea that they should marry, and Mahomet immediately agreed. The bridegroom was twenty-five, the bride forty; and so generous were the happy pair to the guests who attended the wedding, that even Mahomet's old wet-nurse returned home the richer by a flock of forty sheep.

Women and perfumes, Mahomet once said, were his favourite sensual pleasures. His taste for the former was to be reflected in the permissive paradise he promised to his followers, and Gibbon preferred to leave in the obscurity of a dead language the tributes of the Prophet's contemporaries to his virility. By Khadija Mahomet had three sons and four daughters, her menopause having been miraculously delayed to permit conception. Though he was to limit to four the number of legitimate wives allowed to Moslems, he gave himself more latitude; but 'if we remember the seven hundred wives and three hundred concubines of the wise Solomon, we shall applaud the modesty of the Arabian, who espoused no more than seventeen or fifteen wives. . . .' All but one of these, strangely enough, were widows, ten of whom, still more strangely, though 'of mature age and approved fertility, were barren in his potent embraces'.

As the husband of a rich woman Mahomet could now afford to lead a more leisurely life. It seems that he became a partner in a greengrocery business in Mecca; but this left him plenty of time to pursue a taste he had always had for religious speculation, and periodically he would withdraw to a cave near Mecca to meditate with prayer and fasting. One night when he was thus employed an angel appeared to him, bearing a piece of silk and ordering him to read what was written on it. Mahomet replied that he could not read; but he found to his surprise that he could, and that he was receiving the first of many instalments of what, edited after his death, became the Koran – the religious and political code of Islam. 'Oh Mahomet!' said the angel, 'thou art the prophet of God, and I am his angel Gabriel.'

Mahomet was now forty – an age, say the doctors, at which epilepsy often first manifests itself. One of Mahomet's wives and one of his disciples were later to describe his symptoms at moments of ecstasy such as this, and according to Dr Gustav Weil they tally exactly with those of an epileptic during an attack: 'He would be seized with violent trembling, followed by a kind of swoon, or rather convulsion, during which the perspiration would stream from his forehead even in the coldest weather; he would lie with his eyes closed, foaming at the mouth and bellowing like a young camel.' Gibbon, however, speaks of Mahomet's 'epileptic fits, an absurd calumny of the Greeks'.

ABOVE LEFT *Mahomet preaching his farewell sermon*

Mahomet himself, as next morning he hurried back to Mecca to report to Khadija, began to wonder whether it had all been nothing but a dream; but Khadija immediately accepted the reality of the angelic visitation and from that moment became his first and most ardent disciple. For a time, however, converts were few, ridicule undisguised and opposition vigorous. When he tried to preach the One God and the wickedness of idolatry he was howled down; when he prayed in public he was pelted with garbage. He was challenged to work a miracle; but (according to Grotius) when a dove descended from heaven, alighted on his shoulder and seemed to whisper revelations to him, his enemies maintained that the bird had been trained and was merely collecting a grain of corn previously concealed in his ear.

The strain of all this hostility began to affect Mahomet's health, reducing him to a morbid state which induced further visions, the most famous of which was his

The Dome of the Rock Mosque, Jerusalem

so-called 'Nocturnal Journey' to Jerusalem and thence to the seventh heaven; this has provided the theme for what has been described as the 'most imaginative painting ever produced in Persia'. On a night splendid with stars the angel Gabriel appeared to Mahomet, leading a mythical horse-like, human-headed animal, Burak, and inviting him to mount. Mahomet did so, and his steed immediately rose into the heavens and headed in a north-westerly direction.

After touching down briefly on Mount Sinai and at Bethlehem they reached the Temple in Jerusalem, where they joined Abraham, Moses and Isa (Jesus) in prayer. Then, ascending by a ladder of light and with the speed of lightning, they passed successively from the first to the seventh heaven, where Mahomet went forward alone until he found himself within two bow-shots of the throne of God, from whom he received many of the doctrines later incorporated in the Koran. The Deity demanded that believers should pray to him fifty times a day, but after some oriental bargaining was finally persuaded to reduce the number to five. The wonders of these seven heavens, which are described in every detail, make those of St John's Holy City (on which they are undoubtedly based) almost suburban by comparison. Descending now to the Temple, Mahomet remounted Burak and in an instant was back again in his bedroom in Mecca; and some idea of the speed at which the whole excursion was effected may be gauged from the fact that he returned in time to prevent the complete overturn of a vase of water which Gabriel had struck with his wing at they were setting off.

Inevitably the Prophet's Nocturnal Journey has provoked innumerable commentaries and disputes among Moslem theologians. Some insist that he made it corporeally, others that it was no more than a vision. Gibbon, who quotes this and other wonders, comments, 'The vulgar are amused with these marvellous tales; but the gravest of the Mussulman doctors imitate the modesty of their master, and indulge a latitude of faith of interpretation.'

The faithful Khadija had died in 619, probably shortly before the Nocturnal Journey, and while she lived Mahomet had taken no other wife. Three years later came the turning-point in his career. A conspiracy had been formed to seize and murder him, but 'either an angel or a spy' gave him warning and he made his escape to Yathreb (afterwards called Medina), where he already had many converts. This was the famous Hegira[1], from which moment the Moslem era (A.H.) dates. At the age of fifty-two, with only ten more years to live, Mahomet was about to set in motion the conquest of an empire which within a century was to stretch from the confines of China to the shores of the Atlantic. None of the legendary miracles recorded of him is more miraculous than the plain fact of this astonishing dissemination of Islam during the first century of the Hegira.

The Prophet had been without honour in his own country; at Medina he was accepted as a spiritual and a temporal leader, and soon the fervour of his followers was testified 'by the eagerness with which they collected his spittle, a hair that dropped on the ground, the refuse water of his lustrations, as if they participated in some degree of prophetic virtue' (Gibbon). His followers advanced with the Koran in one hand and, unashamedly, the sword in the other; 'The sword', said Mahomet, 'is the key of heaven and of hell; a drop of blood shed in the cause of God, a night spent in arms; is of more avail than two months of fasting or prayer: whosoever falls in battle, his sins are forgiven: at the day of judgment his wounds shall be resplendent as vermilion and odoriferous as musk: and the loss of his limbs shall be supplied by the wings of angels and cherubim.'

By the time of Mahomet's death in 632, all Arabia had acknowledged him. He was succeeded by his father-in-law, Abu Bekr, proclaimed the first Caliph (Arabic *khalifa,* successor); it was, however, under the second Caliph, Omar, who ruled from 634 to 644, that the initial great conquests – of Syria, Palestine, Persia and Egypt – were effected. This fearless warrior and giant of a man – it is said that his walking-staff struck more terror into the hearts of beholders than another man's sword – had been among Mahomet's most dangerous enemies until his sudden and

[1] In Arabic *hijra.* The word does not, as often stated, mean 'flight' but 'separation' (from his native city or his family).

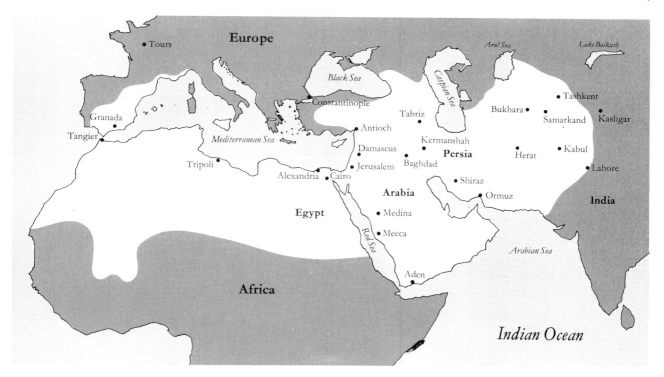

The Moslem Empire at its
greatest extent

miraculous conversion. Sweeping westwards across North Africa the Arab
armies reached Morocco and in 711, at their second attempt, invaded the Iberian
peninsula and finally advanced into France as far as Tours. Here in 732 was fought
one of the decisive battles of the world, after which the defeated Arabs withdrew
behind the protective barrier of the Pyrenees, still, however, retaining the greatest
empire that the world had so far seen.

In their advance eastwards it was the rout of the Persians in 641 at Nahavend,
called by the Arabs the 'victory of victories', that opened the way to Central Asia
and the Punjab. 'The Caliph Othman [644–56] promised the government of Chora-
san [Khurasan] to the first general who should enter that large and populous
country, the kingdom of the ancient Bactrians. The condition was accepted; the
prize was deserved; the standard of Mahomet was planted on the walls of Herat,
Merou [Merv] and Balch; and the successful leader neither halted nor reposed
till his foaming cavalry had tasted the waters of the Oxus' (Gibbon).

But during the latter part of the seventh century the eastward advance of Islam
was delayed by tribal strife among the Arabs. Merv was firmly held; but Balkh,
Samarkand and Bukhara changed hands more than once. Of the innumerable
Arab generals and local rulers who crowd the pages of Skrine's account of the
period till it becomes unreadable, one may be singled out for closer inspection:
the beautiful Princess Khatun, Queen-Regent of Bukhara during the minority of
her son. Khatun fled before the Arab armies to Samarkand, shedding in her haste
one of her slippers; it fell into the hands of the invaders, who estimated its value

at two hundred thousand direms – the equivalent in 1899, according to Skrine, of £4,166 sterling and surely the most expensive slipper of all time.

But Khatun remained a problem: when the Arabs were victorious and menacing, she grovelled and promised anything they asked; but as soon as they were in difficulties she revolted and re-established herself in Bukhara. The day came when she heard than an Arab general named Salem ibn Ziyad, Governor of Khurasan, was advancing on Bukhara with a force of six thousand picked troops. Khatun panicked and offered her hand in marriage to a powerful neighbouring ruler, Tarkhum Malik of Soghd, if he would get her out of the fix she was in. He gladly agreed, and sent to her assistance an army of a hundred and sixty thousand men which was at first victorious, then annihilated. This was Khatun's Waterloo; she had had a considerable nuisance value while she lasted, but now she made her final surrender and, one must hope, married her Tarkhum and lived happily ever after.

Salem, incidentally, seems to have been one of the more amiable Arab generals; so popular was he in Merv during his time there as Governor of Khurasan, that two thousand children were called after him. This custom of naming children after distinguished visitors or popular heroes long continued in Merv, where the Irish newspaper correspondent Edmond O'Donovan found himself in 1880 confronted one day by a number of proud fathers holding new born infants bearing, he was informed, the names O'Donovan Beg, O'Donovan Khan, O'Donovan Bahadur, and so on; the practice is not unknown in England today.

Though Transoxiana was often raided it remained for many years unconquered. The great Arab general destined firmly to establish the rule of Islam in the heart of Asia was Kutayba ibn Muslim, formerly a cameleer, who came to Merv in 705 as Governor of Khurasan and called upon its inhabitants to unite in a *jihad* (holy war). There was a great response, and in the autumn Kutayba captured the prosperous town of Baikand, known as the 'city of merchants', and with it an enormous quantity of gold and silver. A fifth part of this loot was sent home to Kutayba's chief, Hajjaj, the remainder being divided among the troops who, having never before known such wealth, spent it wildly on fine horses and arms. The greatest treasure was two pearls, each the size of a pigeon's egg, which formed the eyes of a golden idol and which were said to have been carried to Baikand in the beaks of two birds; these pearls were also sent to Hajjaj – a diplomatic gesture which was gratefully acknowledged. Kutayba treated the citizens of Baikand humanely; but as soon as his back was turned they revolted. He reappeared, massacred the men and carried off the women and children into slavery.

Various petty rulers and townships now surrendered to the Arabs; but a formidable stand was made by the Bukhariots, and it was to take three years – from 706 to 709 – and four campaigns before they were finally brought to heel. In 712 Kutayba built a large mosque at Bukhara on the site of a former fire-temple; but as soon as the initial curiosity had worn off, the Bukhariots lapsed back into idolatry. Kutayba dealt with this by ordering the payment of two direms a head to all who attended Friday worship – a stratagem which soon filled the mosque to overflowing and one which might usefully be attempted to augment the shrinking congregations in English churches today. Further, Kutayba quartered on every household an Arab whose duty it was to act in the dual role of missionary and spy.

In 711 Khiva fell and Kutayba marched on Samarkand. Legend relates that on the arrival of his forces outside Samarkand the inhabitants shouted from the walls that all attacks on the city would fail: 'You are wasting your time,' they said. 'We have found it written in a book that our town can only be captured by a man whose name is "Camel-Saddle".' It was bad luck; being ignorant of Arabic they did not know that that was exactly what 'Kutayba' meant. So Samarkand fell. Its Zoroastrian fire-altars were destroyed and their idols burnt, Kutayba himself putting the first torch to them.

In his last great campaign Kutayba struck eastwards, as far (it is said) as Kashgar, which was at that time close to country under Chinese control. According to the ninth-century Arab historian Tabari, the 'King of China', hearing of Kutayba's approach, dispatched an envoy inviting him to send an officer who could explain the tenets of Islam to him. Kutayba selected a dozen eloquent Moslems of distinguished appearance, provided them with magnificent horses, weapons and ceremonial robes, and instructed them to tell the King that he had sworn not to go away before he had trodden Chinese soil, fettered[1] Chinese officers, and received tribute money.

The twelve emissaries arrived at the Chinese court and, having bathed and perfumed themselves and put on long white garments with belts and sandals, appeared before the King, who ordered everyone to be seated. Complete silence reigned until the Moslems had withdrawn; then the King invited his ministers to give their impressions of the visitors. The ministers answered, 'They look, and they smell, just like women. We all began to feel quite amorous.' Next day came a second audience, at which the Moslems appeared splendidly dressed in the gayest colours and wearing silk turbans. 'And this time?' asked the King when the emissaries had retired. 'Now', replied the ministers, 'they look more like men.' At the third audience the Moslems arrived on horseback, dressed in magnificent armour and bristling with weapons. The King saw them approaching and was so seized with fright that he did not even invite them to dismount and be seated. 'And this time?' he asked. 'By God!' said his ministers. 'We've never seen such terrifying soldiers.'

The King felt that he would rather discuss business with a single representative of this formidable team, and a man named Hobaira was chosen as spokesman. Asked for an explanation of these charades, Hobaira replied that he and his friends had successively worn dress for family occasions, for ceremonial occasions, and for battle. The King, we are told, was astonished by this answer – so astonished, apparently, that he quite forgot to inquire about Islam. 'Tell your master', he said, 'that if he doesn't go away I shall exterminate the lot of you.' But it was obvious that he was scared and only bluffing, for soon he was asking what he could do to propitiate Kutayba.

'My master', said Hobaira, 'has sworn not to go until he has trodden Chinese soil, fettered Chinese officers and received tribute.' 'Very well,' replied the King, 'he can keep his oath. We will send him a handful of our soil so that he can put his

[1] Perhaps we should understand, 'marked with his seal'.

foot on it; we will send him four princes for him to fetter, and we will send him a handful of silver.' So the emissaries returned to Kashgar with a golden casket filled with Chinese soil, a considerable sum of money, plenty of silks and satins, four expendable princes, and handsome *douceurs* for themselves. Kutayba accepted the gifts, scattered the soil and trod on it, and fettered or sealed the princes before returning them to China.

This pleasant story may not be wholly without foundation, for Chinese records show that Kutayba did send an embassy to the Chinese court in 713.

Hajjaj had died in 712, and Caliph Welid two years later. Both had befriended and supported Kutayba; both were succeeded by men who had a grudge against him and who seemed likely to bring about his downfall. Certain that he was about to be deprived of his Governorship, he decided to revolt and sent a defiant message to the new Caliph – who had, in fact, just given orders for Kutayba to remain in office. But the damage was done; it was too late for explanations. So Kutayba addressed his soldiers, asking them to throw in their lot with his, reminding them of the victories they had won together and the loot of which they had always received a generous share. He was greeted by a stony silence; the soldiers, like those of Alexander a thousand years before, wanted to go home to their families, not to become involved in a campaign that might end badly for them.

Kutayba had always had an ugly temper and, confronted by this ingratitude, he completely lost it – denouncing his men as 'cowardly Bedouin, infidels, and hypocrites'; then he stormed off in a fury to his tent, where all the efforts of his friends and relations failed to persuade him to retract the insults he had poured on what they called 'decent people', or to send his troops home. 'Decent people!' he cried. 'They are not better than fifth-rate camels! The Beni-Bekr bin Wail are just like tarts, ready to offer their services to the first-comer. The Beni-Tenim are mere baboons, the Abdu'l-Kair are desert devils. By Allah! if I ever come to rule over them I'll treat them like dirt.'

Then Kutayba harangued his troops a second time, and even more insultingly; his last chance of recovering the ground he had lost and of regaining their sympathy had vanished, and they now decided to kill him. It was difficult to find a leader, but eventually a Bedouin named Waki was chosen. Somebody cried, 'We must breakfast off Kutayba before he dines off us!' and a number of men went off to fire his stables. Others then rushed to his tent, where they shot him with an arrow and then hacked him to pieces with their swords. So, in his forty-sixth year, died one of the greatest of Moslem leaders – the man who had carried the faith of Islam into the heart of Asia and established it there for all time.

CHAPTER FOUR

Jenghiz Khan
The Mongols in Central Asia

The trains of the Trans-Siberian railway, on the fourth day after leaving Moscow, skirt the southern shores of Lake Baikal and a day later cross an unimpressive river called the Onon. It has, however, some claim to fame: on its banks, in the year 1167, was born to the wife of a petty Mongol chieftain a boy who was named Temuchin, but whom the world was to know as Jenghiz Khan.

And who were these Mongols (or 'Tartars' as they came to be miscalled in Europe)? All that can safely be said about them, wrote Stanley Lane-Poole, is that they were 'a clan among clans, a member of a great confederacy that ranged the country north of the desert of Gobi in search of water and pasture; who spent their lives in hunting and the breeding of cattle, lived on flesh and sour milk (*kumis*), and made profit by bartering hides and beasts with their kinsmen the Khitans, or with the Turks and Chinese, to whom they owed allegiance.' But, thanks to the information brought back to Europe by two Franciscan Friars – John of Pian de Carpine and William of Rubruck, whose missions to the Mongols in 1245–7 and 1253–5 respectively are the subject of a later chapter – and of course to Marco Polo's immortal *Travels,* we know a good deal about the Mongol way of life in the thirteenth century, a way that was in fact to continue almost unchanged down the centuries.

The Mongols lived in circular tents (*gers* or *yurts*) constructed of light wooden frames covered with greased felt whitened with lime; to avoid the prevailing wind they were set up with the entrance turned towards the south, and seen from a distance an encampment looked like a field of mushrooms. These small tents were dismantled during migrations between summer and winter camping sites; but there were also big tents, sometimes as much as thirty feet wide, which were permanent structures carried on enormous wagons drawn by teams of oxen; Rubruck mentions that the door-flaps of the tents were often painted or embroidered with 'vines, trees, birds and beasts'. The floors were strewn with dried grass on which skins and rugs were laid, and the internal arrangement followed a standard pattern, the women being to the right of the entrance and separated from the men, and the master on a couch behind the hearth, which was directly under the central smoke-hole.

The religion of the Mongols was a form of Shamanism – the *shaman,* or priest, being at once a controller of spirits, a medicine man, a procurer of oracles and a watch-dog for the observance of taboos. Inside each tent hung idols of felt – 'the master's brother' (above the master's couch), 'the mistress's brother', and so on. Carpine writes:

> They have certain idols made of felt in the image of a man, and these they place on either side of the door of their dwelling; and above these they place things made of felt in the shape of tits, and these they believe to be the guardians of their flocks, and that they insure them increase of milk and colts. They make yet others out of silk stuffs, and these they honour greatly. Some people put these in a handsomely-covered cart before the door of their dwelling, and whoever stealeth anything from that cart is without mercy put to death.

These idols were manufactured at organized religious sewing-parties:

Tartar idols made of felt, and a kumis churn

> Now when they want to make these idols, all the noble ladies in the camp meet together, and make them with due reverence; and when they have made them they kill a sheeep and eat it. . . . And when any child falls ill, they make in this same fashion an idol and tie it over its couch. . . . To these idols they offer the first milk of every flock and of every herd of mares; and when they begin to eat or drink they first offer them of their food or drink. . . .

Not that their food was very palatable. It was, said Carpine,

> everything that can be eaten; for they eat dogs, wolves, foxes and horses, and when pushed by necessity, human flesh. . . . I have also seen them eat lice, for they say, 'Why should I not eat what eats my son's flesh and drinks his blood?' I have also seen them eat rats. They use neither tablecloths nor napkins. They have no bread, no oil and no vegetables – nothing but meat, of which, however, they eat so little that other people could hardly exist on it.
>
> They get their hands covered with the grease of the meat, but when they have finished eating they wipe them on their boots, on the grass, or something else; but the more refined have little bits of cloth with which they wipe their hands after eating. . . .

These, surely, could reasonably be described as napkins.

The drink was better than the food, the *kumis* (which Rubruck calls 'cosmos'), made of the fermented whey of mares' milk, being 'pungent on the tongue like rapé wine when drunk; and when a man has finished drinking, it leaves a taste of milk of almonds on the tongue. It makes the inner man most joyful, intoxicates weak heads, and greatly provokes urine.' Among other drinks was 'black cosmos', which was reserved for 'great lords'. Rubruck thus describes a drinking party, and the curious procedure employed for stimulating a thirst:

> When the master begins to drink, then one of the attendants cries with a loud voice, 'Ha!' and the guitarist strikes his guitar; and when they have a great feast they all clap their hands and dance to the sound of the guitar, the men in front of the master and the women in front of the mistress. When the master has drunk, the attendant cries as before and the guitarist stops playing. Then everyone starts drinking, and sometimes they continue until they are disgustingly drunk.

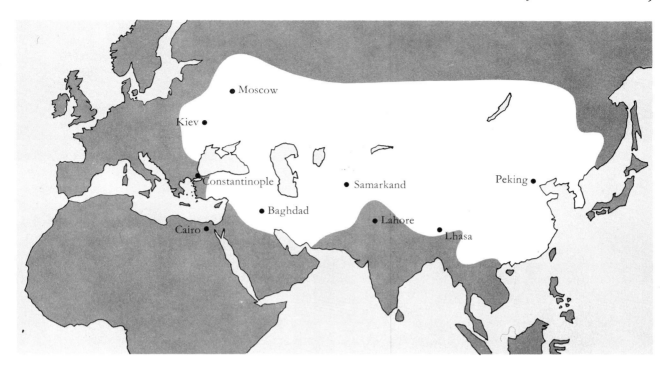

The Mongol Empire under Jenghiz Khan

When they want to challenge anyone to drink they seize him by the ears and pull them so as to distend his throat, then clap their hands and dance before him. In the same way, when they want to make a great feasting and jollity with somebody, one person takes a full cup and, supported by two others, one on his right and the other on his left, they come singing and dancing towards him. But as soon as he puts out his hand to take the cup they quickly withdraw it. This they repeat three or four times, until he has become so excited and so eager to drink that they give him the cup. And while he drinks they sing and clap their hands and stamp with their feet.

This harmless frolic might well be introduced into the West to enliven the tedium of cocktail parties.

Of the women we are told that they were 'wonderfully fat, and she who has the least nose is considered the most beautiful. They disfigure themselves horribly by painting their faces'; one can hardly blame the men for attaching greater value to their horses, or for finding the pleasures of the chase more rewarding than those of the bed. Women, in addition to the household chores, the sewing and the milking, did a good deal of the heavy work; they drove the carts, set up the tents, and even fought side by side with the men. They were dressed, too, in much the same way as the men, wearing over the upper part of the body a nondescript garment fastened over the breast, trousers below, and felt or leather boots. Furs were worn throughout a large part of the year (for snow, even in August, is not uncommon), but in warm weather the rich made use of silks and cottons from China. Women of rank wore an elaborate plumed headdress, called a *boktag,* which at a distance looked like a warrior's helmet.

Wives were bought, and if parents held out initially for too big a sum a girl might grow 'very stale' and finally have to be remaindered. When a man died, one of his sons would often take over (without marriage) all the widows except his own mother. Carpine describes Mongol women as 'chaste, but foul-mouthed', and Rubruck adds the information that they gave birth in a kneeling position.

Such was the world in which the infant Temuchin passed his childhood. Life was hard and dangerous, and for many 'nasty, brutish and short'.

Yesugei, Temuchin's father, had named his child after an enemy chieftain whom he had just defeated in battle – a strange practice: it is hard to imagine an English Field-Marshal of the Second World War naming his son Adolf. Temuchin was only nine years old when his father died – of poison, it was believed. He was the eldest son; but there was reluctance to accept a mere child as Yesugei's successor, and there followed lean and difficult years for him during which he was on one occasion taken prisoner. But he showed signs of remarkable powers of endurance and skill in local fighting; his hairbreadth escapes at this time, his courage, and his ingenuity in a crisis, are described in a work entitled *The Secret History of the Mongols.*

As his fame spread, he gathered round him a body of ambitious young warriors ready to accept his leadership. He also enjoyed the protection of a certain Toghril, Khan of the neighbouring Mongol tribe of the Keraits, who had been an ally of Yesugei. Many of the Keraits had been converted to Christianity by Nestorian missionaries, and this same Toghril is to be identified with the Prester John whose fabulous adventures became almost as widely disseminated as those of Alexander the Great himself.

Temuchin's chance came in 1194 when Toghril invited him to take part in a joint attack on the Buyr-Nur Tartars, a tribe whose pasture-lands lay to the east of the Mongols' territory. It was these Tartars who were believed to have poisoned Yesugei, and the young man must have been eager to avenge his father's death. They fought under the banners of the Kin Emperor of Northern China, and in this campaign Temuchin so distinguished himself that he was awarded an honorific Chinese title. Later, however, Toghril and Temuchin fell out, and in 1203 the former was defeated by the Mongols and killed.

The years between 1194 and 1206 were a time of almost uninterrupted fighting, during which Temuchin gradually asserted his ascendancy over all the neighbouring tribes; according to the Persian historian, Mirkhwand, he soon had at his disposal an army of such a size that 'the neighing of their steeds made Heaven shut its ears, and their arrows converted the whole sky into one great sea of reeds'. Among the prisoners taken in these campaigns was a man named Tatatunga, Chancellor of the Uighur clan. The Uighurs, unlike the Mongols, had a written language, and Temuchin appointed Tatatunga tutor to his four sons – Jochi, Chagatai, Ogedei and Tolui. These were the children of his first and principal wife, Bortei, to whom he had been betrothed when they were both still children. Bortei had for a short time been held prisoner by the Merkits, and there is reason

Yulun, the mother of Temuchin (Jenghiz Khan), pursuing rebellious tribes after the death of Yesugi, his father

to believe that Jochi, born soon after her rescue by Temuchin, was illegitimate.

By 1206 Temuchin felt himself strong enough to summon, to a point near the source of the River Onon, a *Kuriltai,* or Diet of Nobles, at which he assumed the title of Jenghiz Khan, the Ocean-great Khan. Alexander the Great had died before his thirty-third birthday; the empire of Mahomet at the time of his death extended no further than Arabia; but this middle-aged Mongol, who was as yet no more than the ruler of a confederacy of nomad tribes beyond the Gobi, was to die ruler of an empire that stretched from the Pacific to the Dnieper.

It was probably soon after the holding of this *Kuriltai* that Jenghiz Khan began to draw up and dictate his famous *Yassa,* or legal code, which has come down to us only in a mutilated form. The *Yassa,* which covered a very wide field and was compulsory for all the Great Khan's subjects, ordered them to love one another and to respect the old and the poor; it forbad theft, adultery, treachery against the State, the bearing of false witness, and so on. All this the Christian will applaud, though he will be puzzled by the capriciousness of the penalties imposed for infringements of the Code. For example, death was the penalty for urinating into water or ashes (which infringed a Shamanist taboo), whereas murder invited no more than a fine, graded according to the status of the victim – twenty gold coins for a Moslem, one donkey for a Chinese, and so on. Other serious crimes included gluttony and choking when eating, washing clothes before they were in tatters, and getting drunk more than three times a month; in fact many Mongols were drunk a good deal of the time. One reads with pleasure that the clergy of all faiths, and all scholars, were exempt from taxation. The *Yassa* was engraved in the Uighur script on iron tablets, but these have never been found.

China was at this time divided into two kingdoms. The native Chinese Sung dynasty still ruled over the south. But the north (Cathay) was in the hands of the Kin (or Golden) Tartars, who a century earlier had wrested it from the Mongol Kitai (or Cathayans) – themselves invaders after the fall of the T'ang dynasty; their capital was Chung-tu, on the site of the modern Peking, and their culture Chinese. Ta-shih, a Kitai Prince, had escaped westwards after the invasion of his country and there founded the important kingdom of the Kara-kitai (Black Cathayans); other Cathayans had remained to collaborate with their conquerors.

Soon after the *Kuriltai* Jenghiz Khan began to turn greedy eyes towards the vast riches of the Kin empire, lying beyond the Gobi and defended by the Great Wall of China. Having himself fought side by side with the Kin, he had no illusions about what was involved in the invasion of a highly civilized people with strongly fortified towns, modern weapons and siege-trains, and a long tradition in the art of warfare; but he trusted in the speed and daring of his cavalry and in the tactics – the feigned attacks, cunningly calculated retreats and swift encircling movements – that had stood him in such good stead in his earlier battles.

Immediately to the south of the Gobi, in what is now Kansu, lay the Tangut empire of Hsi Hsia, with a population part sedentary and part nomad and an army of one hundred and fifty thousand trained on Chinese lines; it was a vassal of the Kin, and its inhabitants were for the most part Buddhists. Before invading

A Tartar warrior

China it was essential for Jenghiz Khan to eliminate what would otherwise constitute a permanent threat to his right flank; in 1209, therefore, after some exploratory raids in the previous year, he marched with a considerable army across the Gobi and attacked the Tanguts. Though he failed to take their capital, he soon brought them to their knees. The way to China now lay open to him.

Jenghiz gave the Kin a sign of the mood he was in when in 1209 he curtly refused to pay the customary tribute. But he was busy at the time in the West, invading the kingdom of the Kara-kitai (to the south of Lake Balkash) and reducing it to vassaldom; it was not, therefore, until the spring of 1211 that he struck the first blow against the Kin. Crossing the Gobi with three armies he drove deep into Chinese territory, the central army, which he led in person, getting to within twenty-five miles of Peking and annihilating a large Kin army. In 1212 and 1213 came further invasions in which the Kin again fared badly; but the Emperor refused to discuss peace terms, and was shortly afterwards murdered by one of his generals in an army revolt which led to several other generals defecting to the Mongols.

The new Emperor realized that the situation was hopeless even though the capital, with its forty-foot-high walls and elaborate system of moats, still defied the besiegers. In May 1214 he sued for peace, and was obliged to hand over enormous quantities of gold, silks and horses, five hundred boys and girls to become slaves, and a princess to be a wife of the conqueror. Most of the innumerable prisoners taken in these campaigns were put to death, it being impossible to march them all back to Mongolia across the Gobi.

The Emperor, feeling far from secure in Peking, now took the cowardly and foolish decision to abandon his capital and take refuge in the south. Rebellions broke out, and Jenghiz Khan, suspecting that the Emperor was plotting mischief, made up his mind to take his revenge by sending two of his generals to capture Peking. A year later its citizens were starved into surrender; the city was sacked and a 'most glorious slaughter' (wrote a Mongol historian) followed. Vast booty was taken and sent to Jenghiz Khan, who had returned home with the loot of previous victories. With it went a number of high Peking officials among whom was a philosopher named Chu-tsai who made so great an impression on Jenghiz Khan that he took him into his service, where he became a power behind the throne and finally rose to the position of Chancellor. His civilizing influence on the Mongols cannot be exaggerated.

The extension of Jenghiz Khan's conquests westwards had brought him a new and powerful neighbour: the great Khwarazmian (or Khivan) empire – a Moslem kingdom which, under its ruler Shah Sultan Muhammad, had expanded till it comprised Turkestan, Afghanistan, most of Persia and even a part of northern India. Muhammad, himself a Turk, thus controlled the trade-routes between China and the West. In 1209 he had taken Samarkand and made it his capital.

Jenghiz's relations with the Shah were at first amicable. An embassy sent by Muhammad in 1215 was made welcome by Jenghiz, who discussed the furtherance of trade between their two countries. Even a small frontier incident the following year seems to have left no permanent ill-feeling, for in 1218 Jenghiz sent a return

Probably of the 11th century, a Seljuq ewer in white glaze

embassy to Muhammad offering 'his dearest of sons' a treaty of peace. For envoys Jenghiz chose three Moslems, for gifts large ingots of silver, jars of musk, pieces of jade and rich garments. He acknowledged (he wrote) that the Sultan ruled over 'a large part of the world', but thought it only fair to remind him of his own not inconsiderable achievements – his conquest of northern China and various other victories, including, none too tactfully, that over several Turkish tribes. 'My kingdom', he added, 'is swarming with soldiers.' In fact, the letter was a good deal less pleasant than at first sight appeared, for the reference to Muhammad as his 'son' carried disagreeable implications of vassaldom.

The Shah detached one of the three envoys from his companions and, slipping a large jewel into his hand, asked him for an honest estimate of Jenghiz's strength. The envoy gave a tactful, and what he may well have believed to have been a truthful answer: the Mongols were strong, but the armies of the Shah were stronger. For the moment, however, Muhammad, a man of straw, preferred to swallow the veiled insult; to ignore the threats of Jenghiz's letter and to return a friendly reply.

Later in the same year Jenghiz sent to Khwarazm a large caravan of Moslem merchants with five hundred camels loaded with goods for barter.[1] At Otrar, soon after entering the territory of the Shah, the merchants were arrested by the Governor of the town, who reported to Muhammad that they were spies (which they no doubt were) and asked what should be done with them. On the Shah's orders – or at all events with his connivance – the men were put to death and their goods impounded.

Jenghiz Khan is said to have shed tears of rage when he learned what had happened. After three nights and days of prayer to Tengri, the great god of Heaven, he decided to send an ambassador (he chose a Turk) and two Mongols to the Shah, demanding full compensation and the immediate surrender of the offending Governor, the alternative being war. Muhammad, confident in his military strength, and misguidedly imagining that he would only have to deal with a horde of barbarians, put the ambassador to death and sent back the two Mongols without their beards. He had thrown down the gauntlet. If, as seemed to him probable, his armies were victorious, he would gain the credit; if they were beaten he was perfectly ready to leave them in the lurch and save his own skin.

Though small raiding parties might pounce like lightning on an unsuspecting and unprepared enemy, there was no such thing in the thirteenth century as 'instant' large-scale warfare. Almost a year was to pass before Jenghiz Khan, having set his house in order at home and arranged for the security of his empire in his absence, had assembled his sons and his armies on the upper reaches of the River Irtysh, ready to march against the Shah of Khwarazm. The Mongol forces probably numbered between one hundred and fifty thousand and two hundred thousand men, all cavalry. In addition Jenghiz Khan had been able to call upon a large body of Kin engineers, equipped with up-to-date siege machines – ballistae, mangonels, catapults, and the deadly *ho-pao* or 'fire-gun' whose operations (it was rather wildly asserted) were audible 'at a distance of thirty miles'.

[1] Accounts of this episode, as given by different authors, vary considerably in detail.

ABOVE *A Minai jug of the 12th or 13th century, similar to pieces of pottery shown in the miniature on the left*

LEFT *Jenghiz Khan obliged to drink water squeezed from mud after being driven to the desolate borders of Mongolia*

Spies were of course soon active in both camps, and the reports that the Khwarazmian agents brought back to their master were far from reassuring. The Mongols, they said, were

> all compleat Men, vigorous, and look like Wrestlers; they breathe nothing but War and Blood, and show so great an Impatience to fight, that the Generals can scarcely moderate it; yet tho they appear thus fiery, they keep themselves within the bounds of a strict Obedience to Command, and are entirely devoted to their Prince; they are contented with any sort of Food, and are not curious in the choice of beasts to eat. . . . As to their numbers (they concluded), *Genghizcan's* Troops seem'd like the Grass-hoppers, impossible to be number'd. (Pétis de la Croix)

But it was too late now: the die had been cast. In fact the armies of Muhammad were probably twice as large as those of Jenghiz; they were, however, less mobile, and far less disciplined.

More than a thousand inhospitable miles separated the Mongols on the Irtysh from Otrar, their first objective. So that the troops might live the more easily off the land, the horde advanced over a wide front; thus it came about that a division led by Jochi suddenly found itself confronted in a narrow valley by a strong enemy force under the personal command of the Shah and his son, Jelal ad-Din. The general who accompanied Jochi urged flight; Jochi ignored his advice and, though badly outnumbered and with no room to manoeuvre, attacked. The famous *Mangudai,* or suicide squad – the word means 'God-belonging', so that we might translate it as 'God's Own Regiment' – led the charge, and before the day was out the Khwarazmians had been cut to pieces.

The Shah, who narrowly escaped with his life, now acquired a healthy respect for the bravery and tactical skill of these barbarians. He no longer felt inclined to challenge the enemy in the open, preferring to surrender the initiative and to use the bulk of his troops to garrison his principal cities. To besiege a well-fortified city was apt to be a long and a costly business; perhaps the Mongols would be content to ravage the countryside and then return home with their plunder. So fifty thousand Khwarazmians were rushed to Otrar, double that number to Samarkand and thirty thousand to Bukhara. Muhammad himself retired to Balkh, which was not likely to be attacked in the immediate future.

This change of strategy, immediately reported to the Mongols by their spies, suited Jenghiz Khan admirably. He wanted to deploy his forces; he saw that he could now do so without the risk of exposing a small body of men to attack from the full strength of the enemy. To Ogedei and Chagatai he assigned the storming of Otrar; Jochi was to strike northwards while he himself and his youngest son, Tolui, advanced on Bukhara. To several of his generals he allotted the siege of lesser towns.

Otrar put up a brave resistance, and the attackers, though they succeeded in filling in the moat, failed for several months to breach the walls. Ogedei and Chagatai were in favour of starving out the garrison; but Jenghiz Khan, impatient for results, ordered a direct assault, and finally the besiegers forced an entry into the city, whose defenders still resisted street by street. The Governor and his body-guard made a last stand in the castle, from whose summit, when arrows had given out, they hurled down stones upon the heads of the enemy. Jenghiz Khan had given strict injunctions for the Governor to be taken alive; he wanted a personal revenge. At last, after five months of siege, the castle was carried and the Governor brought in chains to Jenghiz Khan, who ordered molten silver to be poured into his ears and eyes.

Meanwhile Jenghiz Khan and Tolui were laying siege to Bukhara, which had become, under the Iranian Samanid dynasty in the tenth century, the greatest Moslem religious centre in that part of Asia, and had continued pre-eminent under their successors the Seljuq Turks and the Khwarazmians. There was an old proverb which ran, 'In all other parts of the world light descends upon earth; from holy Bukhara it ascends.' Lord Curzon wrote in his *Russia in Central Asia:* 'Students flocked to its universities, where the most learned *mullahs* lectured; pilgrims crowded its shrines. . . . Well-built canals carried streams of water through the city; luxuriant fruit-trees cast a shadow in its gardens; its silkworms spun the finest silk in Asia; its warehouses overflowed with carpets and brocades; the commerce of the East and West met and changed hands in its caravanserais; and the fluctuations of its market determined the exchange of the East.'

Within the besieged city the will to resist soon weakened. One night a body of soldiers and their officers, believing their situation to be hopeless, broke out and attempted to slip through the Mongol lines under cover of darkness; they were detected, pursued and virtually annihilated on the banks of the Oxus. Soon afterwards – it was in March 1220 – the leading citizens of Bukhara, seeing themselves betrayed and receiving a promise that their lives would be spared, opened the city gates. The Governor and such troops as had remained loyal shut themselves up in the citadel, determined to fight to the last.

Curiosity overcame fear, we are told, as the Mongol horsemen with Jenghiz at their head surged into the city. The Khan reined his horse before a fine building which he understandably mistook for the royal palace. On being informed that it was the house, not of the Shah, but of God, he entered it – some accounts say that he did not dismount until he was inside the building – and, ascending to the reader's desk, introduced himself, through his interpreter, to the worshippers as the 'Scourge of God' and ordered them to open their storehouses for his men. The order came a little late: soldiers were already breaking in everywhere, ransacking the granaries, looting the houses, and stabling their horses in the libraries where, 'by an unexampled Profanation [wrote a Moslem historian], the Leaves of the glorious *Alcoran* served for Litter to their Horses and were trod under foot'.

Jenghiz Khan, it was said, fancied himself as an orator, and his address in the mosque was followed by another harangue in the main square, in which he explained that it was the wickedness of their Shah that had called down the wrath of Heaven upon the Khwarazmians. Then he commanded the citizens to hand over their treasure, torture soon persuading the hesitant to comply. He had also given a severe warning against harbouring deserters, but many people had taken a chance and hidden relations and friends in their houses; when this was reported to him he took a savage revenge by firing the city. Only the public buildings, which were of brick, escaped destruction.

But the citadel still held out, the Mongols being more immediately interested in loot than in glory. At last, however, the Governor, 'seeing himself and Friends overwhelm'd with Pots thrown in full of Naphta and Fire, and the Gates of the Castle in Flames, surrender'd at Discretion. . . . The City of *Bocara* was the more regretted,' wrote Pétis de la Croix, 'because the Arts and Sciences had flourish'd there as much as in any Place in the World. Several learned Men had render'd it famous; amongst whom was the learned *Avicen*[1] . . . who [the Orientals] assure us did publish more than a hundred Volumes both in Prose and Verse. . . . They also observe that he extremely loved Wine and Women'. A Bukhariot historian who was fortunate enough to escape from the city summed up the devastation wrought by the Mongols in a single powerful line which recalls Caesar's 'Veni, vidi, vici':

Amadand, u kandand, u sukhtand, u kushtand, u burdand, u raftand.
They came, they uprooted, they burned, they slew, they despoiled, they departed.

Now came the turn of Samarkand, where Jenghiz Khan hoped to catch the real villain of the piece, Muhammad himself. But the cowardly Shah had fled to Balkh and so, perpetually harassed by Mongol flying columns sent in pursuit, to Nishapur, Qazvin, Hamadan and, finally, an island in the Caspian, where before the year was out he died, in utter destitution, of pleurisy, 'leaving behind him a reputation for pusillanimity which has rarely been paralleled in history'. He was succeeded by his son the courageous Jelal ad-Din, to whom in his lifetime he had stubbornly refused to hand over the command of the army.

Jenghiz and his main force, joined now by his other sons and their victorious armies, marched up the lush and fertile valley of the River Zarafshan (the 'Gold-Scatterer') to Samarkand. With them were innumerable prisoners from Bukhara who were to act as a screen during assaults and who in the event served the additional purpose of giving from a distance an exaggerated impression of

[1] Avicenna (ibn Sina), Arab physician and philosopher, 980–1037.

Mongol strength. In Samarkand were more than a hundred thousand troops –
Turks, Afghans, and 'brave *Taqis*, each of whom upon an Exigence would not
have shrunk back or trembled at the Sight of an angry Lion, or an Elephant in
Fury'. So wrote Pétis de la Croix, who (quoting native chroniclers) tells of the
strength and the beauty of Samarkand:

> It was wall'd round as well as *Bocara* when the *Moguls* laid siege to it, with this
> Difference, that the Walls of *Samarcand* were much more regularly built, and had
> more fortifications than those of *Bocara*. It had twelve Gates . . . made of Iron, and at
> every two Leagues there was a Fort. . . . The Walls were likewise fenced with
> Battlements and Towers, to fight under shelter, and were surrounded with a very
> deep ditch, through which an Aqueduct was laid that carried the Water from a little
> River in leaden Pipes, which convey'd it into all Parts of the City in such a manner,
> that there was not a great Street but what had Water running through it, or a House of
> any consequence without a Fountain. Besides this, there was a rising ground from
> whence several Rivulets descended, forming Spouts and Cascades of Water, which
> served to adorn their publick Places, and please the Eye. The Inhabitants were very
> curious to have fine Gardens, and every House had one belong to it.

Jenghiz Khan, anticipating a long siege, began operations by attacking
Samarkand from several sides simultaneously, hoping thus to intimidate its
defenders. These attacks were countered by spontaneous sorties of the populace,
during one of which a large number of them were ambushed and killed. Despondency set in, and soon there was a party in the city, led by the *imams* and the
judges, who advocated surrender and who on the fifth day of the siege, on
receiving a promise that their lives would be spared, opened the gates to the
enemy. Some accounts say that the Governor and a body of loyal cavalry fought
their way through the Mongol lines and escaped. The Turkish soldiers, hoping for
clemency, threw down their arms and were duly massacred. All the craftsmen,

*Miniatures from a 14th-
century Persian manuscript
by Rashid ad-Din* LEFT
*Jenghiz Khan receiving
dignitaries after his capture
of Bukhara,*
RIGHT *The armies of
Jenghiz Khan and Jelal
ad-Din face to face in battle*

مراجعت چنگگرخان

از ولایت ختای وفرمودن بجودار دوهانی

چنگگرخان بعد از آنک ولایات وبلاد ومزارع مذکور از ممالک ختای درین سه چهار سال کرده شد بزرمجی که شرح داده آمد
سبخر رسخاصر کرد واند مطغر ومنصور از آنجا به مراجعت بنود وهم در نولایه بسلم مذکور کامران با رزمانجوس زاول فرمود

فرستادن چنگگرخان سوبودای بهادر را با لشکر محکر بوم ملکت وآخر

حال ودولت آن قوم

چون چنگگرخان بزرجی که ذکر رفت از ممالک ختای نایغ شده مراجعت بنود شنید از قوم مرکیت که هر آنها که کرده شد تذکرات
با آنها زنگ کرده بود وبعد ازانها اسار استا یکی وسطی مران وبهادران و کوشک را کنند وکوشک ها انیان را کرده آند دیکر یار برادر
بونای کی روده لبس وحلاون وما بادر مرکان کرویه سوبند ومرجه ولایت ایمان مز منی دنده که درمر کوه زمرسته سبخ ترخ آنها رأست ها
دسوارست الی اجمعتی ساحده اند واین ارنصل خواست کرد درزاب نماک ایان آندیه فرنود ودرزابا کار سه وقف شهرسته اس عز و
ستا سوبودای بهادر را با لشکر بنا را محر بوم و راذان ادرشاد وفرمود باجتک آنک نفاس اند رنیب کرده سبخ آفنین
اسفاد کرد استا نادر بان سبخر رود شکسنه نزد وطوعونجا را بار دار ازرا ازقوم مقاتن کونت عزبه خنای اورا بهزار دهزار مرد قراول
سرشته کیاسته بود تا عز وقفا وار وردها ماکا با کا دار ازدر شدی مدتی منلیم بود وملک برشنه فرونزبا سوبودای بهادر بهزند حوزبا نابان
برنشته بارور ماروزه اند حمران که درر وکا کان رسیا مغولستان است ودرا بجده باوفود دا مصاف مرکیت با نونم مرکیت را شکسنه دا شنامت را کشنه
آنیان سبدار ملک مربکلتین سرکانه آبی ویرا نماری نبات بود ودرا رکسه بسی حوح آوردند وحسنه در بعز اماری
عظیم بود ولاو آلجی هنده بواسطه امک بکرات ارنشان رنجیان دیده بود اندشیه فرستادد وجان اورا بخواست

An ordu, *or encampment,*
of Jenghiz Khan: from a
14th-century Persian
manuscript by Rashid ad-Din

artisans and able-bodied citizens were carried off to work as slaves in various capacities; the other inhabitants, after being heavily fined, were given permission to live on in what remained of the city after the Mongols had sacked and looted it. That the destruction of Samarkand was far from total is attested by a Chinese who was there a year later; and the great Moorish traveller, Ibn Battuta, who passed that way in 1333, considered that even in its ruined state it was still one of the finest cities in the world.[1]

After the fall of Samarkand there was no more holding the Mongols, though Jelal ad-Din, who energetically attempted to raise an army in southern Afghanistan, had a brief moment of victory and displayed a heroism that won the admiration even of Jenghiz Khan himself. One after the other during the next two years the great cities of Transcaspia, Afghanistan and northern Persia – Khiva, Urganj, Balkh, Merv, Herat, Kandahar, Bamiyan, Nishapur, Ardebil, Qazvin, Tabriz, Qum and Maragha – fell. Some put up a show of resistance, many capitulated almost at once, almost all were razed to the ground and the inhabitants massacred to the last infant. In Nishapur, where not a dog or cat was spared, the only monuments standing when the Mongols departed were pyramids of human skulls.

Most brutal of all the generals was Tolui, the Khan's youngest son, who at a conservative estimate put half a million people to death in Merv, where peasants from all the surrounding districts had taken refuge. Like Bukhara, Merv was a great centre of learning. 'Its children were men, its youths heroes, and its old men saints,' wrote the famous geographer, Yakut, who escaped from Merv in the nick of time. Its splendid palaces 'were effaced from the earth as lines of writing are effaced from paper, and these abodes became a dwelling for the owl and the raven'.

In 1222 an army under two of Jenghiz Khan's most able generals, Chebe and Subutai, having subdued north-west Persia swept through Georgia to cross the Caucasus by the Caspian Gates (which no army had passed since the days of Alexander the Great) and overran the Ukraine and the Crimea. After wintering on the shores of the Black Sea they struck north again, overcoming the attacks of three armies mobilized by Muscovite princes. The exploits of these Mongol divisions have been described as 'probably the greatest feat of cavalry in human annals'.

Meanwhile Jenghiz Khan, after driving Jelal ad-Din across the Indus, returned to Sogdia, where he rested or enjoyed the pleasures of the chase; 'he did nothing at *Bocara* worth mentioning', as Pétis de la Croix put it. Then in 1223 he began the long march home to hold a *Kuriltai,* to which his sons and his principal generals were summoned by couriers. Thus, for the moment, Russia was to be spared further humiliations.

When Jenghiz Khan had mobilized his armies to march against Khwarazm, all the countries which were vassals to the Mongols had been ordered to contribute troops; and all had complied – except the Tanguts. Jenghiz Khan had neither forgiven nor forgotten this impertinence, and the time had now come for him to take his revenge. In June 1226 he led an army of one hundred and fifty thousand men against the truculent Tangut commander, Ashagambu. With him rode two

[1] See page 136.

of his grandsons, Kubilai and Hulagu, sons of Tolui; though still mere children – Kubilai (one day to become Emperor of China) was ten and his brother a year younger – they showed great courage in the face of the enemy.

A bad fall from his horse, followed by a sharp attack of fever that he could not throw off, should have served to remind Jenghiz Khan that a man of sixty is too old for the rigours of a campaign; but he made light of his troubles and continued with his armies, which captured an important Tangut city and in the autumn routed and annihilated the main enemy force on the flooded frozen plains beside the Huang Ho (the Yellow River). Soon afterwards the King of the Tanguts sued for peace, and was eventually put to death.

Yet even now Jenghiz Khan would not rest. It was while he was encamped on the frontiers of southern China, celebrating the recent victories and preparing to invade Honan, that news was brought him of the death of his eldest son, Jochi. Hard upon this blow came another severe attack of fever, and soon he saw that he was dying. Having summoned all the available members of his family, 'he set himself upright, and notwithstanding the Pains that racked him, he put on, as much as possibly he could, that majestick look which had always to that moment both awed and gain'd respect even from his Children and the Sovereigns of the East.'

His successor, he told them, was to be his third son, Ogedei, while his widow, Bortei, would act as regent until a *Kuriltai* had been held. Under Ogedei, Jochi's son Batu was to govern his western dominions, Chaghatai those to the east, while Tolui was given the Mongolian homeland. Above all, Jenghiz Khan urged his family to remain united. The chroniclers relate that to drive this lesson home he

OPPOSITE *Temuchin proclaimed as Jenghiz Khan, with his sons Ogedei and Jochi on his right*

BELOW *The family of Jenghiz Khan*

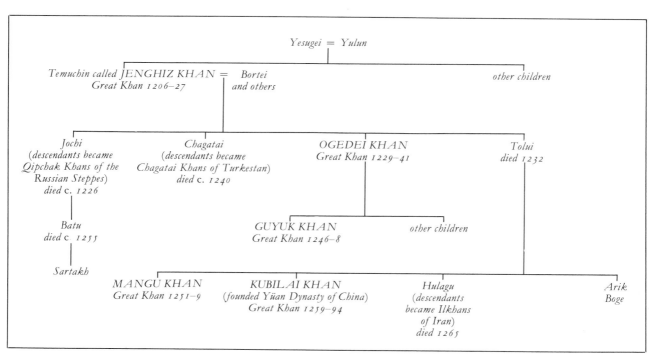

*Jenghiz Khan and his wife
Bortei enthroned before
their sons and courtiers:
a Persian miniature of
the 14th-century*

handed to his sons a bundle of arrows and told them to break them. When they had failed to do this he made them take each arrow separately, and now of course they were easily broken.

Then, on 24 August 1227, he died.

When the news of his death was made known, 'there was then nothing to be heard in every Place but Shrieks. All the Royal Family were drowned in Tears, the Officers of the Court in a general Consternation, the Soldiers overwhelmed with Grief; and all the Officers made the Air echo with their Lamentations.' The body was taken back to Mongolia and buried on a hill-top in the forests where he had spent his boyhood. Those in the funeral cortège, and all who met it on its way, were put to death in order to prevent the place of burial being disclosed.

So ended the reign of one of the most amazing of all Asiatic conquerors. It is, of course, easy enough to condemn the brutalities of Jenghiz Khan and his generals, but the circumstances of all this bloodshed must be seen in true perspective. The Mongols formed only a small minority in the lands which they captured and occupied; any leniency would have been disastrous, and the establishment of a reign of terror, however odious, was a military necessity. Moreover, it must be remembered that Jenghiz Khan founded a great empire where the *Pax Tartarica* was kept so long as he lived, and in which, it was said, a woman could walk from end to end with a bag of gold in her hand and not be molested.

CHAPTER FIVE

The Princes of Christendom
Panic in the West

In the year 1238 the bottom suddenly fell out of the Yarmouth herring market, fish becoming so cheap that (wrote the English contemporary historian Matthew Paris) 'forty or fifty sold for a piece of silver, even at places far away from the coast'. The reason for this unexpected slump was as simple as it will now seem improbable: so great had become the fear of the Mongols in western Europe that Scandinavian merchants did not dare to cross the North Sea for the herring fishery.

Western Europe had remained in almost total ignorance of the earliest Mongol conquests in Asia; of even the subsequent invasion of southern Russia, as far north as Kazan, hardly more than a murmur had reached the West, where Anglo-French rivalry and the feud between the Emperor Frederick II and Pope Gregory IX seemed of paramount importance. In Asia great empires crumbled, ancient dynasties went down in a sea of blood. Towns and villages were burned to the ground and their inhabitants – men, women and children – brutally butchered. Smiling countryside was turned into a desert wherever the Mongol hordes passed. Of all this the West, preoccupied with its parochial squabbles, knew little or nothing; and had it known it would not have cared.

Then, in the year 1238 and without warning, the Mongols, under the brilliant military command of the veteran Subutai, irrupted a second time into the West. Russia bore the first blow. Moscow, an unimportant city at that time, fell in 1238, and two years later great Kiev was captured and sacked by Mangu and Batu, grandsons of Jenghiz Khan. In the early spring of the following year the Golden Horde, using tactics with which the West were unfamiliar, broke through the Carpathian passes. The Poles, with the Teutonic knights they had summoned to their aid, were defeated at Liegnitz where, it would seem, the Mongols used some kind of poison-gas.[1] Batu laid waste all Hungary; Silesia and Moravia were ravaged. In Asia and Eastern Europe, it was said, 'scarcely a dog might bark without Mongol leave, from the borders of Poland to the Amur and the Yellow Sea'.

Only recently, wrote J. B. Bury at the close of the nineteenth century in his notes to Gibbon's *Decline and Fall*, have historians come to appreciate that these Mongol victories

[1] A chronicler relates the sudden appearance of a repulsive bearded human head, on the top of a lance, which emitted 'evil-smelling vapours and smoke' that threw the enemy into confusion and hid the attacking Mongols from sight.

were won by consummate strategy and were not due to a mere overwhelming superiority of numbers. . . . The vulgar opinion which represents the Tartars as a wild horde carrying all before them solely by their multitude, and galloping through Eastern Europe without a strategic plan, rushing at all obstacles and overcoming them by mere weight, still prevails. . . . Such a campaign was quite beyond the power of any European army at the time, and it was beyond the vision of any European commander. There was no general in Europe, from Frederick II downward, who was not a tyro in strategy compared to Subutai. It should also be noticed that the Mongols embarked upon the enterprise with full knowledge of the political situation of Hungary and the condition of Poland – they had taken care to inform themselves by a well-organized system of spies; on the other hand, the Hungarians and the Christian powers, like childish barbarians, knew hardly anything about their enemies . . .

It seemed, in short, that nothing could now save all Europe from being overrun.

RIGHT *A Tartar beneath the feet of Henry II, Duke of Silesia, carved on his tomb at Breslau*

OPPOSITE *Batu Khan, the son of Jochi*

It was probably a mission, sent in 1238 by the Moslem Ismaelians (or 'Assassins' of northern Persia) to Louis IX appealing for help against the Mongols, that first brought the new menace, something as potentially dangerous as the invasion of the Huns eight centuries earlier, to the notice of the West. One member of the mission came on to England and was received in audience by Henry III. The Bishop of Winchester, who was present, announced that he saw no cause for alarm, and rejected out of hand the suggestion of this unholy alliance. He was no doubt voicing the general opinion when he advocated letting dog bite dog; when Mongol and Moslem had exterminated each other, he continued 'then we shall see, founded on their ruins, the universal Catholic Church'.

Carpine and Rubruck had of course not yet brought back to Europe the information about the Mongols and their way of life which was given in the previous chapter; but from merchants and traders in the Near East there soon began to leak enough facts to rouse the complacent West from its lethargy. The new knowledge thus gained is summed up by Matthew Paris in his *Chronica Majora* under the date 1240:

In this same year a detestable nation of Satan – to wit, the countless army of the Tartars – broke loose from its mountain-environed home and, piercing the solid

*A Mongol warrior wearing
a coat of layered armour*

rocks [of the Caucasus], poured forth like devils from the Tartarus. . . . Swarming like locusts over the face of the earth, they have brought terrible devastation to the eastern parts [of Europe], laying it waste with fire and carnage. After having passed through the land of the Saracens, they have razed cities, cut down forests, overthrown fortresses, pulled up vines, destroyed gardens, killed townspeople and peasants. If perchance they have spared any suppliants, they have forced them . . . to fight in the foremost ranks against their own neighbours. . . .

For they are inhuman and beastly, rather monsters than men, thirsting for and drinking blood, tearing and devouring the flesh of dogs and men. They are dressed in ox-hides and armed with plates of iron. They are short and stout, thickset, strong, invincible, indefatigable, their backs unprotected,[1] their breasts covered with armour; they drink with delight the pure blood of their flocks. Their horses are big and strong, and eat branches and even trees; they have to mount with the help of three steps on account of the shortness of their thighs.

They are without human laws, know no comforts, are more ferocious than lions or bears, have boats made of oxhides which ten or twelve of them own in common. . . . They can cross the largest and swiftest rivers without let or hindrance, drinking turbid or muddy water when blood runs short. They are wonderful archers. . . . They know no other language than their own, which no one else knows, for until now there has been no access to them. . . . They roam with their flocks and their wives, who are taught to fight like men. And so they came with the swiftness of lightning to the confines of Christendom, ravaging and slaughtering, striking everyone with terror and incomparable horror. . . .

At long last the Pope and the kings and princes of the West became alive to the danger at their doors; but they had left it too late, and even now they responded with exhortation rather than with action. Everyone not already involved hoped that someone else would bear the brunt of the actual fighting; hoped and prayed that it might not be *his* turn next. The Emperor sent to the English King an appeal for help which was in reality a battle-call to all Christendom – 'to Germany, ardent in warfare; to France, who nurses in her bosom an intrepid soldiery; to warlike Spain; to England, powerful by her warriors and her ships; to Sicily; to savage Hibernia, to frozen Norway'. He, who at that very moment was invading Italy, called for unity; it was hardly surprising, therefore, that it was alleged in certain quarters that he had invented his 'plague of Tartars' to serve his own ends against his old enemy the Pope, and neither men nor money were forthcoming. The Count of Lorraine implored immediate assistance from the Duke of Brabant, who merely passed on his letter to the Bishop of Paris. German priests ordered fasts and prayers and preached a crusade. The aged Pope told King Bela of Hungary how sorry he was and urged him to go on fighting. Most ineffective of all was King Louis of France, who, when asked by his mother whether nothing could be done to save Europe from these devils, replied, 'We have the heavenly consolation that, should these Tartars come, We shall either be able to send them back to Tartarus whence they have emerged, or else shall Ourselves enter Heaven to enjoy the rapture that awaits the elect.'

What saved western Europe was the sudden death, in December 1241, of Ogedei after a long day's hunting followed by a long night's drinking. As soon as the

[1] This discouraged them from running away.

news reached the Golden Horde, the Commander-in-Chief, Batu, and the other members of the royal family hurried back to Karakorum to be present at the *Kuriltai* at which his successor would be elected. They were obliged by law to attend; but no one would have wanted to be absent on an occasion so favourable to the jockeying for position, for the descendants of Jenghiz were already involved in those family feuds which were eventually to lead to the break-up of the Mongol empire. The tension that already existed is clearly shown by a letter from Batu to Ogedei, written from southern Russia at a moment when several of the invading armies had come together and were celebrating their successes. Batu tells his uncle, the Great Khan, that at the feast

> I, as the eldest, drank one or two cups of wine before the others. Buri and Guyuk [his cousins] sulked and left the feast, abusing me as they mounted their horses. Buri said, 'Batu has no authority over us; why did he drink before me? He's just an old woman with a beard. I could knock him down with a single kick, and then stamp on him.' Guyuk screamed, 'I shall issue orders for him to be beaten up,' and someone else said that he ought to have a wooden tail nailed on to his behind.

In the West, Pope and Emperor, kings and princes were awaiting the *coup de grâce*; they saw, with relief and amazement, that the Mongol armies had halted their advance.

The transportation of Mongol yurts

Ogedei Khan with his sons Guyuk and Kadan

Gregory IX had also died in 1241, as too did his successor, and two years later Innocent IV was elected Pope. An ardent supporter of missions, Innocent decided to try a direct appeal to the better nature of the 'King of the Tartar people'; he therefore chose two Franciscans to bear letters from himself to accessible Mongol leaders, who might be prevailed upon to forward them or communicate their contents to the Great Khan, and to bring back as much information as possible about the Mongols and their intentions. Thus the mission was to be in the nature of both a religious and a political reconnaissance. In fact, no new Great Khan had as yet been elected, Ogedei's widow having been chosen to act for the time being as Regent. Friar John of Pian de Carpine, near Perugia, was to go to the Golden Horde in Russia, Friar Lawrence of Portugal to the Mongols in Armenia. Of the latter mission we know virtually nothing; Carpine, however, wrote a short but most valuable account to which his companion, Friar Benedict the Pole, added some further information.

Carpine (as he is generally called) set out in April 1245 and after a hard journey during which he fell seriously ill reached Batu's *ordu* (camp) on the Volga a year later. From here he was ordered to continue his journey to distant Karakorum, where Ogedei's eldest son, Guyuk, was about to be enthroned as Great Khan. The friars were present at the ceremony, which took place in a palace near Karakorum called the Golden *Ordu* – but they never actually entered the capital. Guyuk, who had a number of Nestorian Christians among his advisers, gave them a friendly reception; but to the suggestion that he himself might become a Christian he replied that the first step should be a visit to Karakorum by the Pope and the princes of the West to acknowledge his suzerainty. It was clear, reported Carpine to the Pope on this return in the autumn of 1247, that he was interested only in conquest.

Meanwhile the Pope had held a Council at Lyons for the purpose of 'finding a remedy for the Tartars . . . who will assuredly come back' – the remedy being an exhortation to all Christian peoples 'to block every road or passage by which the enemy could pass, either by means of ditches, walls and buildings, or by such contrivances as they might deem best', and to give immediate notice to the Pope of any sign of impending invasion. The Church was also prepared to contribute towards the cost of these 'Home Guard' defences. In 1247 Innocent sent another mission to the Mongols in Asia Minor; this was entrusted to a Dominican, Friar Ascelin, and a brief account of it has survived. The missionaries were much provoked by Mongol boorishness and arrogance; but Ascelin did his cause no good by his tactlessness, which resulted in his being given a highly offensive letter to carry back to the Pope.

Soon after their return from Mongolia, Carpine and his companion were sent by the Pope to Louis IX, who was about to set out for the Holy Land. Among those friars of mendicant Orders who were much in the company of the French King was a French Franciscan named Guillaume de Rubrouck (usually referred to by English authors as 'Rubruck' or 'Friar William'); it seems almost certain that Rubruck now met Carpine and his companion, and that what he heard from them of their journey first inspired him with a desire to visit the Mongols. Rubruck was with Louis in Cyprus in December 1248 at the time of the arrival of a Mongol envoy from Persia, a man with suspect credentials but who painted so glowing a picture of a people eager to become Christians – indeed already in part converted – that Louis immediately sent a French Dominican, Friar Andrew of Longjumeau, to return the compliment.

Much had happened to Louis before Friar Andrew returned in 1251. The King had sailed to Egypt with an army of Crusaders; he had been taken prisoner by the Saracens, but had later been ransomed. The friar, who had carried from Louis some valuable gifts including holy pictures, a splendid altar and a fragment of the True Cross, described his disastrous reception at Karakorum by the Empress-Regent (for Guyuk Khan had died in 1248, after a brief reign of two years, and his successor had not yet been elected). It appeared that the Empress had accepted the presents as a token of the submission of the King of the Franks, and had publicly announced the good news at court. To Louis's letter she replied in the most haughty and insulting terms, suggesting that next time the King should come in person to pay homage to her and bring the tribute money that was now due. Such gifts as she sent for the King were for the most part of little value, but a piece of Chinese asbestos aroused considerable interest in France and was eventually forwarded to the Pope to be cherished as a relic.

The mission had not, however, been entirely fruitless, for the friar brought back up-to-date information about the Mongols, including the exciting news of the presence on the Volga of a great Mongol Christian chieftain, Sartakh, son of the yet greater Batu, Commander-in-Chief of the Golden Horde. Yet further encouraging information came from a man named Philip of Toucy – an emissary sent by the Emperor Baldwin II to southern Russia, who visited Louis at Caesarea. Rubruck, who had been at the King's side ever since his release, listened excitedly to the stories of Philip's adventures; he was now fully determined to go to the Mongols.

Louis readily agreed and provided him with money and with letters for Sartakh and the new Great Khan, Mangu – Tolui's eldest son; but since he was anxious to avoid a further snub from the Mongols he made it plain that Rubruck's mission, though sponsored by him, was unofficial. He gave Rubruck a bible, while his wife, Margaret of Provence, added a beautifully illuminated psalter and probably some fine vestments also; it was important that Rubruck should make an impressive appearance at the Mongol court. In the early spring of 1252 Rubruck embarked for Constantinople, where he was joined by his future travelling-companion, Friar Bartholomew of Cremona. Here they remained for nearly a year in careful preparation for the journey; there will no doubt have been much cross-questioning of merchants who had personal experience of the Mongols, and probably Rubruck also had an opportunity further to improve his conversational Arabic.

Virtually nothing is known of Rubruck beyond what can be read between the lines of his *Journey to the Eastern Parts of the World* – the account of his travels which he wrote for King Louis; the only positive fact that he tells us about himself is that, like Carpine, he was 'a very heavy man'. But internal evidence, wrote Yule, shows him to have been

> an honest, pious, stout-hearted, acute and most intelligent observer, keen in the acquisition of knowledge; the author, in fact, of one of the best narratives of travel in existence. His language, indeed, is Latin of the most un-Ciceronian quality – a dog-Latin we fear it must be called; but, call it what we may, it is in his hands a pithy and transparent medium of expression. In spite of all the difficulties of communication, and of the badness of his *turgemanus* or dragoman, he gathered a mass of particulars, wonderfully true or near the truth, not only as to Asiatic nature, geography, ethnography and manners, but as to religion and language. . . .

Carpine's account of his journey to Mongolia and back is a straight and factual report; Rubruck's more discursive work might be described as a travelogue, and it is for that reason that we have preferred the author of this 'Jewell of Antiquitie' (as Purchas called it) as our companion on the journey – a journey that innumerable captives 'dumb to posterity' also made, in the middle of the thirteenth century, from Europe into the vast heart of Asia.

CHAPTER SIX

William of Rubruck
A Friar from the West

On Palm Sunday, 1253, Rubruck preached in Santa Sophia. In the course of his sermon he mentioned his forthcoming journey and stressed that, though he was the bearer of letters from King Louis to Sartakh, he would be travelling as a missionary, not as an ambassador. A month later he and his companion left Constantinople by sea, reaching Soldaia (Sudak), on the southern shores of the Crimea, on 21 May. The port was an emporium where Russian 'vaire and minever, and other costly furs' were bartered for Turkish 'cloths of cotton or bombax, silk stuffs and sweet-smelling spices'. Here they found that some Constantinople merchants, also bound for Sartakh's camp, had arrived ahead of them and had unfortunately been putting it about that the friars were official envoys of the French King. Though warned that he might endanger their journey by denying this, Rubruck felt obliged to make their status plain.

Preparations now began for the overland journey to Sartakh's camp. On the recommendation of the merchants Rubruck chose to take carts with him, a decision he later regretted because it doubled the time it would have taken had they travelled with horses only. He purchased four carts 'such as the Ruthenians carry their furs in', filling one of them, as advised, with 'fruits, muscadel wine and dainty biscuits' by means of which to purchase the good will of Mongol officials encountered on the way. He was also given the use of two more carts to carry bedding, and five horses for himself and his four companions – Friar Bartholomew, Gosset 'the bearer' (or clerk, who was in charge of the stores), Homo Dei the dragoman (probably an Arabic-speaking Syrian whose real name was Abdullah, 'servant of God'), and a slave-boy named Nicholas whom Rubruck had redeemed in Constantinople. There were also two men to drive the carts and look after the oxen and horses. Then on 1 June Rubruck and his party set out – presumably in the company of the merchants, though he makes no further mention of them – heading towards the north-east.

On the third day they came upon their first Mongols – 'and when I found myself among them it seemed to me of a truth that I had been transported into another century'. Here Rubruck interrupts his narrative to give the account of Mongol life and customs from which we have already quoted. This was of course compiled from knowledge subsequently acquired; for the moment he knew only that they were surrounded by a number of wild horsemen who cross-questioned them, pried everywhere, and immediately began begging. Rubruck distributed biscuits and wine, only to find that 'when they had drunk one flagon they demanded another, saying that a man enters not a house with one foot only'. This was refused; but the nuisance continued, the men 'begging of our bread for their little ones, admiring everything they saw on our servants, knives, gloves, purses and belts, and wanting everything. . . . It is true they took nothing by force; but they beg in the most importunate and impudent way. . . . They consider themselves the masters of the world, and it seems to them that there is nothing that anyone has the right to refuse them.' That evening Rubruck sampled what he called 'cosmos' (kumis) for the first time – observing rather strangely that 'at the taste of it I broke out in a sweat with horror and surprise. . . . It seemed to me, however, very palatable, as it really is.' Christians in those parts were forbidden by their priests to drink kumis.

The local governor was a man named Scatay, for whom the friars carried a letter of recommendation from the Emperor at Constantinople. This fact seems to have impressed the Mongols, who had at first denounced Rubruck as an impostor, and they agreed to conduct him to Scatay's camp. Next morning 'we came across the carts of Scatay carrying their dwellings, and it seemed to me that a city was coming towards me. I was also astonished at the size of the herds of oxen and horses and flocks of sheep.' Then Scatay's interpreter arrived, demanding (without success) a gown in return for his services and asking what gifts were destined for his master. He took a poor view of the wine, biscuits and fruit which

Opening page of a 13th-century manuscript of William of Rubruck's Journey to the Eastern Parts of the World

he was shown, and it was 'in fear and trembling' that Rubruck arrived in the presence of the governor, whom he found 'seated on his couch, with a little guitar in his hand, and his wife beside him. And in truth it seemed to me that her whole nose had been cut off, so snub-nosed was she; and she had greased this part of her face with some black unguent, and also her eyebrows, so that she appeared most hideous to us.'

However, the audience passed off well enough. Scatay accepted the gifts and appeared satisfied with Rubruck's explanation that a poor friar had nothing finer to offer; he also received the letter which, being written in Greek, had to be sent to Soldaia for translation. Scatay was curious about the contents of the letter which Rubruck was taking to Sartakh, and was assured that its tone was friendly. 'And what', he asked, 'will you say to Sartakh?' 'Words of Christian faith,' replied Rubruck. Scatay insisted upon hearing what these were, and through his incompetent dragoman Rubruck attempted to explain the basic facts of Christianity. Scatay 'remained silent, but wagged his head'.

Rubruck stayed with Scatay until the return of the courier from Soldaia. He spent a part of the time conversing with various Christians – Ruthenians and Hungarians among others – who were in the camp. An attempt was made to baptize a Moslem who initially expressed much eagerness; but when all was prepared for the ceremony he decided that he must first consult his wife, who warned him that as a Christian he would no longer be able to drink kumis. Rubruck told him that this was nonsense, but nothing could now persuade the man to take the risk.

On 7 June, which was Whit Sunday, Rubruck and his party continued on their way, led by guides who robbed them 'in the most audacious manner' until 'vexation made us wise'. It was a desolate journey over barren plains 'with nothing to be seen but the sky and the ground' except an occasional distant glimpse of the Sea of Azov. At night they slept in the open, or under the carts. By day, nomads were constantly appearing from nowhere and demanding a share of their food, which was soon running dangerously low. 'When we were seated in the shade under our carts (for the heat was intense at that time of year) they pushed in most importunately among us, almost crushing us in their eagerness to see all our things. If they were seized with an urge to void their stomachs, they went no further from us than one can throw a bean.' Even more annoying was the fact that all Rubruck's efforts to preach the Gospel to these people were frustrated by the incompetence of the dragoman; later, when the friar had come to understand something of the language, he realized that often the man made no attempt at translation but simply said the first thing that came into his head.

About the middle of July they reached the River Don – 'as broad at this point as the Seine is in Paris' – and were ferried across by Ruthenian boatmen established there for the purpose by Batu and Sartakh. Here the guide made the foolish error of sending back the horses which had brought them this far, only to discover that on the further bank it was impossible to hire all that were needed. This meant that for a time the friars had to go on foot. But the country beyond the Don, with its rivers and great forests, was delightful after the barren plains, and eventually they

OPPOSITE *Jenghiz Khan giving an address in the mosque at Bukhara: from a Shahinshahnama of 1397–8*

OVERLEAF *Mongols and Hungarians fighting on a bridge over the Danube*

seignor · m · CC · xl iiij

cerét homes qui iauoiet
noer ʒceaux entrerent

The Gobi Desert: TOP
an arid waste, and
BOTTOM *an oasis about
200 miles* SW. *of Ulan
Bator, the capital of Mongolia*

were able to get more horses and oxen. On the last day of July, after nearly two months on the way, they reached Sartakh's camp, where they were taken in hand by an important official, a Nestorian Christian named Koiac.

Koiac did not at first show himself in his true colours. He gave the travellers milk to drink, and accepted the biscuits and flagon of muscadel that they offered him in return. The following day he asked to be shown the books and vestments, alarming Rubruck by his assumption that all these were destined for his master. Then Rubruck and his party were ordered to get ready to appear before Sartakh.

> I put on the most costly of the vestments, with a most beautiful cushion (*pulvinar*) against my breast, and took the Bible which you had given me, and the lovely Psalter which my lady the Queen had presented me with, and in which were more beautiful pictures. My companion took the missal and the cross, while the clerk put on a surplice and took the censer. And so we came before Sartakh's dwelling, and they raised the felt which hung before the entry, so that he could see us. . . . Then they enjoined us . . . to chant some blessing for him, so we went in singing '*Salve, regina!*' In the entrance was a bench with kumis and cups, and all Sartakh's wives had come thither and the Moal [Mongols] came crowding in around us.

Sartakh and his principal wife, who sat beside him, examined everything with great attention, showing particular interest in the crucifix because Nestorian Christians never had the figure of Christ on their crosses, and asking various questions. The King's letter, of which Rubruck had had translations into Arabic and Syriac made in Acre, was handed to him, and these were re-translated into Mongol by some Armenian priests. 'When Sartakh had heard them, he caused our bread, wine and fruit to be accepted, and our vestments and books to be carried back to our lodgings. All this took place on the Feast of St Peter in Vinculis [1 August].'

Of Sartakh Rubruck wrote, 'I do not know whether he believes in Christ or not. But this I do know, that he will not be called a Christian, and it even seemed to me that he mocked the Christians.' Many Christians passed through his camp on their way to Batu's, and if they brought him gifts he showed himself 'most attentive'; but when Saracens arrived with richer presents they were immediately given preferential treatment. Koiac explained that Sartakh was '" not a Christian, but a Mongol", for the name of Christian seems to them that of a nation'.

Next day Koiac informed Rubruck that King Louis's letter contained 'certain difficulties' which made Sartakh unable to reply to it without reference to his father, Batu; Rubruck was therefore to proceed to his camp, which was on the banks of the Volga. He was to leave behind the two carts containing the books and vestments, because 'my lord wishes to examine them carefully'. Rubruck was given permission to retain the vestments they had worn when appearing before Sartakh, so that they might wear them in Batu's presence; but in the event almost everything was forcibly taken from them. All Rubruck could do was surreptitiously to abstract his bible and one or two of his favourite books; but the illuminated psalter had attracted too much attention and he did not dare to remove it from the cart. Some of the books he was able to recover on his way home, but he had to give Sartakh the psalter.

On 3 August the party, now reduced to four because the servant was made to remain behind, set out on horseback with a guide. The journey to the Volga, though short, was known to be dangerous because the countryside was infested by brigands, but on the third day they reached the river without incident at a point a few miles to the south of the modern Saratov. Here the river was four times the breadth of the Seine at Paris, 'and when I saw its waters I wondered from where away up in the north so much water could come down'.

Batu, who had encamped here during the summer, had now begun to move southwards towards his winter quarters; the travellers therefore followed him by boat and soon caught up with the slow-moving camp. Rubruck was amazed at the size of Batu's *ordu*, 'which seemed like a great city stretched out about his

William of Rubruck before Batu, from an 18th-century French work containing an account of his travels

dwelling, with people scattered all about for three or four leagues'. Next day came an audience with Batu, the procedure following the familiar pattern. 'Then they led us before the pavilion, and we were warned not to touch the tent-ropes, for they are held to represent the threshold of the door. So we stood there in our robes and barefooted, with heads uncovered, and we were a great spectacle unto ourselves.' Of Batu, Rubruck wrote, 'He looked at us intently, and we at him, and he seemed to me to be about the height of my lord Jean de Beaumont (may his soul rest in peace!). And his face was all covered at that time with reddish spots.' He may perhaps have been recovering from smallpox.

After the audience Rubruck was informed that Batu wished him to remain with his people, but that only Mangu Khan himself could give the necessary permission;

Rubruck must therefore go to Mangu, who was encamped near Karakorum – an enormous journey (as Carpine will have told him) and one that would have to be made in steadily worsening weather. He was informed that he must leave all his companions behind, but after much protesting he finally got permission for Friar Bartholomew and the dragoman to accompany him. Gosset, however, had to return to Sartakh's camp.

Five weeks were to pass before the friars embarked on their long journey. During this time they continued with Batu's *ordu* as it moved slowly southwards down the east bank of the Volga, travelling now on foot because their allotted 'host' was not prepared to do more than the bare minimum for men who could not afford to bribe him. The market followed in the wake of the *ordu*; but it was too far off for them to visit and they were often half starving. 'Sometimes my companion was so hungry that he would say to me, almost with tears in his eyes, "It seems to me that I shall *never* get anything to eat." ' But before long they made the acquaintance of two educated Hungarians who took pity on them and from time to time gave them food and drink; both were clerks, and one of them sang charmingly. In return, Rubruck copied out for them the hours of the Blessed Virgin and the office for the dead.

In the middle of September an important Mongol appeared one day and told Rubruck that he had been ordered to escort them to Mangu Khan. 'It is a four-months' journey,' he said, 'and the cold is so intense that it splits stones and trees. Do you think you can stand it?' Rubruck replied that he trusted that, with God's help, he and his companions 'would be able to bear what other men could bear.' 'If you cannot,' said the Mongol, 'I shall abandon you on the road.' Next day their wardrobe was checked and found to be quite inadequate against the cold; they were therefore each provided with 'a gown and breeches of sheepskin, felt stockings, and boots and hoods such as they wear.' Then on 16 September, with two pack-horses between the three of them, they set out with their escort towards the east.

A glance at the map will show how vast is the distance from Batu's *ordu* to Karakorum: some two thousand six hundred miles as the crow flies and probably more than three thousand by the way they went. Twelve days took them to the banks of the River Ural, which, like the Volga, flows into the Caspian. It was from this land, Rubruck noted, that Attila and his Huns had set out to invade Europe. From now on for many long weeks there were no more towns, and at night came the first frosts heralding the onset of winter.

For six weeks they continued across the Kirgiz Steppe, covering each day (according to Rubruck) 'about the distance from Paris to Orleans, and sometimes more, according to the supply of horses'. But since he admits that his party, 'as foreigners', often got wretched mounts and that sometimes he and Friar Bartholomew had to share a horse, it is hardly possible that they covered sixty miles a day. No doubt it often felt as much as that to the portly friar.

It was a terrible journey. 'Times out of number we were hungered and athirst, cold and weary. They gave us food only in the evening; in the morning we had something to drink or millet gruel, while in the evening they gave us meat – a shoulder and ribs of mutton – and some pot liquor.' Often the meat was nearly raw, especially when they did not reach their camping site until it was too dark to collect ox or horse dung for fuel. On Fridays Rubruck fasted till evening, when, though he hated doing so, he had to eat meat. 'At first our guide showed profound contempt for us, and was disgusted at having to act as escort to such poor folk; but after a while, when he began to know us better, he would take us to the *yurts* of rich Mongols, where we had to pray for them. If only I had had an efficient interpreter I could have done much good.' These Mongols 'asked about our countries, if there were many sheep, cattle and horses there,' and whether the Pope was really five hundred years old, as they had been told.

Early in November the travellers came to mountainous deserts where the wild ass roamed; 'our guide and his companion chased them a great deal, but without getting one, on account of their fleetness.' A week later they descended into an irrigated and cultivated plain; and here at last was a town – a small 'town of the Saracens called Kinchat' – whose governor came out, as was the custom when travellers arrived from Batu or Mangu Khan, to welcome them with mead. At Kinchat Rubruck saw vines, 'and twice did I drink wine'. Grapes have been raised in this part of Turkestan for more than fifteen hundred years.

They now entered territory under Mangu's direct control, where the people they met 'everywhere sang and clapped their hands before our guide, because he was an envoy of Batu'. Then crossing the River Ili they came to 'a goodly town called Equius, in which were Saracens speaking Persian although they were a very long way from Persia', and continued, keeping to the south of Lake Balkash, over a cultivated plain to the more important trading town of 'Cailac' (or Kayalik, near the modern Kopal). Here nearly a fortnight was spent awaiting the arrival of a secretary of Batu's who was to accompany them to Mangu Khan's *ordu*. The country was at this time inhabited by Turkomans, and now Rubruck made his first acquaintance with an unfamiliar brand of 'idolators, of whom you must know there are many sects in the East'.

These particular idolaters were Buddhists, for Buddhism had recently reached that part of Turkestan and Mongolia. Rubruck who entered some of their temples both here and later at Karakorum, describes the colossal images of Buddha ('as large as we would paint St Christopher'), the saffron robes and shaven heads of the monks, the structure of their buildings and the ritual of their worship. Finally he got into conversation with some of the monks and cross-examined them about their conception of God. He was doing splendidly and just coming in for the kill when, unfortunately, his interpreter, who had actually been quite cooperative, 'got bored and refused to go on translating'. Rubruck also attempted to force his way into the house of one of the Shamanist soothsayers, but was forthwith 'most rudely' ejected.

While waiting at Kayalik Rubruck picked up a good deal of miscellaneous information about Central Asia. He learned about the yak, whose cows 'will not allow themselves to be milked unless sung to', and which, like bulls in Europe, always attacked anyone dressed in red. In Tibet, he was told, were 'a people in

*Louis IX of France: a
statue in Maineville
Cathedral*

the habit of eating their dead parents, so that for piety's sake they should not give their parents any other sepulchre than their bowels'. This practice had by then been discontinued; but they still used the skulls of their parents as libation bowls, 'as was told me by one who had seen it'. He wrote about China and the silk trade, and was also remarkably well informed about the various languages of Asia and their relation to one another.

The travellers left Kayalik on St Andrew's Day (30 November) and soon afterwards came upon a village consisting entirely of Nestorians. 'We entered their church, singing joyfully and at the tops of our voices: "*Salve, regina!*" for it had been a long time since we had seen a church.' Three days later they reached the Ala Kul, a small lake to the east of Lake Balkash where the violent wind in spring and autumn is notorious. 'Often', wrote Woodville Rockhill (who edited Rubruck's travels for the Hakluyt Society), 'it carries such masses of snow and sand with it, that whole camps have been buried under them.' Rubruck says that the ground was covered with snow, and that because of the intense cold they turned their sheepskins 'with the wool inside'. They were now entering Mongolia.

On 13 December they came to 'most terrible rocks' – so terrible, indeed, that the guide implored Rubruck to say prayers to exorcize the devils who frequented the gorge and who 'were wont suddenly to bear men off, and no one could tell what they might do. Sometimes they seized the horse, and left the rider; sometimes they tore out the man's bowels and left the body on the horse. . . . So we chanted in a loud voice, "*Credo in unum Deum*", when by the mercy of God the whole of our company passed through.' Such was Rubruck's prestige from now on that he found himself obliged to write 'charms' for his two Mongol fellow-travellers to wear on their heads. These charms consisted of the Creed and the Lord's Prayer, and he briefly described to them what he had written down; 'I could do no more,' he said, 'because it was very dangerous, not to say impossible, to speak on questions of faith through such an interpreter, for he did not know how.'

When the travellers were within five days of Mangu's *ordu*, an attempt was made, by the officers at a station where they passed the night, to send them forward by a roundabout way which would have added ten days to their journey. This was a well-known trick 'to magnify their own importance', and it was only with difficulty that the guide won permission to take the direct route. 'Again we ascended mountains. . . . Finally, on the day of the Blessed Stephen [26 December] we entered a plain vast as a sea, and on the Feast of St John the Evangelist [27 December] we arrived at the *ordu* of the great lord,' who was camped at a spot about a week's journey south of Karakorum. From Batu's *ordu* to Mangu's had taken them just over three and a half months; Rubruck seems to have come through the ordeal well, but poor Bartholomew was almost at the end of his tether.

The friars remained for about seven months with Mangu Khan, the first three of which were passed in the camp and the remaining four at or near Karakorum. On their arrival at the camp their guide was given a large *yurt* whereas Rubruck and his companions found themselves crowded into a tiny tent in which they could not even stand upright. He was much visited and much cross-examined about the purpose of his journey; his explanation, that he came only to preach the word of God, was considered unconvincing, and it was generally maintained that the French King had sent him to make peace – 'for they are already so puffed up in their pride, that they believe the whole world must want to make peace with them. Of a truth,' Rubruck adds, 'were it allowed me I would, to the utmost of my power, preach war against them throughout the whole world.'

On their first day at the camp the friars were summoned to court, though in fact only to be turned away from the door of the palace. They had gone barefoot, and were consequently stared at 'as if we were monsters' and perhaps for this reason not admitted. On his way back Rubruck, to his great satisfaction, came upon a small building surmounted by a cross. 'I entered boldly, and found an altar right beautifully decked. Embroidered on a cloth of gold were pictures of the Saviour, of the Blessed Virgin, of John the Baptist and of two angels, the body and the garments being outlined with pearls. There was also a great silver cross with gems in the corners and centre, and many other church ornaments, and an oil lamp having eight lights was burning before the altar.'

Sitting in the church was an Armenian monk named Sergius – 'swarthy and lank, and dressed in a tunic of the roughest hair-cloth which reached half way down his shins. Over it he had a stole of black silk lined with vair, and under his hair-cloth tunic he wore an iron girdle.' Sergius informed him that he had arrived from Jerusalem a month before, after God had appeared to him three times in visions, telling him to go to Mangu. He said that he had been ordered to tell Mangu that, if he became a Christian, the Franks and the Pope would obey him, and he advised Rubruck to adopt the same line. Rubruck, much shocked, felt that Sergius must have misunderstood his instructions. He then returned to his icy tent and cooked a scrap of meat; he and Bartholomew had eaten nothing all day, and their guide, who had gone to court and got drunk, took no further interest in them. Next morning Rubruck woke to find that, not surprisingly, the tips of his toes were frostbitten, and thereafter the friars wore shoes.

On 3 January Rubruck and Friar Bartholomew, after shaving their beards 'so as to appear before the Khan in the fashion of our countryside' (which led to their being taken for idolaters), were conducted to Mangu. They found him in the *ordu* of one of his daughters by 'a certain Christian lady whom he had much loved . . . a very ugly, full-grown girl called Cirina' who on her mother's death had inherited all her property. After being frisked for weapons the friars entered the *ordu*, which was 'all covered inside with cloth of gold, and there was a fire of briers and wormwood roots – which grow here to great size – and of cattle dung, in a grate in the centre of the dwelling. Mangu was seated on a couch, dressed in a skin spotted and glossy, like a seal's skin. He is a little man, of medium height, aged forty-five years, and a young wife sat beside him. . . . Cirina, with other children, sat on a couch below them.'

The friars were motioned to a bench 'near where the ladies were sitting', and offered a choice of four different kinds of drink; they left the decision to Mangu, who gave them *terracina* (rice wine), which Rubruck considered to be like the best

Auxerre wine except that it lacked a bouquet. The interpreter found himself placed next the bar and was soon pretty drunk, 'and Mangu himself appeared to me to be tipsy'. After the usual interrogation, Rubruck asked that he and Friar Bartholomew be allowed to remain until the weather was warmer, his companion being 'so feeble that he cannot with safety to his life stand any more the fatigue of travelling on horseback'. Permission was given for them to stay for two months either in the camp or at Karakorum, and to avoid even this relatively short journey they chose to remain where they were. They were then conducted to a large and cold *yurt* which was now to be theirs.

Besides the *soi-disant* monk Sergius (for Rubruck was to discover on his homeward journey that the man was really a cloth-weaver and had never taken orders), a number of other persons figure more or less prominently in Rubruck's account of the time he spent with Mangu. There was Kutuktai, Mangu's first wife, and his second wife, Kota, with both of whom he came into frequent contact. There was also a brilliant Parisian goldsmith, Guillaume Buchier, who had been taken prisoner in Hungary in 1242, and his adopted son who was an able interpreter; but at the time of Rubruck's arrival both of these were at Karakorum, where the father was constructing an ingeniously-contrived wine-fountain for Mangu. Other characters who flit in and out of the story include Mangu's 'grand secretary' or Chancellor, Bulgai, who was a Nestorian Christian, and an Alsatian woman named Paquette who had been taken prisoner in Hungary.

The number of Christian prisoners in the camp must have been considerable, and it is believed that among them was a man of English parentage named Basil, also captured in Hungary. There was a good deal of hostility between the Nestorian Christians and those of other denominations. Rubruck mentions 'a great number of Christians – Hungarians, Alans, Ruthenians, Georgians and Armenians – none of whom had seen the sacrament since their capture; for the Nestorians would not admit them into their church, so they said, unless they were re-baptised by them'.

Sergius, although Rubruck did not at this time realize that he was an impostor, was often the source of annoyance and embarrassment to him. Rubruck caught him one day condoning Shamanist methods of divination (sometimes practised by the Nestorians too) and was much disgusted by the bad example he was setting. In Lent Sergius boasted that during the fast he was eating only on Sundays, but it was discovered that he kept hidden under the altar 'a box full of raisins, prunes and various other fruits, which he dipped into all day through when he was alone'. He also boasted that Mangu had agreed to be baptized by him on the feast of the Epiphany, but nothing came of it. 'He did many things which did not please me. Thus he made for himself a folding chair, such as bishops are wont to have, and gloves and a cap with peacock feathers. . . . He showed himself most presumptuous in his speech,' causing unnecessary trouble by denouncing the Moslems as 'low hounds' to their faces. Rubruck took a particular dislike to his finger-nails – 'rough claws, which he tried to improve with unguents,' perhaps henna. Mangu kept the friars supplied with wine, which Sergius (and indeed everyone else too) was constantly 'borrowing', allegedly to entertain guests – 'and what a martyrdom,' lamented Rubruck, 'is the charity of the poor!'

By the middle of January the cold had become almost unbearable and the friars accepted with gratitude gowns of 'papion' skins[1] sent them by Mangu. The Khan also arranged for them to move into Sergius's more comfortable *yurt*. One day the friars set out with Sergius and several of the Nestorian priests on a round of visits to various members of the royal family who, whatever their religious beliefs, usually displayed great devoutness on such occasions. First they waited on Mangu, in whose *ordu* a most unfortunate thing happened. It was a criminal offence, inviting the death penalty, for anyone to step on the threshold of the Khan's *ordu* when entering or leaving it, and of this the friars had already been warned. Poor Friar Bartholomew, still very shaky on his legs, found walking away backwards from the Khan too much for him and trod upon the threshold. He was immediately arrested and led before Bulgai, who had power to order his execution; in the end, however, the friar successfully (though untruthfully) pleaded ignorance, and was pardoned.

Meanwhile the others went on their way to the Khan's eldest son, who 'had as a master a certain Nestorian priest, David by name, a great drunkard'. The young man rose from his couch when they arrived and 'prostrated himself on the ground, striking the ground with his forehead and worshipping the cross' – one of the sacraments of the Nestorian church. From there they passed on to Kota, 'an idolater', whom they found ill in bed. Though 'so feeble that she could hardly stand on her feet', she was forced by Sergius to get up and make prostrations, and to worship the cross. Then they came to Cirina, as devout as she was ugly, who needed no goading. Finally they visited one of Mangu's discarded wives, 'whose dwelling was old and she herself little pleasing'; though an idolater, she too was ready to go through the formalities of worship. At each port of call the party had been regaled with wine, so that all the way home the priests 'sang with great howling in their drunkenness, which in those parts is not reprehensible in man or in woman.'

Kota may or may not have derived spiritual benefit from her supposed devotions, but Sergius's rough treatment of a very sick woman was, from a medical point of view, probably a mistake. Her condition steadily deteriorated, and when the royal sorcerers had failed to drive out the devil that possessed her, Mangu sent for Sergius. The monk rashly announced that if he did not cure her the Khan might cut off his head; then he panicked and implored the friars to save him. Sergius's sovereign remedy for the expulsion of devils was an infusion of finely chopped rhubarb in holy water, a purgative that loosened the bowels so spectacularly that it seemed to the Mongols a miracle; Rubruck, on the other hand, preferred bedside Bible readings to laxatives. So Kota drank Sergius's potion while Rubruck read to her from St John's Gospel, and within a few days one or other treatment had completely cured her. Sergius, who of course claimed most of the credit, took advantage of his newly-won prestige to get Mangu's permission for him to carry the cross high on the top of a lance for all the camp to see, while Rubruck accepted for his reward the offer of lessons in conversational Mongol from his patient, who may have found his regimen at all events less distasteful. A month or two later Kota had a relapse and sent for Sergius, but he refused to go

[1] *Papion* is French for baboon, but Rockhill thinks the skins were more probably those of badgers or foxes.

to her: 'She has called back the idolaters around her,' he said; 'let them cure her if they can.'

Though Mangu remained true to the faith of his fathers, Shamanism, neither racial nor religious discrimination was practised at court. His mother, who had recently died, had been a Christian, but one so broadminded that she had even founded a Moslem religious college at Bukhara.

Like many an Oriental despot, Mangu amused himself by playing one religious sect against another. It so happened that the day of the feast of Epiphany had been proclaimed by his soothsayers an auspicious one on which to hold a great feast:

> On such days first come the Christian priests with their apparel, and they pray for him and bless his cup. When they have left, the Saracen priests come and do likewise. After them come the priests of idols, doing the same. Sergius told me that Mangu believed only in the Christians, but he wanted all to pray for him. But he lied, as you shall learn hereafter, and they all follow his court as flies do honey, and he gives to all, and all believe that they are his favourites. . . .

Sometimes the Khan, if he had nothing better to do, would drop in on the church, when a gilded couch would be brought for him to recline on and he would ask to be shown the pictures in a Bible or a breviary. Kutuktai and some of her ladies also came one day, armed with gifts of money and clothing for the Christians – gifts which Rubruck would not accept for himself. After she had worshipped, 'drink was brought in – rice wine, a red wine like that of La Rochelle, and kumis. Then the lady, holding a full cup in her hand, knelt and asked a blessing, and the priests all sang with a loud voice, and she drained the cup. Likewise I and my companion had to sing when she wanted a second cup. When everyone was pretty drunk, food was brought in consisting of mutton, which was at once devoured, and then some large carp, but without salt or bread; of these I ate. And so they passed the day until evening, when the lady, already tipsy, got into her palanquin and, while the priests continued singing and howling, was driven away.'

On a later occasion – it was at Karakorum on the eve of Pentecost – Mangu ordered a great religious debate at which a Christian, a Moslem and an idolater were to put forward their respective points of view. Rubruck, who was elected to speak for the Christians, gives a full account of the proceedings, at which three of Mangu's secretaries acted as umpires. It seems to have been a surprisingly good-tempered but – like all religious discussions – an inconclusive affair. Rubruck wrote that everyone listened politely to what he had to say, but added sadly, 'no one said, "I believe; I want to become a Christian"'; during the whole of his time with Mangu he was only to baptize six persons. When the debate was at an end 'the Nestorians as well as the Saracens sang with a loud voice, while the Tuins [priests of the idolaters] kept silent.' Then, needless to add, 'they all got drunk'.

One day it was reported to the Khan that Rubruck had described him as an idolater (which of course he was), and the friar was summoned to the palace to defend himself against the charge. Mangu readily accepted his explanation that the fault lay with Rubruck's incompetent interpreter:

Then Mangu held out toward me the staff on which he leaned, saying, 'Fear not.' And I, smiling, said in an undertone, 'If I had been afraid I should not have come here.' He asked the interpreter what I had said, and the man repeated it to him. After that he began confiding to me his creed. 'We Mongols,' he said, 'believe that there is only one God, by whom we live and through whom we die. But just as God gives us the different fingers of the hand, so he gives men divers ways. God gives you the Scriptures, but you Christians do not order your lives by them. For example, they do not tell you to find fault with one another, do they?' 'No, my lord,' I said; 'but I told you from the first that I did not want to wrangle with anyone.' 'I was not referring to you personally,' he said. 'Then, too, you do not find in them that a man should depart from justice for the sake of money.' 'No, my lord,' I said, 'and truly I did not come here to obtain money; on the contrary, I have refused it when it has been offered me.' A secretary who was present confirmed this. . . . 'I don't mean you personally,' said Mangu again. 'God gave you the Scriptures, and you do not keep them. He gave us soothsayers; we do what they tell us, and we live in peace.'

Rubruck sighed. 'Had I had Moses' power to work miracles,' he wrote, 'perhaps I could have convinced him.'

While in the camp, Rubruck made the acquaintance of a Tibetan lama from whom he gathered further miscellaneous facts about China. He was told about the paper money in use there, and how the people wrote with a brush, 'making in one figure the several letters containing a whole word'; this is the earliest reference to Chinese writing in a western work. But not all the lama's tales were so factual. The man's robe was of a rich red colour (which shows that he was a Tibetan), and when Rubruck asked him where the dye came from he replied:

In the countries east of Cathay there are high rocks among which dwell creatures who have in all respects human forms except that their knees do not bend, so that they get along by some kind of jumping motion. They are not over a cubit in length, and their little bodies are all covered with hair, and they live in inaccessible caverns. The hunters of Cathay go carrying highly intoxicating mead with them, and they make cup-like holes in the rocks and fill them with this mead. . . . Then they hide themselves, and these animals come out of their caverns and taste this liquor and cry '*Chin, chin*', so they have been given a name from this cry and are called Chinchin.

Soon the Chinchin were in a drunken stupor:

Then come the hunters, who bind the sleepers' feet and hands. After that they open a vein in their necks, take out three or four drops of blood, and then release them. This blood, he told me, was most precious for colouring purple.

The story was a well-known Chinese fable, the Chinchin (*hsing-hsing*) being a Chinese gibbon. One version reads: 'Some say that when you prick it for its blood, if you ask "How much will you give me?" the *hsing-hsing* will reply, "Would two pints be enough?" In order to get more you must thrash it with a whip, and then you can get up to a gallon.' However, there really *was* a red Chinese dye, in T'ang times and even earlier, called 'gibbon's blood'; but what it was made from is not known. Many fabulous stories about China were fobbed off on travellers; King

دید که در بسیط زمین کدام شهر خوشتر است گفتند بغداد و فرمود مبارکباد آب و رقون شهری منظم نما بنهادند و قدما قورم نام کرد و ما

لایت خنای آن شهر یامی بنیز ازبلیان یام بنهادند و نماز بن یام کردند نام در صریح فرسنگ یام اس و هفت یام مراد در هر منزل نام نزل یا یدا حت

Heythum 1, of Little Armenia, for example, was told of 'a people beyond Cathay whose women had the use of reason, *like men*.'

At the end of March Mangu Khan set out with his light tents for Karakorum, Sergius and the two friars accompanying him. The Khan went there every spring and again in the autumn, at which seasons he held a great drinking festival. There was a blinding blizzard and intense cold as they passed through the mountains, and in the middle of the night Mangu sent a message begging the Christians to pray for better weather, 'for all the animals in the caravan were in danger, particularly since they were heavy with young and about to bring forth'. Then Sergius sent him incense, telling him that he himself should put it on the coals and offer it to God. I know not whether he did this,' Rubruck adds, 'but the storm, which had already lasted two days, abated on the third'.

Karakorum (meaning 'Black Camp') had been chosen by Jenghiz Khan as his military headquarters; it was Ogedei who, in 1235, created a town there with palaces and other permanent buildings. It remained the Mongol capital only until 1256, when Mangu transferred the seat of government to K'ai-p'ing-fu in south-east Mongolia – Marco Polo's Chandu and the Xanadu of Coleridge. In 1889 Russian archaeologists eventually located Karakorum. The site was partially excavated in 1948–50, when enough remains of buildings and utensils were found to establish that it had been an important trading centre and to confirm the description of it left by Rubruck. The friar, who always wrote with a refreshing lack of exaggeration, found the town,

> excluding the Khan's palace, not as big as the village of Saint Denis [near Paris], and the monastery of Saint Denis ten times larger than the palace. It has two quarters. In that of the Saracens are the markets, and here a great many Tartars gather on account of the court, which is always near this city, and of the great number of ambassadors. The other is the quarter of the Cathayans, all of whom are artisans. Besides these quarters there are great palaces for the court secretaries. There are twelve idol temples of different nations, two mahummeries [mosques] . . . and one Christian church at the very end of the city, which is surrounded by a mud wall and has four gates. By the eastern gate is sold millet and other kinds of grain; by the western, sheep and goats; by the southern, oxen and carts, and by the northern, horses.

Near the town wall on the west was a large enclosure containing the Khan's palace and other buildings, all of which stood on artificially raised mounds, and in the summer the courtyard was kept cool by water flowing in little runnels. The palace itself was 'like a church, with a nave and two aisles beyond two rows of pillars, and with three doors to the south'. Evidently, says Rockhill, it was built in purely Chinese style, and must have resembled the halls and pavilions of modern Chinese palaces; the discovery of fragments of green and yellow glazed roof-tiles in the form of dragons confirms this. The Khan sat on a couch, placed on a dais approached by two flights of steps used by his cup-bearer to ascend and descend when serving him. At Mangu's side – 'though not so high as he' – came his first wife; yet lower, on a podium to his right, were his son and brothers, and on another to his left his other wives and his daughters. The centre of the hall was

A pavilion at Karakorum

left clear for the use of ambassadors and distinguished visitors.

But the *pièce de résistance* of the palace was the great wine-fountain which Master William had just completed and which stood at the entrance, 'it being unseemly to bring skins of milk and other drinks into the palace itself'; we may leave Rubruck to describe it. It consisted, he wrote, of

> a great silver tree at whose roots are four lions of silver, each with a conduit through it, and all belching forth white mares' milk. There are also four conduits led inside the tree to its topmost branches, which are bent downwards, and on each of these is a gilded serpent whose tail twines round the tree. From one of these pipes flows wine, from another *caracosmos* [black kumis] or clarified mares' milk, from another a drink made of honey and called *boal*, and from the fourth rice wine or *terracina*. For each liquor there is a special silver bowl at the foot of the tree to receive it. At the top, between these four conduits, he made an angel holding a trumpet, and under the tree he made a vault in which a man could be hidden. Pipes go up through the heart of the tree to the angel. To begin with he made bellows, but they did not give enough wind.

> Outside the palace is a cellar in which the liquors are stored, and servants are ready to pour them in as soon as they hear the angel trumpeting. . . . So when drink is wanted, the head butler calls to the angel to blow his trumpet. Then the man concealed in the vault blows with all his might in the pipe leading to the angel, and the angel places the trumpet to his lips and blows it right loudly. The servants who are in the cellar, hearing this, pour the different liquors into the proper conduits . . . and the butlers draw them and carry them into the palace.

Contrivances such as these were often to be found in oriental courts. Herodotus mentions one, and there was a famous golden tree in the palace of the Emperor Theophilus II in Constantinople in the ninth century, in which 'lions roared and golden birds sang'. Clavijo, the Spanish ambassador to the court of Tamerlane, describes another. Villard de Honnecourt gives in his famous sketch-book a drawing (*c.* 1235) of a very simple wine-fountain, and in the Museum of Cleveland, Ohio, is an actual example of one, believed to date from the fourteenth century.

'Karakorum', wrote Sir Steven Runciman, 'was now the diplomatic centre of the world', and during the time of Rubruck's visit the Khan received embassies

LEFT *A wine fountain in use at a banquet: from an English manuscript,* C. A.D. *1400*

OPPOSITE *A 14th-century French wine fountain, decorated with gilt and enamel*

from the Greek Emperor, the Caliph, the King of Delhi and the Seljuq Sultan, as well as emirs from the Jezireh and Kurdistan and princes from Russia. King Heythum I of Little Armenia was expected daily, but he did not in fact arrive until after Rubruck had left for Europe; he too wrote an account of his experiences.

On the day of their arrival at Karakorum the friars dined 'with great rejoicing' with Master William and his Alsatian wife – a celebration dinner, perhaps, in honour of his masterpiece. The goldsmith was a great supporter of the Christian community. He had made a statue of the Virgin for the church, a silver box to hold the sacrament, and a mobile oratory decorated with religious paintings. He had even tailored certain vestments, which Rubruck was invited to bless; and he also produced, at Rubruck's request, an iron for making holy wafers. He must have been a rich man, for Mangu had paid him very handsomely for his fountain. His son now became Rubruck's invaluable interpreter. Unfortunately Master William soon afterwards fell dangerously ill, and finally nearly died as a result of drinking two cupfuls of Sergius's nostrum under the impression that it was simply holy water. Rubruck sharply rebuked the monk for this, and for a time the two men were not on speaking terms.

The friars had originally been given permission to remain with the Khan for two months only; when May came, and there had been no mention of their leaving, Rubruck thought it time to discuss the situation with him. He asked for an audience, which was granted; but Bartholomew, after his unfortunate lapse in stepping on the threshold, was not allowed to accompany him. Rubruck told Mangu that he and his companion were ready to stay indefinitely at his court, or at Batu's, if he wished it; but if they were to leave Karakorum, then he begged that they might be allowed to start on their journey before winter set in. The Khan was prepared to release them, and there was no more suggestion of their remaining with Batu's *ordu*. He was eager that a Mongol envoy should go with them to Europe, but Rubruck dissuaded him from this; a part of the way, he said, was through hostile territory, and he feared for the safety of an important official. At the last moment it was decided that poor Bartholomew was in no condition to travel, so he remained behind.

Arrogant letters for the French King from 'the One lord of Earth, inspired by the One God of Heaven' were drawn up and arrangements made for the long journey, for which provisions and a guide as far as Armenia were provided by the Khan. Finally, on 18 August 1254, Rubruck 'parted with tears' from Bartholomew and set out with his interpreter, his guide and one servant by the more northerly summer route. Though the worst part of the journey – on which, reluctantly, we must not accompany him – was made in tolerable weather, it was not until a year after leaving Karakorum that Rubruck finally reached Tripoli.[1] Here he learned to his regret that Louis had returned to France, and the Provincial of the Franciscans in Syria would not allow him to go there to report to him in person; we today, however, may perhaps benefit from this refusal, because had Rubruck been able to talk with Louis he might not have compiled so full an account of his adventures.

[1] The Tripoli in what is now the Lebanon.

CHAPTER SEVEN

The Polos and Ibn Battuta
Four Intrepid Travellers

In 1254, the year when Rubruck set out on his return journey from Karakorum, there was born in Venice a boy who was destined to become the most famous of all medieval European travellers in Asia. His father, Niccolò Polo, named the child Marco.

The most famous – but not, one may perhaps think, the greatest; it was because he left to posterity a written (dictated) record of his travels that he stole the thunder from his father and his uncle Maffeo, who made the prodigious journey to Peking twice whereas Marco accompanied them on the second occasion only. Not really the earliest – because Carpine and Rubruck, though they did not actually reach China, had also already fired the trans-Asian trail. And not even the most far-flung: for here pride of place undoubtedly belongs to the Moor, Ibn Battuta, who between the years 1325 and 1354 covered a distance which, if we include his African journeying, has been soberly estimated at not less than seventy-five thousand miles – a record unbeaten until the age of steam. What caught the fancy and stirred the imagination of Europe in Marco Polo's *Description of the World*, what set it apart from all rivals, was his account of the brilliance of the Chinese court at Peking and K'ai-p'ing-fu – places which, unfortunately, lie too far from Central Asia to warrant in this book the consideration they would otherwise merit.

There were three Polo brothers: Niccolò, Maffeo, and another Marco – all prosperous merchants. The elder Marco was one of a number of Venetians who had established warehouses at Sudak, in the Crimea, and about the year 1260 Niccolò and Maffeo, having provided themselves with a large stock of jewels, sailed there (like Rubruck a few years earlier) from Constantinople across the Black Sea, to transact business with traders from Central Asia. Doubtless it was in the hope of finding fresh markets for their wares, and perhaps also to cut the profits made by middlemen, that they decided to proceed to Sarai, on the Volga about seventy miles from its mouths, where the Khan of the Golden Horde, Barkaʿ, the successor of Batu, held his court. It was of Sarai that Chaucer, who was probably familiar with Marco's book, wrote:

HOEUCSREU HOKSVIERGE

Ci apres commence le liure de marc pol des meruailles dise la gant cr dui
er la myaynr esmaurur. Et des diuerces regions du monde
Dur sauoir la puie write de diuerses regions du mon
de. Si prenes ce liure ty et le faites lire. si y trouueres les
grandismes meruailles qui y sont escriptes. De la grut
aumene. et de perse. et des tartars. et dinde et de main
tes autres prouinces. si comme nic liure comptera p
ordres appertanent. de quoy messire marc pol. sages et
nobles citoiens de venise raconpte pour ce que il le

OPPOSITE *Niccolò and Maffeo Polo setting out from Constantinople to trade in Central Asia*

RIGHT *Hulagu Khan, the son of Tolui: from a 16th-century Persian manuscript*

At Sarray, in the land of Tartarye,
Ther dwelte a Kyng that werreyed Russye,
Thurgh which ther dyde many a doughty man.
This noble Kyng was cleped Cambyskan.[1]

Barka accepted the jewels offered him (in such circumstances one made a gift and hoped for the best), and rewarded the Polos with goods of double their value; these they were allowed to sell, and a whole year was spent in profitable trading. They were just about to return home when war broke out between Barka and his cousin Hulagu, Khan of the Levant. This prevented their taking the direct route, which lay across disputed territory; they therefore decided to head eastwards and attempt a large detour. After crossing the Volga (which Marco, who briefly describes this journey in which he took no part, calls the Tigris) they travelled for seventeen days across deserts till they came to 'a large and splendid city called Bucara [Bukhara] . . . the finest in all Persia', whose ruler, Barak, the Khan of Turkestan, had not become involved in the dispute. And here they remained, it being unsafe to go forward, pointless to return to Sarai, and apparently impossible to make the hoped-for detour.

Three years passed – years of which, sadly, we know nothing. Perhaps by the end of that time some kind of a truce had been patched up between the warring Khans, for there now arrived at Bukhara an ambassador from Hulagu on his way to his overlord, the Great Khan Kubilai, at Peking. The ambassador was amazed to find Europeans in the heart of Asia. The Great Khan, he told them, had never seen any 'Latins' and was eager to meet one; if the Polos would accompany his caravan he would guarantee them a safe journey and a warm welcome at the end of it. The two brothers were delighted at this quite unexpected opportunity, and

[1] The opening lines of the Squire's Tale, an eastern story full of magic such as one finds in the *Arabian Nights*. 'Werreyed' means 'made war against', 'Cambyskan' is 'Jenghiz Khan'; Chaucer has of course confused Jenghiz Khan with his grandson, Batu.

Bukhara: the Kalayan minaret, begun in 1127 and called the Tower of Death (see page 261)

a year later, after travelling by way of Samarkand and the oases to the north of the Takla Makan desert, they reached Peking.

Kubilai, a grandson of the half-savage Jenghiz, proved to be a very civilized man who 'had absorbed many of the best elements of Chinese culture, including something of the humanitarian spirit of Buddhism, while retaining much of the simplicity and vigour of the nomad'[1]; his mother was a Christian. He received the Polos hospitably and cross-examined them closely about the state of Europe, in particular about the Pope and the practices of the Roman Church; to all his questions the Polos replied 'well and wisely, like the wise men they were, and with a good understanding of the Tartar language', and agreed to return to Europe in the company of a Tartar ambassador to the Pope. Letters in Turki were immediately drawn up, requesting the Pope 'to send a hundred men learned in the Christian religion, well versed in the seven arts, and skilled to argue and demonstrate plainly to idolaters and those of other persuasions that their religion is utterly mistaken ... men able to show by clear reasoning that the Christian religion is better than theirs'. The Polos were also instructed to procure oil 'from the lamp that burns above the sepulchre of God in Jerusalem.'

So, provided with a passport of the kind given only to VIPs – it consisted of an inscribed tablet of gold authorizing the travellers to receive throughout the Great Khan's dominions such horses, lodging, food and guides as they required – the three emissaries mounted and took to the road. But almost immediately the Tartar ambassador fell ill and had to be left behind; the Venetians, however, continued on their way and three years later, after innumerable delays caused by bad weather and swollen rivers, reached Acre safely. It was April 1269 and they had been absent for about nine years; they arrived to find that the Pope, Clement IV, had recently died, and that his successor had not yet been elected.

The Polos asked the advice of Tedaldo Visconti, the Papal Legate to Egypt, who recommended them to wait until after the election. They therefore returned to Venice, where Niccolò found that his wife had died but that his son Marco, now fifteen, had grown into a sturdy and intelligent lad well fitted to accompany them to China. But because of endless and unedifying wranglings between the pro-French and pro-Italian cardinals the Papal throne continued to remain empty, and when two years had passed the three Polos decided to go to Acre to consult Tedaldo again. Tedaldo now advised them to delay no longer, and provided them with letters to the Great Khan explaining the situation in the Vatican.

Having visited Jerusalem to collect the sacred oil for Kubilai, the Polos set out on their long journey. But at Laias, in Lesser Armenia, news overtook them that a new Pope had at last been elected and that he was none other than their old friend Tedaldo. They swiftly retraced their steps, received at Acre the blessing of Tedaldo (now Gregory X), fresh letters and valuable gifts for the Great Khan, and two Dominican friars – 'assuredly the wisest in all the province', and one of them also a good Arabic scholar – as an interim token offering to Kubilai. It must have been at the very end of the year 1271 that the party of five – the three Polos and the two friars – finally got away from Acre.

[1] Ronald Latham, introduction to *The Travels of Marco Polo*, Penguin, 1958.

The friars may have been wise, but they were certainly lily-livered. On reaching

Laias – in other words, almost before they had started – they found themselves caught up in a little war between the Sultan of Egypt and the King of Lesser Armenia and, 'scared at the prospect of going further', promptly bolted back to Acre, leaving the intrepid Venetians to continue alone on a journey that was in fact to take them three and a half years.

The route they took may be followed on our map. Because of the unsettled state of the country they passed through Erzerum and entered what is now Persia at its extreme north-western corner. Then continuing by way of Tabriz, Kashan, Yazd and Kerman they struck the Persian Gulf at Ormuz, a famous centre of Indian trade which had not yet been transferred from the mainland to the island which now bears the name. From here they had intended to proceed by sea; but on discovering that the planks from which the local ships were constructed were not fastened together with iron nails but with wooden pegs and stitched twine, they thought better of it and chose the overland route instead. This involved returning to Kerman and making the uncomfortable crossing of the Dasht-i-Lut, the Great Sand Desert of eastern Persia which even in Curzon's day (1892) occupied a 'staring and eloquent blank' on the maps. Wells are few and far between, and 'what water there is [noted Marco] is brackish and green as meadow grass. . . . Drink one drop of it and you void your bowels ten times over.'[1]

But the Polos passed safely, though hardly agreeably, over the endless billowing seas of sand to reach Tun, where Marco interrupts his travelogue to give us his famous description of the stronghold of the Assassins (*Hashshashin*) at Mulahet (Alamut), which is in fact near Qazvin.[2] The chief of the Assassins was a certain Ala ad-Din, known to Europe as the 'Old Man of the Mountain', who ran an organization of thugs which also had a subsidiary branch in Syria:

> He had made in a valley between two mountains the biggest and most beautiful garden that was ever seen, planted with all the finest fruits in the world and containing the most splendid mansions and palaces . . . ornamented with gold and with likenesses of all that is beautiful on earth, also four conduits, one flowing with wine, one with milk, one with honey, and one with water. There were fair ladies there and damsels, the loveliest in the world, unrivalled at playing every sort of instrument and at singing and dancing. . . .

And ready, adds Marco, 'to minister to every desire'.

Into this garden the Old Man enticed small batches of carefully selected boys 'between the ages of twelve and twenty' – the cream of the local teenagers – to be trained there in the gentle art of murder. His method of enlisting recruits was to have the boys doped with hashish and then carried unconscious into his garden, where they awoke believing that they were in Paradise. When the Old Man wanted 'some great lord' assassinated he would choose a handful of promising pupils and put them through their paces with the murder of an insignificant local inhabitant. Spies reported on their performance, and those who had scored the highest marks were lavishly entertained and then sent off to do the real job. The Old Man cheered the lads on their way. If all went well, he said, they could return to Paradise; if it did not, and they were killed – why, then they would

[1] Anyone who has visited Kerman, which is still (or at all events was in 1956) outside the Pepsi-Cola zone, will sadly confirm the effect of the local water.
[2] This passage may well have been interpolated into the text by Rustichello, Marco's amanuensis.

regain it all the sooner. They couldn't lose. It was a profitable business for the Old Man, for many of his intended victims, being warned in advance, saved their lives by paying protection money.

The story, though much embroidered, was basically true but, as Marco admits, not quite up-to-date; for the Alamut headquarters, founded in the eleventh century, had been raided and destroyed by Hulagu in 1256 and Ala ad-Din killed. The Syrian branch, however, continued for a time to flourish, and in 1272, the very year the Polos were at Tun, Prince Edward of England (afterwards Edward I) narrowly escaped death in Syria at the hands of one of its members.

'And now', says Marco as he concludes his account of the Assassins, 'let us change the subject.'

The Polos next entered what today is Afghanistan and, probably passing through Herat, came to Balkh, the last outpost of the Khanate of the Levant. 'Balkh', wrote Marco, 'is a splendid city of great size. It used to be much greater and more splendid; but the Tartars and other invaders have sacked and ravaged it. . . . There were once many fine palaces and mansions of marble, which are still to be seen, but shattered now and in ruins. . . . The inhabitants worship Mahomet.'

On reaching Badakhshan Marco fell ill and the party was held up for many months; but recuperation in the good air of the nearby mountains finally restored him to health. His enforced leisure gave him time to describe the ruby mines at Lajwurd, which are still worked, and the local inhabitants of whom he wrote that the men were good archers and keen huntsmen, and that the well-to-do women padded their trousers with 'anything up to a hundred ells of pleated cotton cloth' in order to simulate the plump buttocks so much admired, then as now, by the men.

Now came the perilous crossing of the Pamirs, the 'Roof of the World', where Marco noted that 'because of the great cold' – in fact, because of the altitude – 'fire is not so bright nor of the same colour as elsewhere, and food does not cook well'. In the Pamirs he saw large quantities of the great sheep which today bears his name, *Ovis poli*, but which was not to be scientifically described until 1873. Descending the eastern slopes of the Pamirs the travellers next reached Kashgar, with its 'fine orchards and vineyards, flourishing estates' and close-fisted inhabitants.

Here Marco once again interrupts his story to write of Samarkand, which he had not visited and which lay four or five hundred miles to the west. In particular he relates the legend of the Christian church there whose builders, in the days of Chagatai Khan, had appropriated for use as the base of a pillar a big stone venerated by the local Moslems. When later, under a less sympathetic ruler, the Christians were ordered to return the stone to its rightful owners, they tried at first to offer money in compensation, but were eventually obliged to comply. 'And then the miracle happened. . . . On the day on which the stone was to be handed over, the column that rested on the stone rose up, by the will of our Lord Jesus Christ, to a height of fully three palms and stayed there as firmly as if the stone had still been underneath it. And from that day onwards the column has remained in this position. . . .'

The Great Sheep of the Pamirs, named Ovis poli *after Marco Polo*

From Kashgar the Polos followed the silk road that passed to the south of the Takla Makan desert – the road taken by Hsuan-tsang on his return journey from India. At Yarkand Marco noted the goitres which are still often to be seen there, at Khotan the fruitfulness of the oasis and the pusillanimity of its inhabitants. It was the same at Cherchen where, 'when a hostile army happens to pass through the country, the people take flight, with their wives and children and their beasts, two or three days' journey into the sandy wastes to a spot where they know there is water. . . . And I can assure you that no one can tell which way they have gone, because the wind covers their tracks with sand. . . .'

Now came the 'Great Desert of Lop, said to be so long that it would take a year to go from end to end of it'. There were, however, wells at regular intervals, but of brackish water and enough to supply only a small caravan. Like all other travellers who have crossed the vast wildernesses of Central Asia, Marco describes the will-o'-the-wisps, mirages and ghostly voices that were more feared than the real dangers: 'Yes, and even by daylight men hear these spirit voices, and often you fancy you are listening to the strains of many instruments, especially drums, and the clash of arms. For this reason bands of travellers make a point of keeping very close together. Before they go to sleep, they set up a sign pointing in the direction in which they have to travel, and round the necks of all their beasts they fasten little bells. . . .'

Still following in the footsteps of Hsuan-tsang the Polos reached Tun-huang, with its 'many abbeys and monasteries, all full of idols of various forms to which [the idolaters] make sacrifices and do great honour and reverence': the famous Caves of the Thousand Buddhas which, more than six hundred years later, were to yield up their treasures to Sir Aurel Stein and those archaeologists who followed in his steps.[1]

Beyond Tun-huang our travellers pass out of Central Asia to reach at long last Chandu, the summer palace of Kubilai Khan, and subsequently his winter palace at his capital, Cambalu (Peking). These fabulous buildings, and the luxurious and civilized life at the Chinese court, Marco painted in such glowing colours, in such heavy impasto, that many of his readers considered him a Munchausen; no doubt his figures were often exaggerated – on his return to Venice he earned the sobriquet of *Marco Milione* – but the bare facts were astonishing enough. For the first time the veil which for so long had concealed Cathay from the West had been drawn aside. Like stout Cortez when he stared at the Pacific, like Captain Neil Armstrong when he first set foot on the dusty surface of the moon, Marco, by his book, had written a new chapter of the history of mankind.

The Polos remained for seventeen years in the Far East, for Kubilai simply could not bring himself to part with his remarkable guests. Marco, young and talented, soon rose to a position of considerable importance at Court, and was sent by the Great Khan on missions which took him to southern China, Burma and probably India. At long last, however, the opportunity to return to Europe arose when Kubilai needed a reliable escort for a royal princess who was being sent as a bride to the Khan of the Levant. The journey was made by sea through the Straits of

Illuminations from an English manuscript, c. A.D. *1400*
TOP *Kubilai Khan presenting a golden authorization of passage to Niccolò and Maffeo Polo* BOTTOM *Niccolò and Maffeo Polo, on their return to China with Marco, offering papal letters to Kubilai Khan* OVERLEAF *The three Polos ferried to their ship when setting out from Venice for China in 1271*

[1] See Chapter 13.

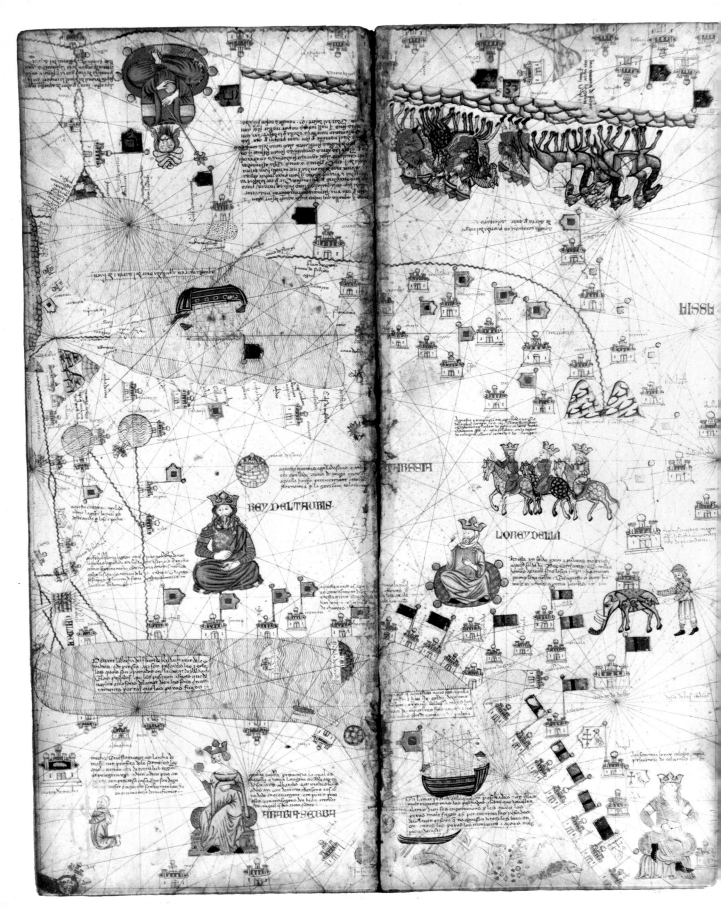

OPPOSITE *Part of the Catalan Atlas, 1375, based on information brought to Europe by the Polos*

OVERLEAF *Kubilai Khan proceeding to the hunt in a litter borne by elephants*

Singapore and across the Indian Ocean and Arabian Sea to Ormuz, continued overland to Trebizond and thence by sea again to Venice, where the Polos arrived 'in the year of the Incarnation of Christ 1295' after an absence of twenty-five years. The Princess had of course been deposited in Persia *en route*, but with the son of her intended husband, the latter having died while she was still on the high seas.

The homecoming of the Polos took their families by surprise, it having long been assumed that they were dead. Indeed they were at first denounced as impostors, for not only had they changed beyond recognition, they had acquired (wrote Ramusio[1]) 'a *je ne sais quoi* of the Tartar, both in their appearance and in their manner of speaking'. But when they produced from the pockets of their outlandish robes handfuls of jewels, they were immediately accepted as genuine and made very welcome.

Not long after his return Marco was given the command of a galley dispatched with a Venetian fleet to repel the Genoese. He was taken prisoner and brought to Genoa, where he became a nine-days' wonder and was able to dictate the story of his adventures to a fellow prisoner, a respectable literary hack from Pisa named Rustichello. Thus by a stroke of good fortune was the record of his astonishing journey preserved for the delectation of posterity. In the summer of 1299 a peace was concluded between Venice and Genoa, and after less than a year of captivity that appears to have been far from rigorous Marco returned to Venice, where he remained until his death in 1324 at about the age of seventy.

*   *   *

A year after the death of Marco Polo in Venice, a pious young Moor of Berber extraction set out from Tangier, light of heart and lighter of purse, to make the prescribed pilgrimage to Mecca. He little guessed that twenty-four years were to pass before he saw his homeland again, or that he was already suffering from an incurable disease not to be found in medical textbooks: *wanderlust*.

Abu Abdullah ibn Battuta came of a long line of *qadis* (religious judges) and had himself been educated as a theologian; when travelling in Islamic countries he was therefore much more fortunately placed than were the Polos or the Franciscan friars. He went first to Alexandria, having married two wives and twice almost dying of fever on the way. Here he was for a time the guest of an ascetic named Burhan ad-Din:

> One day when I went to his room he said to me, 'I see that you are fond of travelling through foreign lands.' I replied, 'Yes, I am' – though I had as yet no thought of going to such distant lands as India or China. Then he said, 'You must certainly look up my brother[2] Farid ad-Din in India, my brother Rukn ad-Din in Sind and my brother Burhan ad-Din in China, and when you find them give them my kindest regards.' I was amazed at his prediction, and the idea of going to these countries having been put into my head, my journeys never ceased until I had met these three that he had named and conveyed his greetings to them.

From Alexandria Ibn Battuta travelled with a caravan of pilgrims to Upper Egypt with the intention of sailing from Aydhab to Jedda. But at Aydhab he learned that because of political unrest no ships were crossing the Red Sea; he

[1] Author of a famous collection of voyages published in Venice in 1559.

[2] Spiritual Brother.

therefore went back to Cairo and from there proceeded to Syria, where he joined the Damascus caravan. The Mecca pilgrimage at an end, he crossed Arabia Deserta with the returning Baghdad caravan and continued on his way through the Bakhtiari country to Isfahan and Shiraz.

Soon it is hard work to keep pace with him. We find him in Tabriz, Baghdad again, and Mosul. He spent three whole years studying theology in Mecca and then explored the trading-stations down the east coast of Africa as far as Mombasa. Sailing to Ormuz (now established on the island) he once again crossed Arabia to perform the pilgrimage of 1332. It was then his intention to go by sea to India; but at Jedda he could find neither a suitable companion nor a suitable craft. So, almost on the spur of the moment, he decided to take a look at Anatolia, after which he crossed the Black Sea in a howling gale from Sinope to the Crimea. He was now in the territory of Sultan Muhammad Uzbek, Khan of the Blue Horde, and about to join that small and select band of medieval explorers of Central Asia.

The Golden Horde was at this time divided into the White Horde and the Blue Horde – the latter, with territory stretching from Kiev and the Caucasus to Khiva and the Aral Sea, being the more important though technically subject to the former. Muhammad Uzbek, who reigned from 1312 to 1340, was a good and capable ruler and in Ibn Battuta's opinion 'one of the seven mighty kings of the world', the other six being the lords of Morocco, Egypt, Syria, the two Iraqs, India and China.

At Qiram, in the Crimea, Ibn Battuta found that the local Governor, the Amir Tuluktumur, was about to go and pay his respects to the Khan:

So I prepared to travel with him, and hired waggons for that purpose. These waggons have four large wheels and are drawn by two or more horses, or by oxen and camels, depending upon their weight. The man who services the waggon rides one of the horses, which has a saddle on it, and carries a whip or wooden goad. On the waggon is placed a light tent made of wooden laths bound with strips of hide and covered with felt or blanket-cloth, and it has grilled windows so that the person inside can see without being seen. One can do anything one likes inside – sleep, eat, read or write – during the march.

Ibn Battuta was greatly impressed by the respect shown by the Turks to their women, who went unveiled:

The first time I saw a princess was when, on leaving Qiram, I saw the wife of the Amir Saltiya in her waggon. The entire waggon was covered with rich blue woollen cloth, and the windows and doors of the tent were open. With the princess were four maidens, exquisitely beautiful and richly dressed, and behind her were a number of waggons with maidens belonging to her suite. When she drew near the Amir's camp she alighted with about thirty of her maidens who carried her train. On her garments were loops, of which each maiden took one and lifted her train clear of the ground on all sides, and she walked in this stately manner. When she reached the Amir he rose and greeted her and placed her beside him, with her maidens standing round her. Skins of kumis were brought and she, pouring some into a cup, knelt before him and gave it to him, afterwards pouring out a cup for his brother. Then the Amir poured out a cup for her, and food was brought in and she ate with him. . .

They found Muhammad Uzbek encamped at Bishdagh, in the Caucasus, and the day after their arrival Ibn Battuta attended the ceremonial audience and banquet held by the Khan in the Golden Pavilion every Friday after the Midday Prayer. The Khan was seated on a 'wooden throne covered with silver-gilt plates, the legs being of pure silver and their bases encrusted with precious stones'. He rose to greet each of his four wives as she entered, then led her by the hand to one of the seats at his side. His sons stood below the throne and his daughters sat at his feet. 'All this takes place in view of the whole people.'

Next day Ibn Battuta called in turn on each of the Khan's wives. The first wife, Taytughli – 'the Queen, and mother of the Sultan's two sons' – he found 'sitting in the midst of ten aged women who appeared to be servants of hers, and had in front of her about fifty young slave-girls with gold and silver salvers filled with cherries which they were cleaning. The Queen also had a tray of cherries in front of her and was cleaning them.' After Ibn Battuta's Koran-reader had recited some *suras,* the Queen ordered kumis to be served. 'It was brought in light and elegant wooden bowls, and with her own hand she offered me one; this is considered among them the highest of honours. I had never drunk kumis before, but I couldn't refuse it. I tasted it, but found it unpleasant and passed it on to one of my companions.' The second wife, Kabak, was discovered reading the the Koran, but interrupted her devotions to offer her guests kumis. The third, Bayalun, was a daughter (probably illegitimate) of the Byzantine Emperor Andronicus III:

> We found her sitting on an inlaid couch with silver legs, with about a hundred slave-girls – Greek, Turkish and Nubian – standing or sitting in front of her. . . . She asked about us and about our journey, and how far we were from home, and wept in pity and compassion, wiping her face with a handkerchief that lay before her. She ordered food to be served, and we ate in her presence while she looked on. When we came to leave she said, 'Don't lose touch with us. Come and see us, and let us know if there is anything you need.' She was extremely hospitable, and afterwards sent us quantities of bread, butter, sheep and money, a magnificent robe and thirteen horses – three thoroughbreds and ten common ones.

But it was the Khan's fourth wife, Urduja, who was the most *simpatica* of all, showering Ibn Battuta with kindnesses that were exceeded only by those he received from one of the royal princesses.

After allegedly making an impossibly long excursion to the north of Bishdagh, Ibn Battuta set out with the Khan and his court for Astrakhan. Here Bayalun, who was pregnant, asked leave to go to Constantinople to have her child among her own people, and Ibn Battuta, eager to seize such a favourable opportunity to visit the great and famous Christian city at not too great risk, immediately begged the Khan to let him go too. The Khan hesitated but finally agreed. Ibn Battuta made the journey and wrote a full and interesting account of Constantinople, where he remained for five weeks. Bayalun had promised to return to her husband after her child had been born; but the temptation to remain in a Christian country was too

Mausoleum of the Samanids,
Bukhara, c. a.d. *900*
(see page 262)

great and she broke her word, leaving Ibn Battuta to go back alone. Perhaps it was fortunate that she did not have to face the journey so soon after her confinement; for it was now mid-winter, and of his crossing of the Kalmuck Steppes Ibn Battuta wrote:

> I wore three fur coats and two pairs of trousers, one of them quilted, and on my feet I had woollen boots, with a pair of boots quilted with linen cloth on top of them and on top of these again a pair of horse-skin boots lined with bear-skin. I made my ablutions with hot water close to the fire, but every drop of water froze immediately. When I washed my face the water ran down my beard and froze, and when I shook it off it fell like snow. . . . Because of the quantity of clothes that I was wearing I couldn't mount my horse, and my companions had to help me into the saddle.

He must have looked rather like an astronaut.

Ibn Battuta arrived at Astrakhan to find that the Khan had moved to his capital, Sarai. This was New Sarai, which Muhammad Uzbek had founded at a point on the Volga some one hundred and fifty miles upstream from the Sarai visited by the elder Polos on the outward journey and also by Rubruck on his way back to Europe. Ibn Battuta followed the Khan to New Sarai, which in a very short space of time had become a big and imposing city with wide streets and fine bazaars. 'One day', he wrote, 'we walked across the breadth of the town, and the double journey, going and returning, took us half a day, this too through a continuous line of houses, with no ruins and no orchards. It has thirteen principal mosques and a large number of others.' Its inhabitants were Mongols who were in part Moslems, Ossetes all of whom were Moslems, and Qipchaqs, Circassians, Russians and Greeks who were Christians.

From Sarai Ibn Battuta struck eastwards and then south to 'Khwarazm', a forty-days' journey most of which was across deserts and by camel. Khwarazm was the name given throughout the Middle Ages to the current principal town of Khoraz-mia, the district later known as Khiva, and at this time Khwarazm was Urganj. Ibn Battuta describes it as 'the largest, greatest, most beautiful and most important city of the Turks. It shakes under the weight of its population, whose movements make it look like a rough sea. One day as I was riding in the bazaar I got stuck in the crowd and couldn't go either forward or backward. I didn't know what to do, and had the greatest difficulty getting back home.'

The people of Urganj were extremely friendly and hospitable to strangers. They also had what Ibn Battuta considered 'a praiseworthy custom, which I have not come across elsewhere, in regard to the prayer-services. Each muezzin goes round the houses near his mosque and warns the occupants to attend. Anyone who absents himself is publicly beaten by the *qadi*, and for this purpose a whip is kept hanging in each mosque. In addition the culprit is fined five dinars, which go towards the upkeep of the mosque or to charity.' Ibn Battuta was so delighted with this idea that he subsequently introduced the practice into the Maldive Islands, whose inhabitants he attempted, like Christian missionaries at a later date, to 'civilize'. ('I tried also to make the [Maldive] women wear clothes,' he added, 'but I couldn't manage that.') Kutayba's method of filling his mosque was equally effective, and more humane.[1]

The Governor who ruled Urganj for Muhammad Uzbek Khan was the Amir Qutludumur. Ibn Battuta, who went to pay his respects, found him 'reclining on a silk carpet with his feet wrapped up, as he was suffering from gout – a malady very common among the Turks'. After the usual formalities, 'tables were brought in with roasted fowls, cranes, young pigeons, bread baked with butter, biscuits and sweetmeats, which were followed by other tables with fruit: pomegranates prepared for the table, some of them served in vessels of gold and silver with golden spoons, others in vessels of glass with wooden spoons, and wonderful melons'. The Amir proved as generous as his subjects, and Ibn Battuta soon had so many horses that he refrains from giving the number for fear of being thought a liar. Among them was a black horse which he favoured above all the others: 'I kept it for three years, and when it died my luck changed for the worse.'

It was an eighteen-days' journey, mostly across the deserts that bordered the Oxus, from Urganj to Bukhara, and winter had now set in. The only town through which Ibn Battuta and his caravan passed was Kait, 'which we reached after four days and pitched camp outside it beside a frozen lake on which boys were playing and sliding'. The Governor of Kait gave a banquet in honour of his guests and

[1] See page 64.

begged them to stay for a few days, but no doubt they were anxious to reach Bukhara before the weather deteriorated further.

Ibn Battuta found Bukhara 'destroyed by the accursed Tinkiz [Jenghiz] . . . and all but a few of its mosques, academies and bazaars lying in ruins. Its inhabitants are looked down upon, and their evidence [in legal cases] is not accepted in Khwarazm and elsewhere because of their reputation for fanaticism and falsehood. There is not a single person there who possesses any theological learning or who makes the slightest attempt to acquire any.' Bukhara the Noble, once famous throughout Asia for piety and scholarship, had fallen low indeed!

The 'Sultan of Turkestan, Tarmashirin', head of the Chagatai Khans, was encamped not far from Bukhara, and on his way to Samarkand Ibn Battuta made a detour to visit this important ruler, who was a devout Moslem. During his travels Ibn Battuta had purchased a number of slaves of both sexes, and that very evening one of the girls gave birth to a female child. 'She was born under a lucky star, and from that moment everything went well for me.' He stayed with the Sultan for nearly two months, and on leaving was presented by him with 'seven hundred silver dinars and a sable coat worth a hundred dinars, which I had asked of him on account of the cold, as well as two horses and two camels'.

Samarkand, even in its decay, he considered

one of the largest and most perfectly beautiful cities in the world. It is built on the bank of a river where the inhabitants promenade after the afternoon prayer. There were formerly great palaces along the bank, but most of them are in ruins, as is also much of the city itself, and it has no walls or gates. Outside the city is the grave of Qasim ibn Abbas,[1] who met a martyr's death at the conquest of Samarkand. The inhabitants go out to visit it every Sunday and Thursday night, and the Tartars also visit it, bringing large votive offerings of cattle, sheep and money, which are used for the maintenance of travellers and of the guardians of the hospice.

Now came Termez, rebuilt on a new site after the Mongol invasion and famous for its fine fruits, meats and milk. 'The inhabitants wash their heads in the bath with milk instead of with fuller's earth; the proprietor of every bath-house has large jars filled with milk, and each man as he enters takes a cupful to wash his head. It makes the hair fresh and glossy'. Balkh he found 'an utter ruin and un-inhabited, but anyone seeing it would think it inhabited on account of the solidity of its construction. The accursed Tingiz destroyed the city and demolished about a third of its [principal] mosque because of a treasure which he had been told lay under one of its columns'. He found nothing.

From Balkh Ibn Battuta travelled for a week through the mountains of Kuhistan to Herat, whose Sultan was 'the illustrious Husayn'. Illustrious, perhaps; but not, one may think, in control of his subjects. A couple of very influential local ascetics had recently taken it upon themselves to clean up the morals of the city, and hearing one day that the Sultan had been drinking they gathered together a body of six thousand men, stormed the palace and personally administered to their master the forty stripes that were the standard penalty for this offence. We learn with some satisfaction that both these killjoys were later assassinated.

Next came Meshed, with its 'noble mausoleum, surmounted by a large and ele-

[1] See page 260.

gant dome and with walls decorated with coloured tiles. Opposite the tomb [of the Imam Reza] is that of Caliph Harun al-Rashid. . . . When a Shi'ite enters the building to visit the former, he kicks the tomb of al-Rashid as he passes. . . .' There was some reason to believe – and all good Shi'ites did believe – that the Imam met his death from eating poisoned grapes given him by Harun's son.

Soon after this there must either have occurred a minor miracle or be a gap in the manuscript, for Ibn Battuta is transported in a sentence from Nishapur to Kunduz in north-eastern Afghanistan – a distance of nearly six hundred miles even as the magic carpet flies. He was heading now for India, but he delayed crossing the Hindu Kush until the worst of the winter was past; he was, incidentally, the first writer to use the name 'Hindu Kush', explaining that it meant 'Slayer of Indians' and that it was given because of the innumerable Indians who perished there from the cold on their way to slavery in Turkestan. Passing through Ghazni and Kabul, in September 1333 he reached the banks of the Indus. 'And here', he concludes, 'ends the narrative of this journey. Praise be to God, Lord of the worlds.'

A minaret of the mosque of Gawhar Shad at Meshed

But only of *this* journey, for many further years of travel still lay ahead for Ibn Battuta. He was in India for about seven years, in Ceylon (where he climbed Adam's Peak), in the Maldive Islands, in Sumatra, and in China where he was sent in 1342 as ambassador by the Sultan of Delhi. Every kind of fortune and misfortune continued to come his way. He was fêted and acclaimed, robbed and left destitute, hunted and shipwrecked. The year 1348 found him at Aleppo at the time of the first outbreak of the Black Death, of which he gives statistics that are gruesome but probably not exaggerated, and in 1349 he was back in Morocco, at long last 'laying down his staff of travel'.

Or so he imagined; but his *wanderlust* was unquenchable. There still remained two Islamic countries which he had not yet visited: Spain, and the Negrolands on the Niger. These he now proceeded to add to his bag, spending some time in Ronda and Granada and then crossing the Sahara to Timbuktu, returning to Morocco by way of the Hoggar country. At Fez he was ordered by the Sultan of Morocco to relate the story of his adventures to the Sultan's secretary, Muhammad ibn Juzayy, who entitled the resultant book *A Donation to those interested in the Curiosities of the Cities and Marvels of the Ways.* Ibn Juzayy concluded his labours on 9 December 1355 with the words:

> Here ends the narrative which I have abridged from the dictation of the Sheikh Abu Abdullah Muhammad ibn Battuta (may God ennoble him!). It is plain to any man of intelligence that this sheikh is the traveller of the age: and if one were to say 'the traveller *par excellence* of this our Moslem community' he would be guilty of no exaggeration.

A number of full texts of Ibn Battuta's great travelogue exist, one, which fell into the hands of the French after the capture of Constantine (Algeria) in 1837, being reputed to be Ibn Juzayy's holograph.

CHAPTER EIGHT

Tamerlane
His Triumph and Death

The life of Tamerlane is one long story of war, butchery and brutality unsurpassed until the present century; and since the recital of atrocities soon palls, in this chapter his military career will be dismissed in a page or so, the bulk of it being devoted to the great celebrations he held at Samarkand in 1404, and to his death the following year on his way to conquer China. The material available for this is abundant and varied: for black-and-white we have the factual report of Ruy Gonzalez de Clavijo, sent by King Henry III of Castile (son-in-law of 'time-honour'd Lancaster') on a return embassy to Tamerlane; for colour there are, principally, the Persian biography of Tamerlane by Ali Sharaf ad-Din and the Arab biography by Ahmad ibn Arabshah, both written (said Sir William Jones) 'with all the pomp and elegance of the Asiatic style' – a style so engaging that no excuse is offered for extensive quotation. Sharaf ad-Din, who wrote under the personal supervision of one of Tamerlane's grandsons, makes his hero a 'liberal, benevolent and illustrious prince', whereas ibn Arabshah can never forget that Tamerlane was 'that viper' – Marlowe's 'monster that hath drunk a sea of blood, and yet gapes still for more to quench his thirst . . .'

Tamerlane, a petty Turko-Mongol prince who claimed direct descent from Jenghiz Khan[1] through the house of Chagatai, was born at Kesh (Shahr-i-Sabz – the Green City), about fifty miles south of Samarkand, in the year 1336. When in his middle twenties he received arrow wounds (in battle, says Sharaf ad-Din; while stealing sheep, says ibn Arabshah) which left him lame in the right leg and with a stiff right arm for the rest of his life: 'Tamerlane' is the English corruption of 'Timur-i-Leng', 'Timur the Lame' – or, since 'Timur' means 'iron', 'The Iron Limper'. But Tamerlane made light of these disabilities; by 1369 he had possessed himself of all the lands which had formed the heritage of Chagatai and, after being proclaimed sovereign at Balkh, made Samarkand his capital.

During the next thirty years he extended his empire by ruthless aggression. In the eighties he seized most of Persia and drove north to Tiflis (now Tbilisi); and within a year he had advanced through Russia as far as Moscow against the Qipchaks, finally defeating their leader, Toktamish Khan, in 1395. In 1398 he conquered northern India and a year later was proclaimed Emperor of Hindustan

[1] His tomb bears an inscription asserting this.

at Delhi. In 1400 he swept into Syria to defeat the Mameluke armies at Aleppo and Damascus, and when Baghdad revolted in 1401 he destroyed the city. The year 1402 saw him in Anatolia, determined to humble the Ottoman Sultan, Bayezid I, whom he decisively defeated and took prisoner at the Battle of Ankara in July of that year, thus postponing the fall of Constantinople for half a century. In February 1404 we find him encamped with his armies on the plains of Karabagh, to the west of the Caspian; 'Never', said a chronicler, 'had been seen a camp so great or so glorious.'

For many weeks the mountain passes had been closed; and even that favoured valley, whose milder climate had more than once attracted Tamerlane to winter there, now felt the lash of the storm. An icy northern wind swept down from the Caucasus across the River Kur, powdering the Amir's great pavilions with fresh snow, bellying out the crimson walls of cloth which enclosed them and tearing at the guy-ropes. 'Sultan Winter polished his black sword and pitched his crystal tents upon the mountain-tops; his mighty winds girt the lakes with the breast-plates of David, and everything in the world, whether frozen or free, was safe from the power of Tamerlane's armies. . . .'; safe till the thaw should release that relentless torrent to flood the earth once more with the waters of its destruction.

To men longing for the coming of spring, for battle glory and fresh conquests, it seemed as if winter would never end. They passed their time in hunting and hawking; in feasting round the camp-fires, plunging their hands deep into the great leathern platters of stewed meat. Their women, who had shared with them the long marches, the hardships and even the battle honours of a four-years' campaign, tended the children and looked after the tents, milked the goats, prepared the meals, and then, when the day's work was over, took up their looms to weave the brightly coloured wools into shawls and dresses for themselves and their families.

Ibn Arabshah has drawn a vigorous and unexpectedly kindly portrait of the Amir as he appeared in old age. He was tall, strongly built and well proportioned, with a large head and broad forehead. His complexion was pale and ruddy, his beard long, his hands dry, his fingers thick, and his voice full and resonant. After mentioning his lameness he says that Tamerlane, though now approaching seventy, was still

A coin struck by Tamerlane, with BOTTOM *the three rings that formed his symbol*

steadfast in mind and robust in body, brave and fearless, firm as a rock. He did not care for jesting or lying; wit and trifling pleased him not; truth, even were it painful, delighted him. He was not cast down by adversity nor over-elated by success. The inscription of his seal was *Rasti, Rusti* – that is, *Truth is Safety*[1] – and for a brand on his beasts and centre mark on his coins he used three rings placed in this manner ⠿ . He would not tolerate obscene conversation in his presence, or talk of bloodshed or captivity, rapine, plunder or violation of the harem. He was resolute and brave, and inspired awe and obedience. He loved bold and valiant soldiers, by whose aid he opened the locks of terror, tore men to pieces like lions, and overturned mountains. He was faultless in strategy, constant in fortune, firm of purpose and truthful in business.

[1] Actually *Rasti Resti* – 'Safety is in Right'.

In a discussion he immediately seized upon the relevant points. He was immune against flattery, no lie could deceive him, and when he had once given an order he never revoked it. Thanks to an elaborate system of spies drawn from all classes of society – 'amirs, fakirs, traders, evil-minded wrestlers, criminal athletes, labourers, craftsmen, soothsayers, physicians, wandering hermits, gossips, strolling vagabonds, sailors, vagrants, elegant drunkards, witty singers, aged procuresses and crafty old women' – he was kept informed of everything that went on in his empire.

Always a keen chess-player, he had invented a more elaborate form of the game with twice the number of pieces on a board of a hundred and ten squares. Night after night in his tent, propped up against golden cushions, he would play interminable games with his boon-companions; and perhaps, as he boldly moved a knight forward into the enemy's camp or advanced his line of pawns to the attack, he was living again the great victories of the past. Now his increasing lameness and his failing sight debarred him from leading his armies into battle, but his lust for conquest was unabated. For one enemy remained: since the establishment of the national Ming dynasty in China he had been treated as a vassal; and though the allegiance was little more than nominal, and the demanded annual tribute never paid, the humiliation rankled. So he began to plot the wildest, the maddest, the most audacious campaign of his whole career: nothing less than the conquest of the Celestial Empire.

At last the thaw came; one by one the passes were reported clear of snow, and soon the army would be on the march. But before camp was struck, Tamerlane ordered preparations to be made for a great hunt. Bows were restrung, swords and lances sharpened, helmets polished and the horses fitted with their high Turkoman saddles. Then, as the long trumpets sounded, Tamerlane's lords rode out of the camp, resplendent in armour inlaid with gold, with silken cloaks fluttering in the breeze and casqued heads held high; the hunt was up. 'None so magnificent had ever been seen before. The trappings of the hounds were of satin embroidered with gold, and the hunting leopards had collars of gold set with jewels. There was an infinite number of Greek greyhounds famous for their swiftness, as well as many of other and valuable breeds; but most conspicuous of all were the European mastiffs, strong as African lions, terrible as tigers at bay, and swift as arrows.' After three days and nights the circle of beaters closed in. Three times the huntsmen drove forward to the kill, and a huge slaughter took place, the bag including lions, stags, gazelles and goats.

At the beginning of April the army set out on the long homeward journey to Samarkand:

When Nature, like a tire-woman, had decked the land in bridal garments, and the adorner of the dry earth had raised the season to its zenith; when the sap flowed again, and the mountain-tops had put on their apparel; when the fires of spring had been kindled, and serpents crawled once more; – then that Viper [Tamerlane], roused himself, and with his armies spat venom at the dead serpents of winter.

And lo! when that *Viper* began to move, the drums were beaten till the sound of them echoed like the crash of thunder; from the corslets of the soldiers the sunbeams

Using scaffold-work to build a palace for one of Bahram Gur's wives: Persian miniature, c. 1494

flashed like lightning, and the glitter of their shields threw a rainbow round the hills. Then the squadrons of his cavalry advanced in their armour, as it were dunes of sand, curvetting among the roses and fragrant herbs in that distant country. Camels strode forward, and mountains passed by like clouds; squadrons marched with spears stretched out, raising clouds of dust where they passed. . . .

Now all the land was spangled with flowers. Spring with her thunderbolts was as the lightning of his armies; her thunder was as his thunderstorms; her soft hills and groves as his couches and divans; her anemones as his banners; her flowering trees as his tents and their branches as his spears; the storms of his commands and interdicts as her winds; his black squadrons as her green sand-dunes; her blue flowers as his gleaming spears, and her rushing torrents as the surge of his army. The very fields were shaken by the tempestuous sea of his forces, and ever raged the wind of his destruction.

Thus steadily marching amid those fragrant herbs and laurels, with a mind free from care, with joy for his familiar, gladness for servant, mirth for boon-companion and hilarity for nightly gossip, he returned to Samarkand.

*   *   *

Ahead stretched a green sea topped by turquoise domes and glittering minarets: Samarkand, the chosen city of Tamerlane. Thirty-five years earlier he had found it still ruinous from the destruction wrought by the armies of Jenghiz Khan; he had then resolved to make it once again the finest city in Central Asia:

> Then shall my native city, Samarcanda . . .
> Be famous through the furthiest continents,
> For there my palace-royal shall be placed,
> Whose shining turrets shall dismay the heavens,
> And cast the fame of Ilion's tower to hell.
> Thorough the streets with troops of conquered kings,
> I'll ride in golden armour like the sun;
> And in my helm a triple plume shall spring,
> Spangled with diamonds, dancing in the air,
> To note me emperor of the threefold world. . . .
> Then in my coach, like Saturn's royal son,
> Mounted, his shining chariot gilt with fire,
> And drawn with princely eagles through the path
> Paved with bright crystal and enchased with stars,
> When all the gods stand gazing at his pomp,
> So will I ride through Samarcanda streets,
> Until my soul, dissevered from this flesh,
> Shall mount the milk-white way, and meet him there.[1]

Sarmarkand, with its population of a hundred and fifty thousand, had under his direction become a thriving city which netted half the commerce of Asia; Clavijo estimated that even without its large suburbs it was bigger than Seville. In its markets were bartered leathers and linen from Russia and Tartary; nutmegs, cloves, cinnamon and ginger from India; silks, musk and diamonds from China, and the rich produce of her own orchards, melon-beds and vineyards. Under the cool arches of its bazaars, merchants fingered rubies from Badakhshan or hag-

[1] Marlowe – *Tamburlaine the Great*, IV iv.

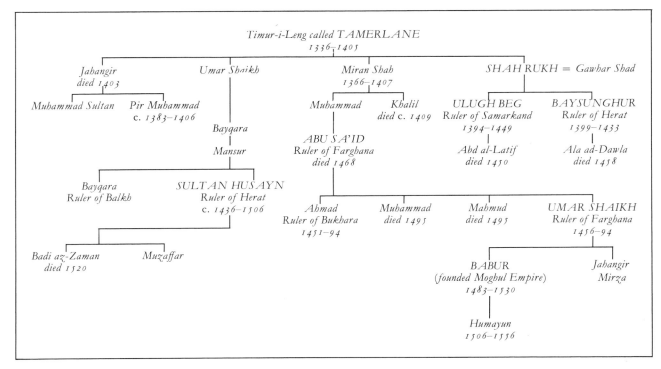

Timur-i-Leng called TAMERLANE
1336–1405

Jahangir
died 1403 — Umar Shaikh — Miran Shah
1366–1407 — SHAH RUKH = Gawhar Shad

Muhammad Sultan — Pir Muhammad
c. 1383–1406

Muhammad — Khalil
died c. 1409

ULUGH BEG
Ruler of Samarkand
1394–1449

BAYSUNGHUR
Ruler of Herat
1399–1433

Bayqara

Mansur

ABU SA'ID
Ruler of Farghana
died 1468

Abd al-Latif
died 1450

Ala ad-Dawla
died 1458

Bayqara
Ruler of Balkh

SULTAN HUSAYN
Ruler of Herat
c. 1436–1506

Ahmad
Ruler of Bukhara
1451–94

Muhammad
died 1495

Mahmud
died 1495

UMAR SHAIKH
Ruler of Farghana
1456–94

Badi az-Zaman
died 1520

Muzaffar

BABUR
(founded Moghul Empire)
1483–1530

Jahangir
Mirza

Humayun
1506–1556

gled over rare pearls from Ormuz and turquoises from the mines of Nishapur.

Now, for the ninth time, Tamerlane was returning to his capital as victor. Huddled in his silk-hung litter, he could picture in imagination that which his tired eyes could not discern – the great, swelling, melon-ribbed dome of the Gur-i-Mir, the still unfinished mausoleum designed to contain the body of his favourite grandson, Muhammad Sultan, in which, almost before the snows of the coming winter had melted, his own shrunken body would be laid; the lesser dome and the towering minarets of the congregational mosque which legend associates with the name of his favourite wife, Bibi Khanum; the roof of his palace in the moated citadel; and outside the city walls the group of mausolea known as the Shah-Zinda, or 'Living King'.

As the royal litter drew still nearer to the town, the sharp-eyed could read the Kufic inscription whose bold white letters belted the drum below the dome of the Gur-i-Mir: 'God is immortality'. Tamerlane, too, had made a bid – a mortal's bid – for immortality; if with one hand he had laid waste the great cities of Asia which had stood in the path of his ambition, with the other he had fashioned in Samarkand his enduring memorial. *Si monumentum requiris, circumspice.* Craftsmen, painters and scholars had been sent to his capital, from cities he had destroyed, to be the instruments of his grand design. There were sculptors, stone-masons and stucco-workers from Azerbaijan, Isfahan and Delhi; mosaic-workers from Shiraz; weavers, glass-blowers and potters from Damascus – in such numbers that 'the city was not big enough to hold them, and it was wonderful what a number lived under trees and in caves outside'. Elephants, brought from India with the plunder of Delhi, dragged the huge blocks of stone into position. Princes of the royal blood had been ordered to superintend the workshops so that no time might

The family of Tamerlane

OPPOSITE *Tamerlane in battle against an Indian army, whose elephants he took back to Samarkand for building mosques and tombs: a miniature from a Moghul copy of a Zafar-nama, 1546*

از طرف برانغار در آمده کمین گرفتند و چون قراول دشمن پیش آمد و ازایشان در گذشت ... روان از کمین ک برون ... شنه لوای شجاعت برافخشت

زین کو بها جست برخاست ... شمشیر غر عدد و کاسته و باشع ظفر شکار جوش شرین عین ... در طلب شکار از پس ایشان در آمد و قریب پانصد ششصد کس را به یک حمله زخاک بلاک

be lost; and Tamerlane himself, in the brief intervals of leisure between campaigns, had seldom been long absent from the building yards.

Nor were his secular buildings less splendid, though in the capital itself little trace of them remains. But at the green city of Kesh, which Tamerlane had at one time considered making his capital, he had built a palace whose ruins still give just a hint of the grandeur of their original conception. Moreover we have a contemporary description of them from the hand of Clavijo, who visited Kesh on his way to Samarkand. Though work had started on the palace twenty years earlier, Clavijo found it still incomplete. Passing through a high arched entrance and along a blue-tiled corridor flanked by guard-rooms, he entered a courtyard three hundred yards wide, paved with white flagstones and surrounded by an arcade. In the centre of this courtyard was a large pool. Before him rose the palace itself, with its great *ivan,* at least 165 feet high, and two smaller *ivans* at the sides – an arrangement which went back to Sasanian times. This central gateway was covered with gold and blue tiles and surmounted, as were the other arches also, by figures of the lion and the sun.

Through the central *ivan* came the big reception hall – a square, domed room whose walls were panelled with tiles and whose ceiling was gilded, The Moghul Emperor Babur, Tamerlane's great-great-great-grandson, who saw the hall some ninety years later, declared that there was not another in the whole world to compare with it – 'not even the Tak-i-Kisra'. This was the famous Sasanian palace at Ctesiphon, on the Tigris a few miles below Baghdad, whose gigantic ruins still astound the visitor today.[1]

'From this room', wrote Clavijo, 'we were taken up into the galleries, and in these likewise everywhere the walls were of gilt tiles. We saw indeed here so many apartments and separate chambers, all of which were adorned with tile-work of blue and gold with many others colours, that it would take too long to describe them here, and all was so marvellously wrought that even the craftsmen of Paris, so noted for their skill, would hold that which is done here to be of very fine workmanship.' Next he was shown the State apartments and the 'great banqueting hall which Tamerlane was having built wherein to feast with the princesses. This was gorgeously adorned and very spacious.' Beyond came a large garden with green lawns, pools and fruit-trees.

Such was the palace at Kesh; and we can be sure that the 'stately four-storey palace' which Babur saw in the citadel of Samarkand was no less magnificent.

The litter bearing Tamerlane had now reached one of the little country palaces which he had had built in gardens on the outskirts of the town. We know the names of a number of these pleasant retreats: the Bagh-i-chinar (plane-tree garden), the Bagh-i-buldi (garden of perfection), the Bagh-i-dilgusha (garden of the heart's delight), the Bagh-i-behisht (paradise garden), the Bagh-i-maidan (garden of the plain), the Bagh-i-shimal (northern garden) and the Bagh-i-naw (new garden).

The Bagh-i-shimal, begun in 1397, was designed by architects from Damascus – 'and what is most remarkable about these able men [wrote Sharaf ad-Din] is that with stones of different colours they made on the walls and floors designs which

[1] The vaulted hall of Ctesiphon – the greatest single span of brick ever raised by the hand of man – was 105 feet high and 150 feet deep, with a span of 84 feet. The span at Kesh would appear to have been about 74 feet.

marquetry workers had made only with ebony and ivory. . . . Afterwards workmen from Persia and Iraq decorated the outside of the walls with faience from Kashan.' Tamerlane personally supervised the building for the first six weeks, and celebrated its completion with a great feast. The Bagh-i-dilgusha lay to the east of the Turquoise Gate of Samarkand and was connected with it by an avenue lined with poplars. It had been laid out by Tamerlane in 1396 for one of his brides, Tukel Khanum. By careful planning, its palace had been finished in a few weeks, the masons and other craftsmen working throughout the night by torchlight. Later, a series of paintings illustrating Tamerlane's Indian campaign was carried out either in the palace itself or in a kiosk in the garden.

No details of the interior plan of these buildings survive, but Clavijo describes that of another of Tamerlane's Petits Trianons:

> The interior was all most richly furnished with hangings on the walls, and within there was a chamber with three arched alcoves which were sleeping-places, each with a raised dais, the walls and flooring being of coloured tiles. As you entered this chamber the largest of the three alcoves was the one facing you, and here stood a silver and gilt screen the height of a man and the breadth of three outstretched arms. In front of this screen was a bed composed of small mattresses, some covered with kincob [gold brocade], some with silk stuff worked with gold thread . . . and this was his Highness's couch. The walls here about were all hidden, being covered by rose-coloured silk hangings ornamented with spangles of silver plate gilt, each spangle set with an emerald or pearl or other precious stone.
>
> Above these wall-hangings hung strips of silk attached to which were a number of coloured silk tassels that fluttered very agreeably . . . in the draught. Everywhere the floor was covered with rugs and reed matting.

Tamerlane's litter was carried to the Bagh-i-chinar. But no sooner had he arrived there than he ordered a horse to be saddled for him; he was impatient to see how his buildings had advanced during his absence, and for all his years and infirmities he was determined to show himself to his people as a hero. Then Tamerlane 'entered Samarkand as the soul enters the body'.

That autumn Tamerlane divided his time between his building, his feasting, and his preparations for the invasion of China. He surveyed the new buildings with a critical eye, rewarding officials who had served him well and dealing summarily with those who had taken advantage of his absence to defraud him or to skimp their work. Finding the Gur-i-Mir – or perhaps some part of it – too low, he publicly reproved the architect, ordered it to be rebuilt in an impossibly short time, and later hanged the two court officials who had been left in charge. To the feast held to celebrate the completion of this building Clavijo and his suite were invited, 'since even the minnows have their place in the sea'.

For the next two months banquet succeeded banquet in a never-ending round, and the Castilian ambassador was present at no fewer than fifteen of these orgies. It was in the garden of the heart's delight, at his first audience with Tamerlane, that he and his suite[1] were introduced to the whole gamut of Tartar hospitality. They were accompanied by an Egyptian embassy and by the Tartar ambassador

[1] Clavijo writes of himself and his suite as 'the ambassadors'.

who had travelled back with them from Castile, the latter, in the dress of a Spanish *hidalgo,* affording a good deal of mirth to his friends.

Passing through a high gateway the ambassadors entered the garden, from which wardens armed with maces were vigorously excluding an inquisitive crowd. After paying their respects to several members of the royal family and handing to the appropriate officials the gifts destined for the Amir, the guests were conducted to the palace, where they found Tamerlane seated on a high dais placed under a richly embroidered canopy. In front of the dais played a fountain in whose basin red apples were floating; no doubt it was the creation of Syrian craftsmen, who were past masters in the art of designing fountains 'whose beauty they enhanced by an endless variety of sprays and jets':

> His Highness had taken his place on what appeared to be small mattresses stuffed thick and covered with embroidered silk cloth, and he was leaning on his elbow against some round cushions that were heaped up behind him. He was dressed in a cloak of plain silk without any embroidery, and he wore on his head a tall white hat on the crown of which was displayed a balas ruby, the same being further ornamented with pearls and precious stones. As soon as we came in sight of his Highness we made him our reverence, bowing and putting the right knee to the ground and crossing our arms over the breast. Then we advanced a step and again bowed, and a third time we did the same, but on this occasion kneeling on the ground and remaining in that posture. Then Tamerlane gave command that we should rise to come nearer before him, and the various lords who up to this point had been holding us under the arms now left us, for they dared not advance any nearer to his Highness.

The royal chamberlains then came forward and conducted Clavijo and his suite to the couch on which Tamerlane was sitting. Here they knelt. 'His Highness, however, commanded us to rise and stand close up to him that he might the better see us, for his sight was no longer good; indeed he was so infirm and old that his eyelids were falling over his eyes and he could barely raise them to see.'

The usual courtesies having been exchanged, the Spaniards withdrew from the dais and were led by the chamberlains to seats below that occupied by the Chinese envoy, who was also present. Observing this, Tamerlane ordered that Clavijo should be given a place above him. A lord came forward, and 'addressing that envoy from Cathay, publicly proclaimed that his Highness had sent him to inform this Chinaman that the ambassadors of the King of Spain, the good friend of Tamerlane and his son, must indeed take place above him who was the envoy of a robber and a bad man the enemy of Tamerlane, and that he his envoy must sit below us; and if only God were willing, he, Tamerlane, would before long see to and dispose of matters so that never again would any Chinaman dare come with such an embassy as this man had brought. . . . This Emperor of China', adds Clavijo, '. . . rules an immense realm, and of old Tamerlane had been forced to pay him tribute; though now, as we learnt, he is no longer willing, and will pay him nothing.'

These Chinese envoys, thought the Spaniards, did their master little credit. They came from some remote province of the empire and were dressed in out-landish costumes. The ambassador himself wore a kind of tabard of old and tattered skins, the fur being outside, while his suite 'might all have been taken for so many blacksmiths who had just left serving the forge'. But they had brought with them gifts of marten and white fox skins and some valuable falcons, and in any case seem hardly to have deserved such discourteous treatment.

Now came the serious business of eating. First, gigantic leather platters piled high with mutton and horse-meat, roasted, boiled and stewed, were dragged into the banqueting hall. The croupe of the horse, with the saddle-meat attached but the leg disjointed off, was considered the most succulent; but sheep's saddle and buttock, with the ham removed, was also a delicacy. When Tamerlane called for any particular dish, the platter was pulled along the ground – it was impossible to lift it – to within about twenty paces of where he sat. Here the carvers, dressed in aprons with leather sleeves, knelt and cut it up. The slices were placed in huge bowls of gold, silver or porcelain, laid out in rows. To each bowl were now added knots of horse-tripe in balls the size of a fist, and a whole sheep's head. Lastly, the cooks came forward with gravy and folded slices of bread. The bowls were then distributed by some of the more privileged courtiers, two or even three men being needed to lift each bowl. 'The amount of meat that was placed before us', wrote the astonished Clavijo, 'was a wonder to behold'.

When the second course – mutton stews and balls of force-meat supplemented by various side dishes – was brought in, the remains of the first were not removed, but pushed to one side for the guests to take home with them; and 'so ample was the store thus provided for our later consumption that had our servants cared to carry it all home it might have lasted us for the space of at least half a year'. Dessert followed, consisting of melons, peaches and grapes on the same lavish scale, washed down with draughts of mares' milk sweetened with sugar and served in goblets of gold and silver – 'an excellent drink that it is their custom to use during the summer season'.

A Persian miniature, c. 1400, of a giraffe – an animal that Tamerlane received as a present from the Egyptian Ambassador to his court

After this gargantuan meal was over, the gifts were brought forward and displayed. The Spanish tapestries, which one of the native chroniclers generously admitted would have put the best work of Mani[1] in the shade, came in for special praise; and the Egyptian ambassador produced a sensation with his nine ostriches, and his giraffe – the first ever seen in Samarkand – which had presumably been obliged to walk the three thousand miles from Cairo.

Such was the regular pattern of the more restrained Tartar banquet; on special occasions, however, when Tamerlane sanctioned the use of wine, it degenerated into an Asiatic orgy. It was the custom to drink before eating, and no feast, says Clavijo (who was a teetotaler), 'is considered a real festival unless the guests have drunk themselves sot'. The service was excellent – the cup-bearers, one to each two or three guests, kneeling and plying them with wine till they grew weary, when others took their places. 'The man who can swallow the most wine is by them called a *Bahadur,* a title which means "valiant drinker". Further, he who refuses to drink must be made to do so, whether he will or no.' Sometimes flagons of wine were sent to the guests beforehand, so that they might arrive at the feast already half intoxicated. At all these banquets, drunken and sober, women were allowed to be present.

[1] The great legendary Persian painter, none of whose work has survived.

Tamerlane, restless as a nomad, could not bear to remain for long in the same surroundings; he was for ever moving from palace to palace, and the Spaniards rarely saw him twice at the same spot. Towards the end of September he set up the royal pavilions by the river bank in the Kan-i-gil meadow, 'where the air is more fragrant than musk and the water sweeter than sugar, as though it were a part of the garden of Paradise which the watchman Razwan had left unguarded'; Babur refers in his Memoirs to this 'excellent meadow: the Samarkand sultans . . . always camped there each year for a month or two'. Tamerlane gave orders that everyone was to assemble here for the crowning festival of the season, the celebration of the weddings of his grandson Ulugh Beg (a boy of eleven) and five other of the royal princes.

Almost overnight the meadow was transformed into a teeming city, where 'near twenty thousand tents, pitched in regular streets' (Clavijo tells us), encircled the royal enclosures; and every day the number was swelled by more tribesmen from the outlying districts:

> Throughout the horde thus encamped, we saw the butchers and cooks passing to and fro selling their roast and boiled meats. Others purveyed barley and fruit, while bakers with their ovens alight were kneading dough and making bread for sale. Thus every craft and art needful for supply was to be found dispersed throughout the camp, and each trade was in its appointed street of the great horde. . . . There were bathing establishments whose proprietors had pitched their tents and built wooden cabins near by, each with its wooden bath supplied with hot water heated in cauldrons . . . with all the furniture necessary to their craft. Thus was all duly ordered, and each man knew beforehand his place to go.

Most splendid of all were the royal enclosures. In each of these a large square pavilion had been set up; 'from a distance, indeed, it would appear to be a castle, it is so immensely broad and high,' wrote the Spaniard. 'It is a wonder to behold, and magnificent beyond description.' These tents were nearly forty feet high, and large enough to hold ten thousand people. The centre part was circular and domed, and supported by twelve blue and gold poles, as thick as a man's chest, made of three pieces of wood artfully jointed; a windlass as big as a cart-wheel was used to hoist them. The outer part of the pavilion was supported on twenty-four smaller poles, and the whole held in position by some five hundred guy-ropes painted vermilion. Inside, each tent was lined with crimson tapestry and hung with silks worked with gold thread. Even more impressive was the roof, on which were portrayed four eagles with folded wings. The outside walls were of silk cloth woven in bands of black, white and yellow; and at the corners of the tent rose four very tall staffs, each crowned with a glittering sphere and crescent and turreted with silk battlements.

Other splendid tents were also to be seen in the royal enclosures. In one of these

> they set roofs of silver, and stairs to ascend, and doors for their houses, and couches on which to recline. . . . They also showed rare treasures, and hung there curtains of marvellous beauty. Among them was a tapestry taken from the treasury of Sultan Bayezid. . . . It was decorated with pictures of all kinds of buildings, leaves, herbs and reptiles; with figures of birds and wild beasts; with the forms of old men and young

The Mosque and Mausoleum of Hodja-Ahmed Yassevi, built by Tamerlane near the town of Turkestan

men, of women and children. There were also inscriptions painted upon it, and rareties from distant lands; joyous instruments of music; and strange beasts exactly portrayed in various colours, their limbs perfect in beauty and well articulated. So lifelike were the expressions of the faces that the figures seemed to be holding secret converse with you, and the fruits seemed to approach as though bending to be plucked. This curtain was one of the wonders of the world, yet its fame is as nought to the sight of it.

In another pavilion the ladies of the court, seated upon silken carpets, enjoyed the performances of singers, musicians and buffoons.

Each guild of craftsmen had been commanded to construct a set-piece for the occasion. In booths garlanded with flowers the jewellers displayed their necklaces of pearl and their rarest rubies, their rings and bracelets of agate, coral and rock crystal. A hundred such booths had been set up, and in each some carnival or display was offered. The cotton-workers made a minaret of cotton on a wooden framework, 'whiter than the houris of paradise' and so high that it served as a landmark for travellers approaching the city. On its summit perched a stork. All were convinced that this tower was made of bricks and mortar, until they saw that it could be moved from place to place. The mat-makers had woven in rushes a gigantic Kufic inscription. The fruiterers sold their wares to the sound of fifes and drums in a garden of artificial almond, apple and pear trees. Never had the tight-rope walkers stretched their ropes so high, or attempted such breathtaking feats.

The butchers' guild had dressed up animals as human beings, while pretty girls masqueraded as goats, sheep, fairies and winged angels. The furriers, not to be outdone, disguised themselves as leopards, lions, foxes, hyenas and tigers, to represent djin who had assumed the shape of animals. The linen-weavers displayed a 'horseman fully equipped and perfectly formed, even to the nails and eyelids'. Everything, even to the armour, bow and sword, was made of linen. Perhaps the most popular exhibit was that provided by the saddlers, who had attached to a camel a couple of litters in which the two loveliest girls of Samarkand were seated, 'posturing most delightfully, both with the hands and the feet, for the entertainment of the crowd'. On visualizes the display as the oriental equivalent of a super-production of the final scene of *Die Meistersinger*.

But there was a note of warning ever present in all this gaiety that was lacking in Nuremberg: here and there among the tents gallows had been set up, and the dangling bodies of the mayor of Samarkand, of the officials who had been left in charge of the construction of the Bibi Khanum mosque, and of a number of shop-keepers convicted of over-pricing their goods, served as a reminder that those who disobeyed Tamerlane's orders could expect no mercy. 'If the culprit be a person of rank,' says Clavijo, 'it is the custom to put him to death by hanging; but the meaner sort are beheaded' – exactly the reverse of the practice in medieval England.

> Then Tamerlane loosed for men the reins of indulgence and pleasure; every suitor hastened to his desire, and every lover to his beloved. . . . And he ordered the jacinths of red wine to be poured out upon the emerald of that verdant meadow, and made it flow for all, so that the nobles and the people alike swam in its waves. Spheres of gaiety were formed in that firmament, and on its horizon angels descended with inspiration of pleasure from the orbs of beauty; and those lions became tame and these gazelles like calves. And from the Hell of combat they went to the Paradise of loving converse, exchanging their roughness and uncouthness for charm and beauty. And now after oppression they practised courtesy and friendship. . . .
>
> Nor was the sword drawn, except the sword of contemplation – and that shattered; nor was the spear brandished, except the spear of love – and that bent by embraces; and you would have seen nothing moving save the lyre, or cups coarse and fine, or singers warbling, or young gazelles drinking, or maidens bringing drink, or flowing streams, or cheeks fragrant with roses, or the roses of the cheeks burning with love, or goblets sipped, or limbs bent to embrace, or the capture of delight, or the moment of chanting and singing. . . .
>
> Everywhere there was security, tranquillity, leisure and comfort. Grain was cheap, needs were satisfied; there was equality of fortune, justice of the Amir, health of body, fair weather, ceasing of enmity, attainment of desire, and the company of the beloved.

*   *   *

The royal astrologers had chosen 10 October as a propitious day for the weddings. The marriage contracts were drawn up, and the ceremonies performed in a crowded pavilion by Sheikh Shams ad-Din Mahmud-i-Jazri and the Chief Justice of Samarkand. Then, as the drums and trumpets sounded, handfuls of gold coins and jewels were scattered upon the six princes and princesses who knelt before the royal throne.

Pir Muhammad, Tamerlane's eldest surviving grandson, had just arrived from India, where he was viceroy, and three days after the marriage feast the Spaniards were ordered to pay their respects to him. They found a swarthy, beardless young man dressed in a fine robe of blue Chinese silk embroidered with a pattern of golden wheels; he was watching a wrestling match, and seems to have paid little attention to the foreigners. Within two years he was dead.

The Spaniards passed on to Tamerlane's great pavilion, where shortly afterwards the Amir himself arrived to witness a display. The royal elephants were brought in, their hides painted red and green, and howdahs on their backs. Clavijo, who had never seen one before coming to Samarkand, gives a gloriously naïve description of them which is unfortunately far too long for quotation. To the sound of timbrels, the bellowing animals were put through their tricks, while the servants, unperturbed, continued with their preparations for yet another feast, bringing in the wine and churning the cream and mares' milk in great skins supported on tripods.

The display was interrupted by the arrival of the Great Khanum, Tamerlane's principal wife, the daughter of Chagatai Khan and the mother of Shah Rukh. She was dressed, Clavijo tells us, in an outer robe of red silk embroidered with gold, sleeveless, cut high at the neck, and hanging loosely in ample folds. Fifteen ladies-in-waiting bore her train. Through a thin white veil could be seen her face, so smeared over with white lead that it had the appearance of a paper mask, and her jet black hair hung down freely over her shoulders. On her head was a huge set-piece consisting of a red, helmet-shaped cap with loosely hanging borders, crowned with rubies and turquoises and encircled by a gold, bejewelled wreath. Above this rose a framework displaying three gigantic balas rubies, and an ell-high white plume bound with gold wire and ornamented at its summit with a knot of white feathers set with pearls and precious stones. This plume swung forwards and downwards, so that the tip swayed in front of her face as she moved. The whole headdress was so massive and so precariously balanced that it had to be held in position by several of her ladies.

She came forward towards the tent under the shade of a parasol of white silk held high above the waving plume. Before her went a number of eunuchs, and behind her train-bearers walked three hundred of her ladies-in-waiting. Then followed Tamerlane's seven other wives and one of the princesses, all dressed and attended in the same manner as the Great Khanum. They took their places in order of precedence, each on a separate dais a little behind that upon which Tamerlane was seated.

After drinks had been served, the display was resumed. First came a troupe of acrobats; then once more the elephants, fourteen of which were made to race against horses to amuse the crowd gathered round the pavilion. When all the elephants charged abreast, it seemed to Clavijo as though the very ground shook; he was full of admiration for the great beasts, each of which he reckoned to be the equivalent of a thousand foot-soldiers on the field of battle. There followed yet another banquet. Clavijo had had more than enough of these orgies; learning that this one was to continue until dawn, he soon followed the example of one or two of the guests and slipped out of the tent unobserved.

On 17 October, the morning after a particularly drunken debauch in Tamerlane's tent, the Great Khanum gave orders for the Spaniards to be shown over her *sarapardeh* (royal enclosure). Clavijo has described in every detail the richness and variety of her pavilions. In one he noticed two large silver doors of Byzantine workmanship, decorated with figures of St Peter and St Paul, which looked strangely out of place in this pagan setting. These doors had come from Broussa (Bursa) as part of the loot taken from Bayezid. In the same tent were more gold cabinets, tables and drinking vessels, and a golden tree:

> Its trunk was as thick as a man's leg, and its spreading branches bore leaves like those of an oak. This tree rose to the height of a man; and below, it was made to appear as though its roots grew from a great dish that lay there. The fruit of this tree consisted of vast numbers of balas rubies, emeralds, turquoises, sapphires and common rubies, with many great round pearls of wonderful orient and beauty. They were set all over the tree, while numerous little birds made of gold enamel in many colours were to be seen perching on the branches. Of these, some with open wings seemed ready to fly, some with wings closed as though they had just alighted upon the twigs; others appeared about to eat of the fruits of the tree, and were pecking with their bills at the rubies, turquoises and other gems, or at the pearls which so to speak grew from the branches.

Thus October passed in unrestrained feasting by the banks of the Zarafshan, the golden river, 'amid zithers, dulcimers, lyres, organs and pipes; amid dances, zither-players, singers, and things wonderful and rare . . .' Then, when the leaves had fallen and the autumn nights grew cold upon the meadow, Tamerlane 'rolled up the carpet of pleasure' and turned his thoughts to the administration of his kingdom. Once more, wine and unlawful pleasures were prohibited. The great pavilions were dismantled and placed upon wagons, the smaller tents folded up and packed on the backs of camels, and in an endless stream the Samarkandi returned to the town. The great festival – the greatest that Asia ever knew – was at an end.

*　　　*　　　*

It was out of the generosity of his heart, so Sharaf ad-Din tells us, that Tamerlane had determined upon the conquest of China; no doubt the prospect of the spoils of Cathay also helped him to make his decision. Marching once again with those 'sisters of victory – murder, pillage, destruction, fire, captivity and loot', he was resolved to tear down the heathen idols, exterminate the idolators, and thus atone for the blood of millions of Moslems which had been shed to gratify his unbridled ambition. More than once that autumn he had been ill, and he knew that this mad adventure would be the last; he would die, then, on the *jihad,* and so pass to eternal bliss among the houris of paradise as surely as if his feet had been set upon the road to Mecca itself.

The princes and commanders listened respectfully as he unfolded his plan of campaign; 'If the Emperor unfurls his standard,' they said, 'we are his slaves. We will follow him; if need be, we will die for him.' When the news became public, everyone rose to the emergency. Provisions were laid in, tents overhauled, affairs set in order. At the arms factory in the citadel hundreds of craftsmen worked night and day to provide the great store of helms and plate armour required for the long campaign, while a thousand Turkish bow-makers and gunsmiths from Damascus fashioned the necessary cross-bows and arquebuses. The troops were mobilized, and soon two hundred thousand men stood ready to march.

Winter was rapidly approaching, but Tamerlane brushed aside the advice of his

OPPOSITE *The Bibi Khanum Mosque, Samarkand, with the* rahla *in the foreground*
OVERLEAF *Persian miniatures showing Tamerlane besieging* LEFT *Herat, and* RIGHT *Urganj*

دلاوران نموده مرد و را زخم رسید و چون اثیا زالشکرگاه همایون آورده بمعالجه مشغول
شدند ایلچی بوخا صحبت یافت و انوشروان در که شب بعد ازآن عساکر نصرت نشان برحسب
فرمان قضاجریان منجنیق ترتیب کرده بر افراختند

دبضرب سنگ قصر یوسف صوفی راخراب ساختند

*The Gur-i-Mir, Samarkand,
where Tamerlane is buried*

generals to remain in Samarkand until the spring. His mind was made up; his armies would advance northwards without delay, encamp at various points near the river Jaxartes while provisions for the campaign were being assembled, and with the first sign of spring strike towards China.

Then Winter unloosed his raging tempests, raising over the world the tents of his swirling clouds and roaring till shoulders trembled. And all serpents for fear of that cold fled for refuge to the uttermost depths of their Gehenna. Fires subsided and were quenched; lakes froze; leaves were torn from trees; avalanches rolled headlong into the abyss; lions hid in their dens and gazelles sought shelter in their lairs. The world fled to God the Avenger because of the Winter's prodigious vehemence. The face of the earth grew pale for fear of it; the cheeks of the gardens and the graceful figures of the woods turned to dust, and all their beauty and vigour vanished; the young shoots shrivelled up and were scattered by the winds.

But Tamerlane, hating the foul voices of these spirits and chilled by the breaths of these winds, ordered coverings to be prepared for the tents, and tunics doubly lined with thick cloth to be kept ready, and defended himself against the broad swords of ice and sharp spears of cold with cloaks for shields and thick shirts for breastplates. Then for a protection against the onslaught of Winter he fitted double breastplates and forged them to the measure of his burning project, and from the abundance of his supplies provided a multitude of shields. Unmindful of censure, he thought himself enough defended against the injuries of Winter by garments and all the equipment which he had had made, and said to his men: 'Fear not that Winter can harm you: truly this is refreshment and safety.'

The main army, under the personal command of Tamerlane, left Samarkand early in January on a day chosen by the astrologers as auspicious. With him went his wives and his grandchildren, his chief amirs and many of his most reliable senior officers, his battle elephants, and five hundred specially constructed iron-plate wagons to carry the baggage. Advancing by long marches in the teeth of the gale they at last reached the plain of Askulat, where Tamerlane pitched camp while the arduous task was begun of assembling the food and munitions necessary for the provisioning of his vast armies. Every general had been given strict orders to check equipment, so that no sudden shortage of essential materials should imperil their safety. By day and night, convoys of wagons dragged by weary horses and shivering soldiers struggled through the snowdrifts to the various depots which had been set up. Thousands of horses and milking camels were driven in; thousands of specially constructed carts were loaded with corn to be sown on the outward march and harvested on the return.

Never had there been seen – never, perhaps, would there be seen again – so mighty an army. Even those who had witnessed the immense and fabulous wealth of the festival at Kan-i-gil were struck dumb with astonishment. The thoughtful reflected upon the Arab proverb which proclaims that when prosperity has reached its peak it approaches a decline. Many people, when they saw the dazzling beauty of this innumerable host and the endless supply of arms and equipment that had been collected together so quickly in the imperial camp, frankly admitted that Tamerlane's glory could rise no higher; they feared, and with reason, that the tide of his fortune was about to turn, that some disaster would overtake him.

Tamerlane's forces attacking a walled town

With each day that passed the cold increased; no one could remember so terrible a winter. But Tamerlane, undaunted, gave orders for the camp to be struck; he would lead his army as far as Otrar, and there await in his palace the coming of spring. When he reached the Jaxartes he found the river covered by three feet of ice. 'So he passed over and stubbornly pushed forward.'

But Winter encompassed them with the fury of his storms, scattered against them his whirlwinds of hail, roused above them the wail of his tempests, discharged against them the full force of his freezing winds, and descending with his herald proclaimed to Tamerlane: 'Why yield to delay, caitiff; why tarry, fierce tyrant? How long shall hearts be burned by your fire, and breasts consumed by the fury of your flames? If you are one of the infernal spirits, then I am the other; we are both old, we have both grown grey in the destruction of men and countries. You should therefore read an ill omen for yourself in the conjunction of our two unfavourable planets. If you have slain souls and frozen men's breath – truly the breath of my frost is colder far than yours; if there are men among your cavalry who have plucked out the hair of Moslems with torture, pierced them with arrows and deafened them – truly in my time, by God's help, have I made men more deaf and more naked. Nor, in God's name, will I lie to you! Mark my warning, therefore, in God's name! The heat of piled coals shall not defend you from the frost of death, nor shall fire blazing in the brazier.'[1]

Then he measured over him from his store of snow, that which could split breast-plates of iron and dissolve the joints of iron rings; and sent down upon him and upon his army mountains of hail from his frosty skies, discharging in their wake typhoons of his searing winds which filled their ears and the corners of their eyes with hail and drove it into their nostrils. And thus that barren wind, which crushed and corrupted everything that crossed its path, drew forth the breath from their bodies. All around stretched the snowbound earth, like the plain of the Last Judgment or a sea of silver forged by the hand of God. When the sun rose and the frost glittered, marvellous was the sight: a sky of Turkish gems and a crystal earth, specks of gold filling the space between.

When the breath of the wind blew on the breath of man (which God forbid!) it quenched his spirit and froze him as he rode; when it blew upon the camels, the weaker died. And so it continued, till fire seemed to exhale a sweet odour of roses and give safety and refreshment to him that approached it. As for the sun, it trembled also; its eye froze and became withered. . . . When any breathed, his breath congealed on his moustache and beard and he became like Pharaoh who adorned his beard with necklaces; or if a man spat, his spittle, warm though it might be, froze to a ball before it reached the ground. The covering of life was removed from them. . . .

Therefore many of his army, both noble and base, perished. Winter destroyed both great and small among them; scorched by the cold, their noses and ears fell off; and their order was confounded. Winter ceased not to attack them, hurling against them wind and storm until, feebly wandering, they were submerged. . . .

Yet Tamerlane cared not for the dying, and grieved not for those who perished. . . .

*   *   *

At last, towards the end of January, Tamerlane reached Otrar. On the very day of his arrival an ominous event occurred: a chimney set fire to the roof of the palace. The blaze was extinguished before much damage had been done; but this pre-

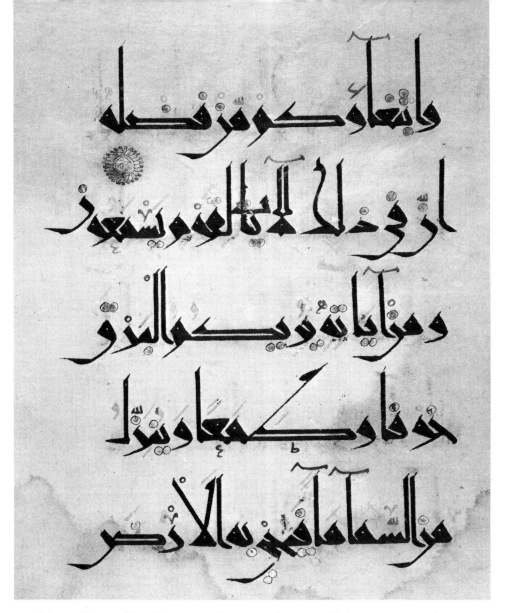

A page of an 11th-century Koran in Kufic script

monition of impending disaster, and strange dreams which were reported on every hand, troubled his family and the Court officials.

Their fears were realized. The Amir's health had suffered from the severity of the journey, and before long he was seriously ill. Yet his mind remained clear; he was in constant touch with his generals, and insisted upon being kept informed about the progress of the preparations for the spring campaign. He ordered scouts to be sent into the mountains to examine the state of the roads, and personally received their report that they were still impassable, with snow two pikes deep.

But each day he grew worse; not all the furs of Asia could now bring warmth to his chilled body, nor arrack laced with drugs and spices allay his shivering fits. When orthodox treatment had failed, his doctors attempted to drive out cold with cold, laying ice packs on his chest and belly till he 'coughed like a strangled camel and foamed like a camel dragged backwards with the rein'. Soon he began to spit blood, and the doctors were obliged to confess that all their remedies were un-availing: 'We know of no cure for death,' they said. For the first time in his life Tamerlane had encountered an adversary stronger than himself.

When he realized that he would not recover, he called his family to his bedside. 'I know that I am dying,' he said. 'Do not weep and rend your garments, but pray God to have mercy on my soul. I appoint my grandson Pir Muhammad my suc-cessor; obey him, serve him, be ready to lay down your lives for him.' Then, summoning all his amirs, lords, generals and senior officers, he required them to take the oath of allegiance in his presence. They begged to be allowed to send for those of the amirs and princes who were at Tashkent, but Tamerlane forbad it. 'There is no time,' he said sadly. 'I only wish that I could see my son Shah Rukh once more before I die, but that is . . .' – and from his parched lips came the word that no one had ever heard him utter: 'impossible'. Then, turning to his grand-children who stood sobbing by his bedside, he said: 'Remember what I have told you. Be strong. Be brave. Grasp your swords firmly in your hands, so that, like me, you may long reign over this great empire. If you quarrel among yourselves, your enemies will rise up against you; irreparable harm will come to our country, to our religion . . .'

The effort of speaking had been too much for him, and a fit of hiccups convulsed him. They stood by helpless as spasm after spasm shook his body. In an adjoining chamber the imams were reciting the Koran, and as soon as he could speak again he ordered one of the readers to approach his bedside and repeat the profession of faith. Outside a storm was raging, and the words were drowned by the roar of thunder; night fell, and the storm grew in violence.

Tamerlane lay silent now, his body wracked with pain. Through tired, half-closed eyes he watched the torchlight that flickered upon the drawn faces of the weeping, hysterical women; not even the lightning could illuminate the blackness of the roof of the great vaulted chamber where the moaning of the wind and the cries of the courtiers mingled and reverberated. Then, suddenly mustering all his remaining strength, he cried out, 'There is no god but God, and Mahomet is His Prophet.'

A great crash of thunder seemed to answer, as his body fell back upon the golden cushions.

The head of Tamerlane, reconstructed from his skull

*   *   *

In 1941 the late Professor M. M. Gerasimov, a distinguished Russian scientist, obtained permission to exhume the body of Tamerlane. He found the skeleton to be that of a 'powerfully built man who, for a Mongoloid, was of comparatively high stature (about 5 feet 8 inches)'. Examination also confirmed Tamerlane's lameness. The bodies of other Timurid princes were exhumed at the same time, and Professor Gerasimov explains in his book, *The Face Finder*, how he was able from a careful consideration of the skulls to reconstruct exact likenesses of them.

There was an old legend that if Tamerlane's body was disturbed, a greater catastrophe than any that he himself had wrought would overwhelm the world. On the very day (22 June) that the body was exhumed, Germany invaded Russia.

CHAPTER NINE

Timurid Princes and the Fifteenth-century Renaissance

A reconstructed head of Shah Rukh

Treading the Central Asian stage during the fifteenth century, ceaselessly jockeying one another to capture the leading roles, were innumerable princes of the house of Tamerlane. Among the more successful of these were, in the first half of the century, Tamerlane's youngest son, Shah Rukh, and Shah Rukh's sons, Ulugh Beg and Baysunghur; in the latter half, after a decade of anarchy, there was the Amir's great-great-grandson Sultan Husayn. During this time Samarkand and Herat became centres of a literary and artistic Renaissance which might be considered the Asiatic equivalent of the contemporary Renaissance in Europe.

This 'golden age', like that of the Italian Renaissance, had its darker side, and it is important to remember when reading what follows that the historians who recorded it found it expedient to stress the glitter and to gloss over the shadows. The Timurid princes were, and remained, Turks. There were witch-hunts and murders in Herat. Even Shah Rukh was often violent and unscrupulous, and perhaps the only reasonably stable member of the family was Ulugh Beg. Painters and poets were near enough to the throne to become involved in political intrigue.

Four years of unedifying family squabbles followed upon the death of Tamerlane, during which Pir Muhammad, his chosen successor, died before he had been able to eject the usurper, his cousin Khalil Sultan. But in 1409 Shah Rukh seized Transoxiana and made Herat his capital, leaving his son Ulugh Beg to govern Samarkand.

Shah Rukh was born about 1378, and it said that his name, which means 'King Castle', was given to him because at the moment of his birth his father was playing chess and had just 'castled'.[1] When he was nineteen his father gave him Khurasan – what is now north-east Iran and a part of Afghanistan – which he proceeded to govern from Herat. Malcolm, author of *The History of Persia* (1815), wrote that Shah Rukh 'inherited no passion for conquest'; during his reign of nearly forty years, however, he managed to expand his dominions until they came to include the whole of Persia:

> He desired not to extend, but to repair, the ravages committed by his father. He rebuilt the walls of the cities of Herat and Merv, and restored almost every town and province in his dominion to prosperity. This prince also encouraged men of science

[1] The word 'rook' (castle) is derived from the Persian. 'Check mate' is *shah mat* – 'the King is dead'.

and learning, and his court was very splendid. He cultivated the friendship of contemporary monarchs, and we read in the pages of his historian [Khondamir] a very curious account of some embassies which passed between him and the Emperor of China.

There were other embassies too – from Cairo, Constantinople and India – and soon Herat became the metropolis of Central Asia. 'From the time of Adam until this day,' wrote Dawlatshah in his florid and fulsome *Biography of the Poets,* 'no age, period, cycle or moment can be indicated in which people enjoyed such peace and tranquillity'; and a no less obsequious Turkish historian adds that 'never knowingly did Shah Rukh commit a major sin'.

To Shah Rukh's court came Persian artists, musicians, painters and calligraphers. Magnificent manuscripts were produced, illustrated with exquisite miniatures painted in the richest colours, under the patronage and often under the personal supervision of Shah Rukh and of his son Baysunghur – one of the greatest patrons of the art of the book that the world has ever seen, and himself a fine calligrapher. The Prince, who lived mostly at Herat where he acted as his father's vizir, was responsible for a new critical edition of Firdausi's famous *Shah-nama* or Book of Kings, of which a number of copies were made. Unfortunately, like so many of his family he became an alcoholic, and died when in his early thirties, fourteen years before his father, of a fall after a drunken orgy.

Ulugh Beg, Shah Rukh's eldest son, survived his father by two years and briefly occupied the throne. He was the scientist of the family, and while Shah Rukh lived was his viceroy in Samarkand, where he built an observatory that soon became world-famous.[1] Dawlatshah describes him as 'learned, just, masterful and energetic. He attained a high degree in the science of astronomy, while in rhetoric he could split hairs.' With the assistance of two other distinguished scientists he reformed the calendar, his calculations bringing him posthumous honour at Oxford, where they were published in Latin in 1652 by John Greaves, at one time Savilian Professor of Astronomy.

Dawlatshah mentions Ulugh Beg's 'fine College in Samarkand . . . in which at the present time more than a hundred students are domiciled and provided for', and which is still one of the glories of the city. He also gives an example of Ulugh Beg's powers of memory. The Prince, when hunting, kept a detailed game-book which on one occasion was temporarily mislaid. When an embarrassed courtier announced the loss, Ulugh Beg told him not to worry since he could reconstruct it from memory. This he did, and when finally the book turned up again the two lists were found to be identical. Ulugh Beg also had the royal memory for faces. Dawlatshah's uncle had been story-teller to Tamerlane, and Dawlatshah as a boy had for several years been 'the Prince's playmate in childish games, telling him tales and stories while he, after the fashion of children, became intimate with me'. Fifty years later the two met again, and Ulugh Beg immediately recognized the playmate of his childhood.

The most remarkable woman of the age was Shah Rukh's wife Gawhar Shad, the daughter of a Chagatai Turkish noble and the mother of both Ulugh Beg and Baysunghur, who rose to a position of power and authority rarely achieved in the

Ulugh Beg: a reconstructed head

[1] See page 260.

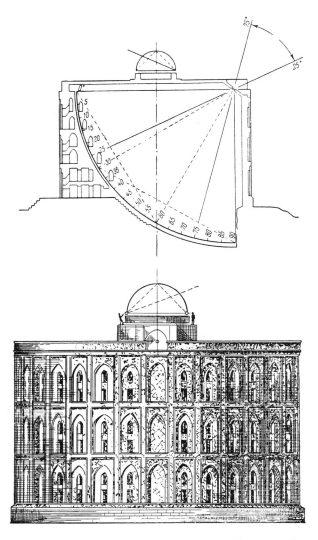

ABOVE *Reconstruction drawings of Ulugh Beg's observatory and his quadrant*

RIGHT *An allegory: the Muse Urania honouring Ulugh Beg (who is seated on her right) as one of six famous astronomers*

Non Verbis,
sed factis
ostenden-
dum quid
per actum

J.Hevelius

Propesse
agere et
cuiq;relin
quere sua
maxime
honorificu
Princ Hass

Vigilanter.

Diligenter.

Synodus Astronomorum,
qui præ Aliis Fixarum Catalogo operam dederunt.

Habet quisq.
omni tempore, quod agat.
quærat, corrigat atq. augeat.

URANIA

Posteritatis bono omnia peregi.
Prolom

Non habere sed esse
Tycho Bra

Labore et Industriâ
Ricciolus

Primus, et quousq. nostrum quilibet sublimem hanc sideralem
m omnium Creatoris Gloriam deduxerit, sincera testabitur

Catalogus Fixarum
Ptolom Ul Beigh
Tycho Princeps
Ricciol J.Hevelius

Prudenter.
Constanter.

IOHANNIS HEVELII
PRODROMUS
ASTRONOMIÆ

Moslem world except by a man. Gawhar Shad is principally remembered as the creator, together with her architect Qavam ad-Din of Shiraz, of her mosque at Meshed (1405–18), and of the group of buildings at Herat – her mosque, college and mausoleum – known collectively as the musalla (1417–37). The latter must, in its heyday, have been the noblest architectural achievement in the whole Islamic world; the mosque at Meshed falls little short of it, and what it lacks in brilliance of conception is amply compensated for by its good state of preservation. Of the buildings at Herat, only a handful of precariously poised minarets and the mausoleum of the Queen still stand.

OPPOSITE *The tomb of Gawhar Shad, Shah Rukh's wife at Herat and* BELOW *Herat: Gawhar Shad's musalla, of which only one minaret now remains*

What is so tragic is that a large part of the destruction of the musalla occurred relatively recently. Arthur Conolly of the East India Company's service, who was in Herat in 1830, wrote of 'an *iwan* built so high that the eye is strained in looking up to it', and of *twenty* minarets, one of which he climbed 'and thence looked down upon the city and the rich gardens and vineyards round and beyond it; a scene so varied and beautiful, that I can fancy nothing like it, except, perhaps, in Italy'. But in 1885 most of the musalla was wantonly demolished, probably on British advice, to avoid the possibility of its affording cover for a Russian army advancing from the north. Of the four minarets of the mosque, two were destroyed by an earthquake in 1932 and the third fell in the early fifties. A double-balconied minaret of the college of Gawhar Shad and her mausoleum are still relatively intact. Four minarets, tottering and mutilated, shedding their tiles like autumn leaves, mark the corners of the college built by Sultan Husayn in the second half of the fifteenth century.

No written description, not even the most brilliant colour photographs, can give any real impression of the beauty of the great court of the mosque at Meshed; but Byron has come as close to it as words will allow, and to attempt to improve upon what he has written would be presumptuous:

> The whole quadrangle was a garden of turquoise, pink, dark red, and dark blue, with touches of purple, green and yellow, planted among paths of plain buff brick. Huge white arabesques whirled above the ivan arches. The ivans themselves hid other gardens, shadier, fritillary-coloured. The great minarets beside the sanctuary, rising from bases encircled with Kufic the size of a boy, were bedizened with a network of jewelled lozenges. The swollen sea-green dome adorned with yellow tendrils appeared between them. At the opposite end glinted the top of a gold minaret.
>
> But in all this variety, the principle of union, the life-spark of the whole blazing apparition, was kindled by two great texts: the one, a frieze of white *suls* writing powdered over a field of gentian blue along the skyline of the entire quadrangle; the other, a border of the same alphabet in daisy white and yellow on a sapphire field, interlaced with turquoise Kufic along its inner edge, and enclosing, in the form of a three-sided oblong, the arch of the main ivan between the minarets. . . .

The latter inscription tells us that Gawhar Shad built the mosque at her own expense, and that 'Baysunghur, son of Shah Rukh, son of Timur Gurkhani [Tamerlane] wrote this inscription, with hope in God, in the year 821 [A.D. 1418]'.

It is interesting to remember how sombre and monochrome by comparison was contemporary architecture in Europe: the cool grey of the late Gothic French and

English cathedrals; the austerity of the early Renaissance buildings in Italy, such as Brunelleschi's Foundling Hospital in Florence, begun in 1419. In the art of the book, on the other hand, East and West have, if allowance be made for oriental conventions of perspective, a great deal in common. In Pol de Limbourg's *Très Riches Heures* made for the duc de Berri at the turn of the fifteenth century, and the *Shah-nama* made in 1429 for Baysunghur and now in the Gulistan Museum in Tehran, we find the same love of detail, fineness of execution and joy in bright colours; and each was commissioned by a great royal bibliophile. The title-page of this copy of the *Shah-nama* bears a calligraphic dedication which reads:

Shah Rukh brought as a child before Tamerlane at Samarkand in 1377: a miniature from a 15th-century Shah-nama

> I adorned the beauties and rarities of these verses, and arranged the pearls and jewels of these sentiments, for the library of the most mighty Sultan, Lord of the necks of the peoples, Defender of the weak places of Islam, the greatest of the Sultans of the time, Protector of the Sultanate of things temporal and spiritual, Baysunghur Bahadur Khan; may Allah perpetuate his power.

The colophon states that the text was written 'by the feeble hand of the weak Ja'far Baysunghuri' – in fact, the finest calligrapher of his day, and Baysunghur's chief librarian. The miniatures are unsigned.

One would like to know much more about Gawhar Shad. The historian Mirkhwand tells us a little, and there is a pleasant story in the *Travels* of Mohan Lal, an Indian who accompanied an English mission to Afghanistan in 1831. Mohan Lal says that on one occasion the Queen, 'accompanied by two hundred beautiful ladies', came to inspect her college at Herat. The students were of course ordered out of the building, but one of them, asleep at the time, did not receive the message:

> He awoke, and peeping fearfully through the window, beheld a ruby-lipped lady, one of the companions of Gauhar Shad. She observed the scholar, and fell in love with him, and leaving her associates, entered the room of the student. Gauhar Shad, on being informed of this, was much vexed, and to get rid of the reproach, she married all her associates to the students of the college, prescribing this rule, in order not to interrupt their studies, that they should meet their wives only once in seven days.

All this, adds Mohan Lal, she did 'to arrest the progress of adultery'.

We know that in the summer of 1419 the Queen took her husband to Meshed to see her new mosque, that he admired what he saw and presented a golden lamp to the shrine of the Imam Riza. A year or so later she visited Samarkand to inspect her son's observatory. Then for twenty-five years we hear virtually nothing of her. But in 1446 she rashly persuaded Shah Rukh, now in his late sixties, to lead an army into western Persia, and though several years older than he she insisted upon accompanying him. With them also went her grandson Abd al-Latif, Ulugh Beg's son – a dangerous young man on whom she wanted to keep an eye.

The old lady, tough like all Turks, survived unscathed the long journey and a bitter winter in camp at Rayy, just south of the present Tehran. But Shah Rukh did not, and before the snows had melted he was dead.

Now came difficult days. Gawhar Shad, who had long been involved in family intrigues, was seized by Abd al-Latif and made to follow on foot, 'with an ordinary linen scarf over her head and a staff in her hand', the litter bearing the body of her

*Ulugh Beg dispensing
justice at Khurasan:
a miniature from a 15th-
century Shah-nama*

husband back to Herat. The story becomes too confused to pursue in detail. Timurid fought Timurid; Samarkand was sacked by the Uzbeks, and most of Persia except the eastern part of the country fell into the hands of the Turkomans. Then, in 1449, Ulugh Beg was murdered by his son Abd al-Latif.

There finally emerged from this chaos of warring Timurids a Prince who in 1452 seized Samarkand and gradually extended his authority over Transoxiana, Afghanistan and northern Persia. This was yet another great-grandson of Tamerlane – Abu Sa'id, a descendant of the Amir's third son, Miran Shah. He was a patron of scholars and men of letters, but his reign was marred by an ugly crime: in 1457, while beseiging Herat, he took his great-aunt Gawhar Shad prisoner and, believing her to have encouraged the citadel to hold out, had her put to death. This spirited old octogenarian, who to the very last had a finger in every pie, may well have rallied the citizens of Herat to resist; but she deserved a better fate. She was buried in the lovely mausoleum she had built, joining other members of her family who had predeceased her, and on her tombstone was inscribed 'The Bilkis of her Age': Bilkis was the Queen of Sheba. Eleven years later her murderer fell into the hands of one of her great-grandsons, who settled an old score by having him beheaded.

Abu Sa'id was taken prisoner by the Turkomans in 1468 and executed. He was succeeded in turn by two of his sons, who ruled in Samarkand; but another, and one of the greatest of all the Timurid princes, Sultan Husayn, now obtained possession of Herat, where he ruled as an independent monarch for nearly forty years (1468–1506). It was under his beneficent direction that Herat achieved the zenith of its glory as a centre of art, literature and scholarship. Babur, a grandson of Abu Sa'id and the subject of the chapter which follows, spent several weeks with his younger brother, Jahangir, in Herat in the autumn of 1506, and it is to his Memoirs that we are indebted for an account of its buildings – he was a sightseer of almost American energy – and, more particularly, of those men who gave lustre to Sultan Husayn's glorious reign.

'His was a wonderful age,' wrote Babur. 'In it Khurasan, and above all Herat, was full of learned and matchless men. Whatever the work a man took up, he aimed and aspired at bringing that work to perfection.' And later he wrote again, 'The whole habitable world has not such a town as Herat had become under Sultan Husayn.'

Of the Prince himself we can form a clear picture, for Babur's portrait in words is supplemented by a miniature attributed to the great Bihzad himself. Babur describes Sultan Husayn as slant-eyed and 'like a lion, slim from the waist down'. Even in his white-bearded old age he wore fine silk clothes of red and green, and on his head a black lambskin cap or Turkoman bonnet; but sometimes on a feast-day he would 'set up a little threefold turban wound broadly and badly, stick a heron's plume in it and so go to prayers'. In old age arthritis prevented him from genuflecting, and he never observed the fasts. He was good company, but quick-tempered 'and with words that matched his temper'.

Of course he took to drink, and during his long reign 'there may not have been a single day on which he did not drink after the Midday prayer; but he never drank before it.' He fathered fourteen sons and eleven daughters by his wives and innumerable concubines, but of these sons only three were legitimate. That he kept catamites also goes without saying, and Bihzad's painting of him feasting in one of his palaces suggests that the party was given for the pretty boy who lolls drunkenly by his side. Thanks to the royal lead, everyone in Herat 'pursued vice and pleasure to excess'; and Babur maintains that it was the direct result of debauchery that within seven or eight years of Sultan Husayn's death his male descendants were extinct but for a single grandson.

Yet in his youth the Prince was manly and athletic, an excellent swimmer and an incomparable swordsman. But 'when once he had in his hands a town like Herat, his only concern, by day and by night, was the pursuit of ease and pleasure'. He was no mean poet, writing in Turki under the pen-name of Husayni some couplets which Babur, a good judge and an honest one, considered 'far from bad', though he regretted that Sultan Husayn stuck monotonously to a single metre. The Prince's Achilles heel, other than alcohol and sex, was his low taste for ram-fighting, cock-fighting and pigeon-flying – occupations hardly suited to a prince, though in fact Babur's own father was an enthusiastic flyer of pigeons.

Babur gives us an account of Sultan Husayn's principal wives, concubines and children. His first marriage, to the ill-tempered daughter of Sultan Sanjar of Merv, was a mistake and he quickly got rid of her; she was the mother of Badi az-Zaman, one of the two sons who were to succeed him jointly. Another of his wives was a daughter of Abu Sa'id; she blotted her copybook by refusing to leave her litter during the battle of Chikmak, when all the other ladies mounted horses and joined in the fray, and was divorced for her cowardice. A third had been a mistress of Abu Sa'id; though silly and feather-brained, she bewitched her husband, became very powerful at court, and was the mother of Muzaffar – the Prince's favourite son and other successor.

The man most directly responsible for the great flowering of the arts in Herat during the closing decades of the fifteenth century was Sultan Husayn's minister, Ali Shir Navoi. He and the Prince had been at school together, and though he was several years the younger they had become very intimate; indeed, says Babur, he remained throughout his life the friend rather than the *vizir* of the ruler.

Ali Shir, having inherited a considerable fortune, took nothing from the Prince; and being a bachelor he devoted his wealth to the good of the community. 'As a patron and protector of men of parts and accomplishments he had no equal.' He supported promising young musicians (two famous lutenists and a flautist are particularly mentioned); it was he who brought forward Bihzad, the most famous of all Persian miniature painters, and Jami, by far the greatest poet of his age. His splendid library was at the disposal of men of letters, among them the historian Mirkhwand. It is said that in Khurasan alone he erected or restored, and endowed, no less than three hundred and seventy mosques, colleges, hospitals and other public buildings. He composed music, including 'some excellent airs and preludes', and a quantity of admirable verse in Turki; but much of what he wrote in Persian, under the pen-name 'Fani', was 'flat and feeble'. His name is much revered today in Tashkent, the capital of Uzbekistan, where there is an interesting museum devoted to his memory.

A Persian poet of the late 13th century presenting a panegyric to a Mongol ruler

*Ali Shir Navoi: a Russian
woodcut made in 1968 for
a book celebrating the 525th
anniversary of his birth*

It was only to be expected that so rich and successful a Maecenas should have enemies, chief among whom was the poet Bana'i, who amused himself by inventing stories intended to make Ali Shir look ridiculous. Babur quotes the following, which seems harmless enough: 'Ali Shir, at a chess party, in stretching his leg accidentally kicked Bana'i and said jestingly, 'A plague on Herat! If you stretch your leg you kick the backside of a poet." "And so you do if you draw it up again," retorted Bana'i.' Anything new in the shops would be given Ali Shir's name to promote its sale. There was, for example, 'the Ali Shir comforter', a blue triangular handkerchief made after the pattern of one that he had been seen wearing round his head during an attack of earache. Bana'i took advantage of this vogue to get a new kind of saddle designed for his donkey and name it 'the Ali Shir ass-saddle'.

The Persian and Turkish ministers, justices, artists, poets and musicians of Sultan Husayn's court live again for us in the little thumb-nail sketches drawn by Babur. We have a glorious and almost complete set of verbal portraits of his Cabinet, which contained, among others, the following ministers (whose names may be ignored):

Mir Murtaz. Philosopher, metaphysician and chess-player. 'When he met with two persons who knew the game, while he played with one of them he would hold on to the coat-tails of the other to stop him running away.'
Badr ad-Din was 'so nimble that he could leap over seven horses at once'.
Shaikhim Beg 'wrote all sorts of verse, bringing in terrifying words and imagery. Here is one of his couplets:

> In the anguish of my nights, the whirlpool of
>   my sighs engulfs the firmament;
> Like a dragon, the torrent of my tears swallows the
>   four quarters of the world.

On one occasion he recited this couplet in the presence of Jami, who asked him whether he was reciting verse or trying to frighten people.'
Zu'n-nun. 'Brave though he was, he was a bit crazy. . . . He was orthodox and regular with his prayers, indeed he said the optional ones also. He was mad about chess but played without art, just as the fancy took him. . . . Avarice and stinginess predominated in his character.'
Khwaja Abdullah was talented and versatile, being a musician, a calligrapher and a poet, and excellent company too. 'On the dulcimer he had no equal, and had invented the shake on that instrument.' But he was a lecher and caught syphilis,[1] 'outliving his hands and feet and tasting the agonies of varied torture' for several years before his death.
Hasan of Ali. A good poet, but 'impudent and shameless, a keeper of catamites, an inveterate dicer and draughts-player'.
Muhammad i-wali was given to charity. 'He kept his servants neatly dressed, and with his own hands gave liberally to the poor and destitute; but he was foul-mouthed . . .'
Maulana Saifi of Bukhara wrote two volumes of poetry, 'one for the use of tradesmen', and a book on Persian prosody which left out everything of importance but dealt at great length with what was not. 'He is said to have been a heavy drinker, nasty in his cups, and very good with his fists'.

[1] *abla-i-farang,* 'the European's pox' – perhaps the earliest reference to syphilis in oriental literature.

Sayyid Badr. 'A very strong man, graceful of movement and with charming manners. He danced marvellously, doing one dance that was unique and, it seems, his own invention.' He was one of the Prince's boon companions.

Mir Husayn 'appears to have had no equal as a maker of riddles, and to have given his whole time to it. He was a curiously humble, disconsolate and harmless person'.

Nuyan Beg. 'A bragging, easy-going, wine-bibbing, jolly person.'

Muhammad Baranduq. 'Exceptionally intelligent, and a leader of men. He was extravagantly fond of his hawks – so much so that if one of them died or was missing he would say (naming one of his sons), "It would have been far better if *he* had died, rather than this bird."'

A Navoi medal struck at Tashkent in 1968

Two Chief Justices are also subjected to scrutiny by Babur, and both condemned – the one for wasting his life on a far-fetched, long-winded and ridiculous tale, the other for writing a mystical work in very doubtful taste entitled *Assemblies of Lovers,* in which 'the Prophets – Peace be on them! – and Saints are represented as subject to earthly passions, each being given a minion and a mistress.' Among musicians Babur mentions the lutenist Husayn, who behaved like a prima donna and had to be coaxed into playing. The Uzbek Shaybani Khan, who seized Herat in 1507, 'saw through him at once and ordered him to be well beaten on the neck, there and then.'

Of poets there was, first and foremost, Jami (1414–92) – 'one of the most remarkable geniuses whom Persia ever produced', wrote Edward Browne; 'at once a great poet, a great scholar and a great mystic.' Babur, who when at Herat piously visited his tomb (and indeed every monument, garden and beauty-spot in the city), describes him as being far beyond the need of his praise, and only introduces his name 'for luck and a blessing'. Probably Jami's best work is his *Yusuf and Zulaykha;* but his *Salaman and Absal,* for having been translated by Edward Fitzgerald, is better known in England. This translation, which has never (and rightly) attained the popularity of his version of the *Rubaiyat* of Omar Khayyam, is none the less sometimes felicitous, as the following lines from it show:

> Sun and Moon are but my Lady's
> Self, as any Lover knows;
> Hyacinth, I said, and meant her
> Hair – her Cheek was in the Rose –
> And I myself – the wretched tree
> That in her Cypress Shadow grows.

But to those who can neither read Persian or Turki nor hope to visit Herat or Meshed, some idea at all events of the splendid achievement of the Timurid Renaissance can be gauged from what are often unhappily described as a country's 'minor' arts, and in particular, of course, in this case its miniature painting. In the art of the book we find not only a vivid picture of the life of the court and illustrations to the Persian classics and the poems and romances of contemporary Herati men of letters, but also calligraphy brought to a new perfection.

The greatest of these miniature painters was Bihzad. And here, just when we might expect Babur to be helpful, he lets us down, for his account of Bihzad is brief and almost puerile: 'His work was very dainty, but he did not draw beardless faces well; he used to exaggerate the length of the double chin. But bearded faces he drew admirably.' Elsewhere he mentions that Shaybani Khan, his bitter enemy whom he often maligns, once had the impertinence to correct Bihzad's drawing: and that is all!

Experts haggle over just which miniatures are the work of the master himself. Some that bear his signature are clearly not by him; others, though unsigned, most probably are. But his *style* is at all events unmistakable, and, as with a painter like Rubens, much that was largely the work of a pupil may have received the touch of the master. Bihzad was not so much an innovator as a perfecter, and it seems safe to say that the more exquisite, subtle and refined a Timurid miniature is, the more likely it is to be by Bihzad himself or by one or two of those other Timurid artists – Qasim Ali, for example – who fell little short of him in brilliance.

In Timurid miniatures (which, it must not be forgotten, were also produced in Shiraz and other Persian towns) we find intoxicating colour combined with purity of line and delicacy of execution. Safavi miniatures of the succeeding century may be more spectacular – just as the high Renaissance paintings of Venice were more spectacular than those of fifteenth-century Florence – but they were not more perfect. Thanks to the admirable conventions of Oriental art which free the artist from the tyrannies of western perspective and the cast and formed shadow, there are no tedious empty spaces, no muddy colours, in Persian art.

The story is told of an Oriental who, on being shown a Western portrait in which the head was strongly lit from one side, asked why Europeans washed only one side of their faces. The point is well made: the whole of a face is face-coloured; why then, when painting it, dirty one side of it merely because an accident has temporarily deprived it of light? As for the conventions of perspective, since a Persian artist is allowed to make a figure in the middle distance as large as one in the foreground, or a floor stand upright like a wall, it is easy for him to render every square inch of his picture-space lively and interesting. We in the West may condescendingly find such an approach naïve; but this very naïveté is no small part of the charm of Persian miniatures.

Little is known of the latter part of Bihzad's long life. It seems that when Herat fell to the Uzbeks he stayed on there for a time; but after the defeat, four years later, of the Uzbeks by the young Shah Ismail, first of the great Safavid dynasty which ruled Persia for two centuries, he moved to Tabriz, where he probably remained until his death about 1535.

Such were the poets, painters, musicians, scholars and patrons of the arts who made Herat in the closing years of the fifteenth century the Florence of Central Asia. But it was not primarily her culture that had brought Babur to Herat in 1506; he had gone there in order to lend Sultan Husayn a hand against the Uzbeks; he arrived to find that the Prince had just died, and what he saw of his two sons and joint successors, Badi az-Zaman and Muzaffar, made him decide that they were not worth helping. 'Ten dervishes may sleep under one blanket,' he quoted from Sa'di's *Rose Garden,* 'but one country cannot contain two kings.' So he left them to their fate.

CHAPTER TEN

Babur
A Soldier of Sensibility

The Memoirs of Zahir ad-Din Muhammad – nicknamed 'Babur', 'the Tiger' – must rank among the most self-revealing of all autobiographies written before the present permissive age which has rendered it almost obligatory upon authors to strip to the buff in public; compiled towards the end of his life from notes made earlier, they have justly been described as 'fit to rank with the confessions of St Augustine and Rousseau and the memoirs of Gibbon and Newton'.

What Babur wrote carries the immediate stamp of honesty. 'I don't write this in a spirit of complaint,' he says on one occasion; 'I have simply stated the facts, with no intention of making myself come well out of the affair. . . . In these Memoirs I have rigidly adhered to my principle of getting at the truth in every case.' And just as he does not attempt to gloss over his failings (drink, for instance), so too – but with all modesty – he allows us to read between the lines his many virtues: his courage, his integrity and his loyalty; his contempt for chicanery and quackery of any kind; his generosity, hatred of meanness and rejection of wealth; and – but for his drinking – his dutiful observance of the (Sunni) tenets of Islam.

Nothing could be further removed from the euphuistic and engagingly absurd hyperboles of Arabshah and Sharaf ad-Din, the biographers of Tamerlane, than Babur's terse Turki in which (to judge from English translations) the author says exactly what he means in the plainest and fewest possible words. Nothing, also, was too trifling or too humiliating to record if he felt so inclined, and it is these tiny touches which make him so human and so modern. He mentions, for example, that he 'could not help crying a good deal' when the town in which he had spent much of his childhood was captured by his enemies. He tells us of his first shave at the age of twenty-two (though admittedly this was considered an event of some importance among the Turki); of his first sight, near Kabul, of the star Canopus – the second brightest star in the sky, but one which would not have been visible further north; of his embarrassment, at a rather smart party in Herat, at having to confess that he couldn't carve a roast goose, and of his satisfaction when the remaining half of a broken tooth finally came out one day while eating. Such trivia are endearing.

The book, as it has come down to us in various copies of the lost original manuscript, records only eighteen years of Babur's life, the longest and most regrettable

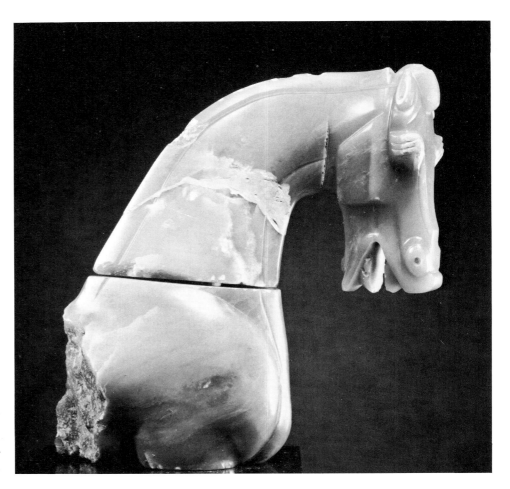

A Farghana horse, in a Chinese jade sculpture of the Han Dynasty (226 B.C. – A.D. 220) revealing that the breed was famous centuries before Farghana became the birth place of Babur

lacuna being that of the period between 1508 and 1519. There seems little doubt that what is now missing was in fact written and that some mischance befell it. Babur was perpetually on the move (he tells us, towards the end of his life, that since the age of eleven he had never kept the Feast at the end of Ramadan for two successive years in the same place); so it is perhaps more remarkable that anything of the Memoirs survives, than that a part of them has disappeared. Some of the pages may have been swept away when Babur's tent was flooded and capsized during a monsoon storm in India in 1529, for he describes how he sat up all night drying sopping sheets; others may have vanished while the original manuscript was in the possession of his son Humayun during his many campaigns and eventual flight from India.

Babur was born on 14 February 1483 in Farghana (later called Kokand), a small kingdom to the east of Samarkand of which his father, Umar Shaikh, was ruler. He was descended on his father's side from Tamerlane, on his mother's from Jenghiz Khan – those two great scourges of Asia.

The Memoirs open abruptly at the time of Umar Shaikh's death in June 1494: 'In the month of Ramadan of the year 899 and in the twelfth year of my age, I became ruler in the country of Farghana.' The boy loved Farghana with its fertile soil, its rich flora and luscious fruits (especially its melons), and its wonderful breed of horses so prized by the Chinese. He bathed in its rivers, hunted the wild ass on its hillsides and flew his hawks for pheasants so fat that one, when served with vegetables, made a meal that four men could not finish. Near Ush – a place famous for its violets, tulips and roses – there was a 'shady and delightful meadow where every passing traveller pauses to rest', whereupon (wrote Babur) 'all the urchins of Ush' would open a sluice-gate of the local river and drench them with water. The young Prince does not tell us whether or not he himself ever took a part in this pleasant, if plebeian, practical joke; but can he really have resisted?

Of his father – 'a very ambitious Prince, always bent on some scheme of conquest' – he has left us one of his characteristic portraits, vivid and unexpected as those of Aubrey:

> Umar Shaikh was short and fat, round-bearded and podgy-faced. He used to wear his tunic so tight that to tie the strings he had to draw his belly in, and when he let it out again the strings often burst. He was not particular as to what he ate or how he dressed. He wound his turban with a single fold at a time when everyone else was winding them with four. . . .

This rather unfilial description is tempered by the relation of Umar Shaikh's good qualities. He was 'a true believer and pure in the Faith', just, generous, 'affable, eloquent and sweet-spoken, daring and bold' – a tolerable archer, and so strong-fisted that he always felled his man. He was fond of poetry and recited it admirably, but – and for those days this was surprising – he was not himself a poet. The sketch concludes: 'As a young man he drank heavily, but later he cut his parties down to one or two a week. He was extremely good company. . . . Towards the end of his life he preferred *ma'jun*,[1] and under its influence often lost his head. He was of an amorous disposition and bore many a lover's mark. He played draughts a great deal, and sometimes even threw dice.'

It was not drink, drugs or draughts, however, but his passion for breeding tumbler-pigeons that brought Umar Shaikh's life prematurely to its close. Babur describes the circumstances with his customary brevity. On 8 June 1494, while tending his favourite birds in the mountain fortress of Akhsi, which he had made his capital, Umar Shaikh 'fell with his pigeons and their house, and became a falcon' – in other words, the pigeon-house collapsed and fell into the ravine, carrying the thirty-eight-year-old King of Farghana with it.

It is Babur the man, rather than Babur the warrior of innumerable and complicated campaigns, who is of interest to us today; his military career will therefore be related very briefly. Three times – in 1497, in 1500, and finally with Persian aid in 1511 – he captured Samarkand, to which, as a descendant of Tamerlane, he believed he had a hereditary right; for a brief moment he had simultaneously held Tashkent, Balkh, Kabul, Samarkand, Bukhara and Farghana. But each time he took Samarkand he was soon ejected by his most formidable enemy the Uzbeks, under another

[1] Sweetmeats containing *bhang,* etc.

A young soldier smelling perfume: from a Timurid miniature of the early 16th century

descendant of Jenghiz Khan, Shaybani Khan (d. 1510), and his successor. Far-ghana, which he loved deeply, was soon lost to him also, and 'having placed the foot of despair in the stirrup of despondency' he abandoned, for ever and 'with a sigh', the hope of recovering his kingdom, and turned his eyes towards the south.

During the first years of his reign he had often been a wanderer, outcast and homeless in the wilderness and enduring much poverty and humiliation; he had even at one moment in these 'throneless times' (as he called them) thought of cutting his losses and going off to China. But in 1504 he had managed to raise a small army and seize Kabul, which he made his capital. From there, between 1519 and 1526, he five times invaded India, on the last occasion capturing Delhi and Agra. Before his death in 1530 he had made himself absolute master of northern India, thus laying the foundations of the great Moghul (Mongol) empire which was to endure for more than three centuries under his descendants Humayun, Akbar, Jahangir, Shah Jahan, Aurangzeb, and their successors.

Babur had been betrothed at the age of five to his cousin Ayisha, Sultan Ahmad Mirza's daughter, and in 1499 they were married in Khojand; Babur was not yet seventeen, and the girl presumably a year or two younger. 'Though I did not dis-like her,' he wrote, 'this was my first marriage, and from bashfulness or modesty I used to go to her only once every fortnight or three weeks. Later on, when even the slight inclination I had felt for her had begun to wane, I became still more embarrassed. But every four or five weeks my mother used to pester me until I agreed to visit her.' It was hardly surprising that two or three years later Ayisha, after bearing him a daughter who died in infancy, walked out on her unsatisfactory husband. Babur married six further wives, and there is mention of two Circassian slaves who became recognized members of the royal household.

The immediate reason for Babur's coldness towards Ayisha would appear to be that, just at the time of his marriage, the young king was experiencing the ecstasy, agony and bewilderment of first love. The object of it was a working-class boy:

In these days, when I had time on my hands, I found myself strangely attracted to a boy in the camp bazaar whose name, curiously enough, was Baburi. I had never been in love before; indeed I did not know, even by hearsay, what love was all about. I wrote some Persian couplets, one of which ran:

Never was lover so wretched, enamoured, abashed as I now;
And never may beauty be found so cold, so disdainful as thou.

Baburi used to come to see me from time to time, but I felt so shy that I could not look him in the face; how then could I hope to entertain him with my conversation? I was so carried away, so distraught, that I could neither thank him for coming nor reproach him for leaving. One day while this passion lasted, I was walking with one or two companions down a narrow alley when I suddenly came upon Baburi face to face. The effect on me of this encounter was so overpowering that I almost fainted: I could not meet his eyes; I could not utter a single word. Overwhelmed with embar-rassment and confusion I passed on my way. A couplet of Muhammad Salih's came into my head:

Whene'er I meet my love, my bashful looks betray
My shame. My comrades stare at me; I turn my face away.

That was exactly how I felt. In the highly emotional state I was then in I used to wander at random, bare-headed and barefoot, through streets and lanes, orchards and vineyards; I was careless of others and careless of myself. . . .

Though bisexuality is endemic in the East, there is plenty of evidence to show that Babur was merely passing through a phase of homosexuality common all the world over in adolescence. He always speaks of pederasty with revulsion. There was his uncle, Sultan Mahmud Mirza, for example, of whom he wrote: 'He carried violence and vice to frantic excess, drank heavily and kept innumerable catamites. If anywhere in his land there was a pretty boy, he stopped at nothing until he had laid his hands on him; he made catamites of his begs' sons and the sons of his sons' begs. This vile practice was considered smart, and not to keep a boy a sign of rusticity.' One is left with the impression that Babur, like Alexander the Great, was not by nature very passionate or highly sexed. Of only one of his seven wives does he even go so far as to say that he liked her, adding that it was *she* who had fallen in love with *him*.

Women have been the cause of downfall of not a few kings; with Babur alcohol was a graver danger than lechery, though for some years he remained a teetotaller. The drinking of wine was of course forbidden to Moslems; but, as Gibbon observed, the wines of Shiraz had always prevailed over the law of the Prophet.

One evening during Babur's visit to Herat in 1506, Muzaffar, the younger of the two brothers who ruled jointly, took him to a party that someone was giving in a little pleasure pavilion called the Tarab-khana (House of Joy). All the guests were drinking wine 'as though it was the water of life', and when Babur's abstemiousness was noticed an attempt was made to persuade him to join in:

Although I had never so far committed the sin of drinking wine and not as yet known the pleasurable sensation of getting mildly drunk, I now felt that I would like to take the plunge and taste it. As a child, I had never wanted to drink. When, as sometimes happened, my father tried to make me, I refused; and after his death Khwaja Qazi kept me straight. Later on, when youthful lusts and sensual passion made me eager to drink wine, there was no one to press it one me – in fact, nobody realized that I desired it; so it was hard for me, though I now wanted to, to take this step.

But then it occurred to me that since the Princes were so insistent, and since we were in a town as refined as Herat, where should I drink if not here – here where all the circumstances were so exactly right. So I made up my mind to drink wine, to cross that stream. But then I realized that as I had not taken wine with Prince Badi az-Zaman, who was like an elder brother to me, he might be offended if I drank it with his younger brother. So I explained how things stood, and they accepted that my objection was reasonable and did not press me further. But it was agreed that when next I was with the two princes together I should accept wine from them jointly.

News of all this reached the ears of Qasim Beg, 'controller of the Gate' to Babur in his youth, who sent the princes a sharp message of protest 'with the result that they stopped pressing wine on me'.

OPPOSITE *Babur depicted reading by the Indian court painter, Bishan Das*

OVERLEAF *Babur making the Garden of Fidelity at Kabul: an Indian miniature, c. 1590*

The shrine of the Sufi
poet Khwaja Abdulla
Ansari, at Gazargah, near
Herat, with many fine
Timurid tombs of the first
half of the 15th century

Babur did not normally allow his attendants to drink, 'and if they ever did it was only about once a month, behind barred doors and in a state bordering on panic'. But when he accepted an invitation from Prince Badi az-Zaman to a party in the World-adorning Garden, he informed his suite that on this occasion the ban would be relaxed. So they drank – 'but taking a hundred precautions, sometimes distracting my attention and sometimes hiding their cups behind their hands'. Babur mentions more than once that he never tried to persuade an abstainer to drink, and also that it was disastrous to have drugs and drink at the same party.

It would appear that Babur's resolution held firm until he was nearly thirty; then he fell, and for many years drank both wine and arak steadily though, unlike some of his boon companions, for the most part he carried his drink well. The Memoirs are full of entries such as 'At dawn we got drunk, slept, and at the Midday Prayer rode from Istalif.' Of a water picnic during his first Indian campaign he wrote:

> We drank [arak] in the boat until the Bedtime Prayer; then, full of drink, we disembarked and, seizing torches, mounted and galloped all the way to the camp, swaying from side to side on our horses and letting the reins hang free. I must have been very drunk indeed, because when they told me this next day I hadn't the slightest recollection of it. When I got in I was extremely sick.

Drinking parties sometimes began in the morning and went on all day. One morning, after having ridden throughout the night in the countryside round Kabul, Babur arrived towards dawn at the house of a man named Tardi Beg, who was in charge of a local waterworks:

> The moment he heard me he ran out. I felt in the mood to have a private and thoroughly uninhibited party, and since it was well known that he never had any money, I gave him a hundred *shahrukhis* and told him to go and fetch wine and make everything ready. At 9 o'clock Tardi Beg brought a pitcher of wine from which we drank in turn; he was followed by Muhammad-i-qasim and Shah-zada, who had heard that he had been sent to get wine, and we invited them to join us. Tardi Beg said, 'Hul-hul Aniga wants to drink with you.' I answered, 'I've never seen a woman drink wine; ask her in.' We also invited a dervish named Shahi, and a man from the waterworks who played the rebek. We drank until the Evening Prayer on the hillside behind the conduit, and afterwards in Tardi Beg's house by lamplight until the Bedtime Prayer; the party was quite informal. Then I lay down, while the others went on to another house and continued drinking until midnight. Hul-hul Aniga came in and made a great nuisance of herself; in the end I got rid of her by pretending to be drunk.

In January 1519 Babur wrote, 'As I intended to return to obedience [i.e. to stop drinking] in my fortieth [lunar] year, I was drinking heavily now that less than a year remained.' But it was not in fact until 25 February 1527, during the last critical stages of his conquest of Hindustan, that he finally brought himself to make the great renunciation. 'The wish to cease from sin had been ever present in my mind,' he wrote, 'for my transgression had set a lasting stain upon my heart'; but it may well be that an almost successful attempt, two months earlier, to poison him, had something to do with his acting now. He was not the man to do anything by halves: after the wine had been poured on the ground, all the gold and silver flagons and cups were broken and the fragments distributed 'among deserving persons and dervishes'. Then a well was dug on the spot and an almshouse erected beside it.

A month later Babur issued a lengthy *farman*, or proclamation, full of Koranic quotations, forbidding the manufacture, sale, and consumption of wine, and three hundred of his begs, attendants and soldiers joined him in publicly taking the pledge. Though many times sorely tempted – 'for two whole years my craving for alcohol was such as often to bring me to the verge of tears', he wrote in 1529 – he never drank again; but he continued to use *ma'jun*. Inevitably there were moments when he regretted his decision:

> Renouncing wine has left me bewildered;
> I am so distraught that I do not know how to work.
> While others repent and make a vow to abstain,
> I made a vow to abstain – and now repent of it.

But it was in fact work – literary work: a verse translation from the Arabic into Turki, and no doubt the writing of his Memoirs – that most helped him to win what may well have been the hardest of all his battles.

Much of Babur's drinking had been done in gardens or beside water – 'after sunrise, under the orange-trees on the bank of the reservoir', for example. 'Beauty spots' seemed to him to cry out for a party. His deep love of nature, in particular of flowers both wild and cultivated, is evident throughout his Memoirs. Of a favourite hillside in the mountains near Kabul he wrote:

> Tulips of all sorts of colours grow in these foothills; I once counted them and found thirty-two or thirty-three different kinds. We named one the 'rose-scented' because it smelt rather like a red rose; it grows all by itself on the Shaikh's Plain, and nowhere else. Another is the hundred-petalled tulip. . . .[1]

Babur was in Kabul in 1519 in what seems to have been an exceptionally golden autumn. One day in the middle of October he visited a garden he had made there – the Garden of Fidelity. He found it

> at the height of its beauty – its lawns a sheet of clover, the leaves of the pomegranate trees turned to autumnal gold and their fruit a rich red. There were quantities of oranges, but they were not yet ripe; the pomegranates, however, were excellent.

A month later, when the autumn was further advanced, his eye was caught by 'a young apple-tree, all golden, with five or six leaves [still left] on each branch – a subject to which no painter could have done full justice'.

Babur made no fewer than ten gardens in Kabul, his favourite being the Garden of Fidelity, of which he once wrote, 'I have mentioned on a number of occasions the extent, the charm and the beauty of this garden, which is most delightfully situated . . .'; and from Agra he sent an urgent order to Kabul for the Belvedere Garden to be planted 'with the very finest young trees', for lawns to be made and borders to be set with herbs and sweet-smelling flowers.

One of the great defects of India, he found, was the lack of running water. 'I

[1] If these flowers were wild (as is implied) they cannot all have been tulips. Possibly some were ranunculuses, anemones or poppies.

Babur dictating his memoirs in a garden: an Indian miniature, c. 1605

OVERLEAF *The Fort, Kabul*

kept on thinking that it might be possible to overcome this by means of water-wheels, and that when I had decided where to live I would make a formal garden. With this in mind, a few days after arriving in Agra we crossed the Jumna to look for possible sites.' Each site examined seemed more unpromising than the last; but in the end a plot was chosen, a well sunk, trees planted, a pool made and a house built. 'So, in that charmless and disorderly Hindustan, gardens were laid out in an orderly manner, with borders and parterres everywhere, with roses and narcissi in their proper place.' The introduction of the Persian-style garden into India was one of the greatest contributions Babur made to the land of his adoption.

Soon he was getting grapes from the vines he himself had planted in the Garden of the Eight Paradises in Agra, and three years later he received young melon seedlings from a nurseryman in Balkh. Melons always reminded him of his childhood in Farghana; in a letter to a friend, written from India in February 1529, he mentions being given one, and that 'cutting and eating it so affected me that I burst into tears'.

Babur was not merely a garden-lover but an all-round naturalist and an observant geographer. The wild life of India fascinated him, and he gives a detailed account of the country's animals, especially of its birds. Of a tame parrot that he kept he reported (on the evidence of a servant) that it apparently talked *intelligently*, quoting as an example that, one very hot day when its cage was covered with a cloth, it cried, 'Uncover my face! I'm stifling.' A sixteenth-century Indian manuscript of the *Babur-nama* (Memoirs) in the British Museum contains some splendid pictures of Indian animals.

If the beauties of Nature seemed to call for a carouse, wine in its turn called for music. Tradition has it that Martin Luther, born the same year as Babur, had advocated 'Wein, Weib und Gesang'; Babur preferred 'Wein, *Natur* und Gesang'. He himself occasionally composed an air, and mentions one 'in four time' which came into his head while under the influence of *ma'jun* at Kabul. Lane-Poole, in his biography of Babur, wrote:

> His friends would gather round him under the Tal trees, among the orange-groves or beside a canal; the musicians played and they drank till they were merry. It was a rule that every man who sang a Persian song – one of Babur's own composition, sometimes – should have his glass, and everyone who sang a Turki song, another: but on rare occasions it was enacted that if a man became drunk, he must be removed, and another take his place.

Babur was a sharp critic, as is evident from his account of the music made at that party at Herat, already mentioned, at which he was tempted to drink for the first time:

> Among the musicians present were Hafiz Haji the flautist and Ghulam Shadi's younger brother who played the Babylonian harp. Hafiz Haji sang well – softly, delicately and in tune, as do the Herati. With Jahangir Mirza [Babur's brother] was a Samarkandi singer, Mir Jan, whose voice was loud and strident and who always sang out of tune. The Mirza, who had had plenty to drink, ordered him to sing, and sing he did: loudly, harshly and vulgarly. The Khurasani are well bred, but one of the

The Mosque of Khwaja Abu Nasr Parsa, built at Balkh in the late 15th century

guests stopped his ears and another frowned; yet out of respect for the Mirza nobody ventured to stop him.

*   *   *

That Tamerlane should have been brutal and callous – it has been estimated that he was responsible for the death of seventeen million men, women and children, many of them massacred with indescribable brutality – causes us little surprise. It comes, however, as something of a shock to find Babur, nature-lover and poet, collecting tulips one day and impaling Afghan prisoners the next; and one might have expected him to have outgrown that unpleasant Mongol habit of making pyramids of human skulls. There are also too many slit noses and floggings to death for petty looting for our present taste. But in general, what was done by his orders was far less horrible than the tortures of the Inquisition or the burnings of Tudor England, and on the one occasion when he mentions acting with almost western severity he had certainly been much provoked.

It occurred in Hindustan in December 1526. Babur, curious to sample Indian dishes, had engaged four native cooks, one of whom allowed himself to be bribed by an 'ill-omened old woman' (an Afghan who – quite unreasonably, as it happened – bore Babur a grudge) to poison his food. The tasters, who sampled the food in the pot, failed to see the poison being added to the dish as it was served:

> On Friday, late after the Afternoon Prayer, I ate a good deal of a dish of hare and also a lot of fried carrots, then took a few mouthfuls of the poisoned Hindustani food without noticing any unpleasant taste, and a mouthful or two of dried meat. I immediately felt sick; but as some dried meat I had eaten the day before had tasted nasty, I thought that that was the cause of my nausea. Again and again my stomach rose, and after retching two or three times I was nearly sick on the table-cloth. At last I had to get up and go, retching all the way, to the water-closet [ab-khana, water-room], where I vomited a great deal. Since eating, even drinking, had never made me sick before,[1] my suspicions were aroused; so I had the cooks arrested, and ordered some of the vomit to be given to one of the dogs and its reactions watched.
>
> The dog was rather out-of-sorts early next morning; its belly was swollen, and however much people threw stones at it or rolled it over it did not get up. It remained like that till midday, then rose and did not die. One or two of my men who had also eaten of that dish vomited a lot next day and one of them was very ill indeed, but all recovered in the end. I ordered Paymaster Sultan Muhammad to go with the cook when he was taken for torture, and the man confessed everything.
>
> Monday being Court-day, I ordered the grandees and nobles, amirs and vizirs, to be present, and that the two men and two women in question should be brought and interrogated; they related what had happened. I had the taster hacked in pieces and the cook flayed alive, one of the women trampled to death by an elephant and the other shot with a matchlock. The old woman I had put under arrest; she will meet the fate that she has deserved.

Babur soon recovered. 'Thanks be to God,' he wrote, 'who saved me from harm! Till now I had never really known how sweet a thing life can be.' The old woman, the most guilty of the conspirators, was in the event the most fortunate; she was despatched to Kabul where no doubt an unpleasant end awaited her, but on the way there she succeeded in jumping into the Indus and was drowned.

[1] But see page 189.

Babur must have been incredibly tough. Sometimes he rode enormous distances in a single day, even in the hottest weather or when sick with fever, and as a boy had walked barefoot in the mountains round Samarkand till the soles of his feet became so hard that 'rock and stone made no difference to them'. Even after a day and a night of steady drinking he would be in the saddle by dawn. He mentions quite casually that one evening his tent was flooded knee-deep, and that he sat up all night 'balanced precariously on a pile of blankets'. During one of his winter campaigns the cold was so intense that the ears of many of his men 'swelled to the size of apples'; but he was not affected. In the exceptionally cold winter of 1501–2, when he was encamped near Khojand, several soldiers were frozen to death; but, he wrote, 'since I needed to make an ablution I went to an irrigation channel which because of the strong current was free of ice in mid-stream, and there bathed, diving in sixteen times. The coldness of the water froze me to the marrow'. In 1529, the year before his death, he swam the Ganges 'counting every stroke. I crossed with thirty-three, then without resting swam back. I had swum other rivers; the Ganges remained to do.'

In January 1507 he led a small force across the Hindu Kush in appalling weather, conducted by an incompetent guide who lost the way. 'I endured more hardships and miseries during those few days than at any other time in my life', he wrote (and he was not forgetting the horrors, so graphically described in his Memoirs, of the six-months' siege of Samarkand in 1501):

We continued for nearly a week, trampling down the snow and not covering more than two or three miles a day; I was one of the ten or fifteen snow-tramplers. We used to go forward for seven or eight yards, sinking in up to the waist or breast at every step, when the leading man would stop, exhausted, and another would take his place. Then a riderless horse was dragged forward; it sank to the stirrups and girth and after advancing ten or fifteen paces was worn out and replaced by another. Meanwhile the rest of our men – even some of the best of them, including many begs – rode along the road we had thus beaten down for them, hanging their heads for shame. It was no time for reproaching them or for using authority; in such a situation, if a man has guts he will volunteer.

At last we reached a cave at the foot of the Zirrin Pass. A terrible blizzard was raging, with a biting, icy wind. We halted at the entrance; the snow was deep and the path so narrow that we had to move in single file. The advance troops began to arrive while it was still light; but when darkness fell the remainder had to stop where they were, and many spent all night in the saddle.

Since the cave seemed to be rather small, I took a spade and cleared a space near the mouth, about the size of a prayer-rug; I dug away several feet of snow, but even then did not come to the ground. This afforded me a little protection from the wind, and I sat down. People kept on calling me to go inside, but I refused. I felt that for me to be warm and comfortable while my men were out in the snow and the storm, would be an unmanly and an uncomradely thing to do; whatever their hardships, it was right that I should share them with them. There is a Persian proverb that says, 'In the company of friends death is a feast.'

So there I sat till the Bedtime Prayer, while the snow fell so heavily that it was four hands thick on my head, back and ears, and gave me ear-ache. Then somebody explored the cave and shouted, 'It's large! there's plenty of room for everybody.' So, shaking myself free of snow, I and some of the men near me went inside, to find that there was room there for fifty or sixty people. Those who had something to eat – stewed meat, preserved flesh, or anything ready – produced it. And so we escaped from that terrible cold and snow into somewhere warm and snug.

Babur's physical strength is proved by his 'strong man' turn of leaping from pinnacle to pinnacle of the ramparts of a fortress in double-soled boots while carrying a man under each arm, and both his strength and quick temper by his striking an incompetent equerry so hard a blow in the face that he dislocated his right thumb. 'It didn't hurt much at the time' – hurt *himself,* of course! – 'but it was rather painful when we reached camp, and for some days I couldn't hold a pen.' Being himself fearless, he despised cowardice, both moral and physical, in others; one of his uncle Sultan Mahmud's amirs is pleasantly dismissed as 'not having the guts to stand up to a hen'. Of the cowardice of one of his cousins, Kupuk Mirza, he wrote 'behaviour such as his outlives the man; how should anyone with any intelligence try to get himself ill spoken of after death? In the honourable remembrance of their names, wise men live a second time.'

It would not be difficult to quote a dozen passages to show Babur's courage and resourcefulness in battle, but one must suffice. During the fighting round Andijan (in Farghana) in 1502 he suddenly came face to face with a certain Tambal, once his friend but now his bitter enemy:

> His horse's mail excepted, he was fully accoutred, whereas I had nothing but my sword and quiver. I released an arrow, aiming at the attachment of his shield, and at the same time I was shot through my right leg. I was wearing only the soft under-cap [of the helm], and Tambal chopped so violently at it that my head lost all feeling under the blow, which made a large wound yet didn't cut a single thread of the cap! I hadn't drawn my sword, and there wasn't time to. I was all alone among so many foes and it was not the moment to stand still, so I turned rein; but as I did so, down came another sword – this time on my arrows. . . .

An Indian doctor was sent to tend Babur's wounds. 'He was a brilliant surgeon; if a man's brains had come out, he could put them back, and he could deal with any kind of severed artery.'

Babur always spoke with affection of the members of his family – or at all events of most of them: of his splendid maternal grandmother ('there were few of her sex who equalled her in common sense and sagacity'), of his mother, and of his eldest sister Khanzada who after being twice widowed joined him at Kabul. While in Herat he dutifully made time to look up a whole bevy of paternal aunts; and he mentions to which of them he bent the knee, to which he did not, according to their rank. (He was, incidentally, a stickler for social etiquette, snubbing anyone who tried to treat him without proper respect – for example, 'he hesitated to kneel, so I ordered them to pull his leg and make him do so'.) But above all he loved his eldest son and ultimate successor, Humayun, who was born on 6 March 1506 in the citadel at Kabul; his mother was a woman named Mahim about whom little is known.

The proud father often refers in his Memoirs to the boy's progress. At twelve he was given a small province to govern, and a year later the kingdom of Badakh-shan (in north-eastern Afghanistan). Babur praised his skill in shooting wild duck, and records his first military success in Hindustan in 1526. After the Emperor's great victory at Panipat three weeks later, in which Humayun also played his part, the young man was sent to occupy Agra, where he received from the family of the defeated Raja vast quantities of jewels including an enormous diamond which was probably the famous Koh-i-Nor. 'Its value', wrote Babur, 'has been estimated at the equivalent of two-and-a-half days' food for the whole world. Humayun offered it to me when I came to Agra; I simply gave it back to him.'

Babur doted on the boy, but he could be firm with him when need arose. In 1527, when Humayun seized the treasures of Delhi without his authorization, he noted angrily in his diary, 'I never dreamed he would do a thing like that. I was furious, and wrote very sharply to him.' More venial was Humayun's reluctance to write letters, and his turgid style of writing when he brought himself to make the effort. In November 1528 Babur felt it necessary to reprove him for this:

> You wrote to me, as I ordered; but why didn't you have your letter read over to you? If you had tried to read it yourself you couldn't have done it, and so you would almost certainly have re-written it. It *can* be read, if one really takes the trouble, but it is very puzzling. Though your spelling isn't too bad, it's not quite correct [Babur gives two examples]. Your remissness in writing seems to result from that which makes your letters so obscure – namely over-elaboration. Write in future without so much hyperbole, using plain, straightforward language; it will be less trouble to you, and less for the reader.

Sound advice to any author, and Babur practised what he preached.

In the autumn of 1530 Humayun was taken ill at Sambhal with a violent attack of fever. He was brought by water to Agra for the best available medical atten-tion, but the doctors there could do nothing for him. His father, in despair, resolved to put into practice a traditional oriental rite: the sacrifice of a man's most valued possession in exchange for the life of a sick man. Someone suggested that the Koh-i-Nor diamond (which, it will be remembered, was really his son's) should be offered for pious uses; Babur chose to barter his own life for his son's. One of Babur's daughters, and his grandson's biographer, are our authorities for what follows:

> Babur made intercession through a saint and moved thrice round Humayun's bed, praying, 'O God! if a life may be exchanged for a life, I, who am Babur, give my life and my being for Humayun.' Even as he spoke he felt the fever grip him, and, con-vinced that his prayer and offering had prevailed, he cried out, 'I have borne it away! I have borne it away!'

Humayun poured water on his head and was able the same day to get up and give audience. But Babur took to his bed, from which he was never again to rise, and within a few weeks he was dead. Such, at least, is the legend; in fact several months elapsed before Babur was struck down by what proved his final illness.

His body was buried temporarily at Agra, in a spot opposite to where the Taj Mahal now stands; but a few years later it was removed to Kabul and re-interred,

OPPOSITE TOP *An avenue of plane trees in one of Babur's gardens;* BOTTOM *his tomb, left open to the sky as he desired*

BELOW *Babur's tomb today*

as he had directed, in a garden of his choice at the foot of the Shah-i-Kabul hill 'in a grave open to the sky, with no building above it and no doorkeeper to watch over it'. He wanted, in death as in life, to commune with nature. To the flat gravestone a marble headstone was added by the Emperor Jahangir and a marble balustrade by Shah Jahan. But misdirected piety has since unhappily provided a 'ludicrously incongruous superstructure, looking much like an expensive bus stop, with red-tiled sloping roof and dormer window' and other discordant appendages.

Thus, as so often, have the clearly expressed wishes of a dead man been disregarded.

CHAPTER ELEVEN

Anthony Jenkinson
An Englishman reaches Central Asia

The first Englishman to reach Central Asia and leave any account of his experiences was 'Master Anthonie Jenkinson, from the Citie of London', a merchant who in December 1558 came with two companions to Bukhara by way of Russia. He could not proceed to Samarkand, with whose ruler the King of Bukhara was at that moment at war, nor could his road truthfully be described as 'golden'; but his adventurous pioneer journey into the land of the Turkomans entitles him to a place in this book. Two and a half centuries were to elapse before the next Englishman reached Bukhara.

To explain the circumstances which sent Jenkinson through the mountainous seas of the Arctic in order to reach a town in a latitude south of that of Naples or Madrid, we must glance back over the previous fifty or sixty years – years during which the English had looked on impotently while the wealth and trade of the New World and the East Indies slipped into the hands of the Spaniards and the Portuguese. True, there had been a flicker of hope when John Cabot, sailing westwards from Bristol, came to what he believed to be Cathay; but this spark was soon extinguished for, like Columbus, he found that he had reached the New World, not the Old. It was Cathay, then cut off by the iron curtain of Moslem hostility from direct contact through Central Asia, which constantly beckoned: Cathay, land of fabulous wealth and infinite mercantile opportunity, a prize that Portugal and Spain were hoping to win.

In 1527 an English merchant in Seville, Robert Thorne, exhorted King Henry VIII to encourage mariners to seek short cuts to the 'Indies' and 'spiceries' by a north-west or north-east passage, or even by sailing over the North Pole – ways 'nearer by almost two thousand leagues' than the passage round the Cape. He optimistically believed that northern cold, like southern heat, had been much exaggerated; that a relatively warm ocean awaited the adventurous seaman, whose voyage would be rendered the easier by the long daylight hours of a northern midsummer. But it was not until 1553 that a north-east passage to the 'backe side' of Cathay was first attempted.

In May of that year a little fleet of three ships, under the command of Sir Hugh Willoughby with Richard Chancellor as pilot-general, sailed on this hazardous enterprise in which only a single ship – Chancellor's *Edward Bonaventure* – survived a hurricane off the Lofoden Islands. In August, after rounding the North Cape, the *Edward Bonaventure,* alone now, entered the White Sea and anchored off land which looked singularly unlike golden Cathay. Here some local fishermen, whom he comforted 'by signs and gestures', raising them up 'in all loving sort', gave him the surprising information that they had reached, not China, but Russia. They had in fact come to the little village of Nenoksa, on the Dvina near the site of the modern Archangel, and so far as is known they were the first Englishmen to set foot on Russian soil.

Russia may not have been China, but it was better than nothing; trade was trade, all the world over, and the Russians, with their bitter winters, might well prove willing purchasers of Hampshire kerseys and woollens, the merchants' principal stock-in-trade. So the party made the 'very long and troublesome' journey to Moscow, where Chancellor was cordially received, wined and dined by the Tsar, Ivan the Terrible.

Ivan the Terrible, painted by B. M. Vasnetsov

Ivan, who was now twenty-three, had been on the throne since infancy and an orphan since the age of seven. His youth had been vicious and his later years, when he murdered his son and threw his disgraced courtiers to his dogs, were to be bloodthirsty; but while he was in his twenties he came temporarily under good influences. Chancellor found him eager to trade with the English, and returned to London with a letter from him to Edward VI (who had in fact died in the meantime) promising 'free Marte' throughout his dominions and safe anchorage in his harbours. Thus encouraged, London's leading merchants obtained from Queen Mary a royal charter for what is generally known as the Muscovy Company – an offshoot of the Merchant Adventurers founded by Cabot.

Chancellor returned to Russia the following year with several other Englishmen and set up trading stations at Kholmogory (seventy miles from Archangel), Vologda, and Moscow, where he spent the winter and found the Tsar as friendly and hospitable as before. Ivan was quite overwhelmed by one of Chancellor's companions, George Killingworth, whose five-foot-two-inch-long 'thicke, broad and yellow coloured' beard was unrivalled even in Russia. One night after the Englishmen had dined in the Kremlin, Ivan took it in his hand as it lay on the table and 'pleasantly delivered it to the Metropolitane, who seeming to blesse it, said in Russe, "This is Gods gift." '

In July 1556, accompanied by a Muscovite ambassador – Osep Napea, Governor of Vologda – Chancellor sailed from Archangel; but his ship was wrecked off the Scottish coast and Chancellor and most of his crew perished. The Ambassador and several of his suite were among the few survivors. Such, briefly, were the events which led up to Anthony Jenkinson's journey to Moscow and its audacious continuation into Central Asia.

Anthony Jenkinson, merchant and sea-captain, a man now in his late twenties, already had wide experience of travel in the Mediterranean and the Near East, and it is no small tribute to his skill in handling Moslems, which subsequently was to stand him in such good stead, that in 1553 he had obtained at Aleppo a 'safe-con-

Suleiman the Magnificent, who granted permission for Jenkinson to trade in Turkish ports

duct or privilege' from Suleiman the Magnificent himself to trade unmolested in Turkish ports. Two years later he had been admitted a member of the Mercers' Company, and in 1557 he was chosen to succeed Chancellor as captain-general of a new trading mission to Moscow. The terms of his commission would seem to suggest that if opportunity arose he was to attempt to push on into Central Asia, perhaps even to Cathay itself.

On 12 May he wrote, 'I embarked myself in a good ship, named the Primrose, being appointed, although unworthy, chiefe Captaine of the same' and of three other ships, and sailed from Gravesend; with him in the *Primrose* were the Muscovite ambassador and his staff, and two lions as a royal gift for the Tsar. After many adventures and delays the little fleet rounded the North Cape and on 12 July anchored at the mouth of the Dvina. Here most of the party set out at once for Moscow, leaving Jenkinson to supervise the discharging and reloading of the ships. This accomplished, he proceeded with his consignment of cloth, kerseys, and pewter to the Company's depot at Kholmogory, the great trading emporium of the north:

> To Kholmogory [wrote E. Delmar Morgan] came the Lapps, the idol-worshipping Samoyedes with their reindeer sledges, the Karelians, the Russians, and the Tartars. They brought salt, stockfish, salmon, train oil, feathers, furs and walrus-teeth from the shores of Lapland and Kola, from Pinega, Mezen and Pechora, from Nova Zemlia and the distant Obi. These wares were carried by the Russians to Moscow and Novgorod, partly for home consumption and partly to barter with the Dutch,[1] who traded at Novgorod for cloth, tin, copper utensils, etc.

Having completed his business, Jenkinson set out with a part of his stock by boat up the Dvina, towed by day and sleeping by night 'in the Wildernesse by the Rivers side'. Ten weeks were spent in Vologda – a 'great Citie' with houses built entirely of wood – presumably in transacting business; thus it was in the bitter cold of the Russian winter that he left 'in poste in a Sled' for Moscow, where he arrived on 6 December. It must have been an efficient service, for he covered some two hundred and fifty miles in five days; the whole journey from Archangel to Moscow was over a thousand miles.

The population of Moscow was at that time more than one hundred thousand – bigger than that of London with its suburbs. The houses were mostly of wood, though some were of stone, and fitted with 'windowes of yron, which serve for summer time'. Jenkinson describes the Kremlin, with its walls and towers, its sixteen gates, its 'fairely gilded' churches full of 'images of golde', and its palaces. The principal market was inside the Kremlin, but in winter, when the river was frozen, there was a second market on the ice.

Soon after his arrival Jenkinson went to the Kremlin to present his credentials to the secretary of the Tsar, and on Christmas Day he was summoned to Court:

> I came into the Emperours presence, and kissed his hand, who sate aloft in a goodly Chaire of estate, having on his head a Crowne most richly decked, and a staffe of Gold in his hand, all apparelled with Gold, and garnished with Precious stones. There sate distant from him about two yards his Brother, and next unto him a Boy of twelve years of age, who was Inheritor to the Emperour of Casan [Kazan], conquered by this

[1] In fact, the Germans

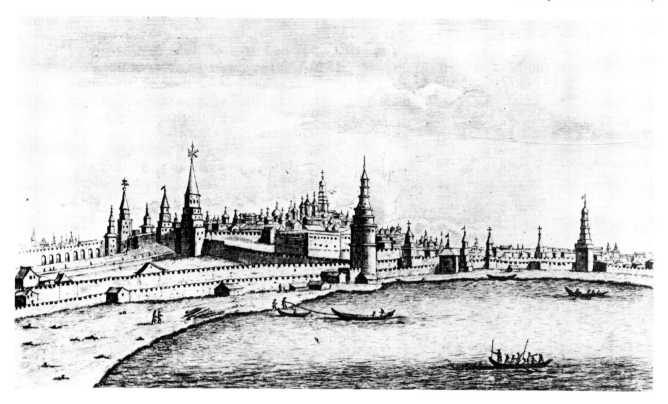

Emperour eight years past. Then sate his Nobilitie round about him, richly apparelled with Gold and stone. And after I had done obeysance to the Emperour, he with his owne mouth calling me by my name, bade me to dinner, and so I departed to my lodging till dinner time, which [was] at sixe of the clocke, by Candle light.

Moscow: the Kremlin, an engraving from Cornelius de Bruin's Travels, 1737

No fewer than six hundred men sat down to dinner in 'a faire, great Hall, in the midst whereof was a Pillar foure square, very artificially made'; this was the famous Granovitaya Palata, built by Italian architects in the fifteenth century. The Tsar and his more distinguished guests were seated on one side of the high table, while Jenkinson found himself

set at a little Table, having no stranger with mee, directly before the Emperours face. Being thus set and placed, the Emperour sent mee divers bowles of Wine, and Meade, and many dishes of Meate from his owne hand, which were brought mee by a Duke, and my Table served all in Gold and Silver, and so likewise on other Tables, there were set bowles of Gold, sét with Stone, worth by estimation 400 pounds sterling one cup, besides the Plate which served the tables.

There was also a Cupboord of Plate,[1] most sumptuous and rich, which was not used; among which, was a piece of Gold of two yards long, wrought in the top with Towers, and Dragons heads, also divers barrels of Gold and Silver, with Castles on the bungs, richly and artificially made. The Emperour, and all the Hall throughout was served with Dukes; and when dinner was ended, the Emperour called mee by name, and gave me drinke with his owne hand, and so I departed to my lodging. . . .

[1] Jenkinson had brought English silver plate for presentation to the Tsar (see Charles Oman, *English Silver in the Kremlin*, Methuen, 1961).

*The Granovitaya Palata,
in the Kremlin, where
Jenkinson dined with the Tsar*

At Epiphany Jenkinson was present at the blessing by the Metropolitan of the River Moskva, for which purpose a large hole was cut in the ice. After the ceremony, at which the Tsar was present, hundreds of naked men, women and children plunged into the freezing water, while they filled pots to take home. Then the Tsar's favourite horses were led to the water's edge to drink. Jenkinson remained in Moscow until April, when the river became open to navigation; then, armed with letters from the Tsar 'directed unto sundry Kings and Princes, by whose Dominions I should passe', he left by boat, heading eastwards. With him, on the orders of the Governors of the Company, went two 'painfull [i.e. painstaking] young men' – the brothers Johnson. His real adventures were now beginning, and it is far from clear whether or not he knew exactly where he was heading.

After passing through (Nijni) Novgorod[1] and Kazan, in the middle of July they reached Astrakhan, near the mouths of the Volga; all these three towns had recently been captured by Ivan from the Tartars, thus making the Volga for the first time a Russian river. Jenkinson found conditions in Astrakhan, where six years after its fall famine and the plague were still raging, 'very pittifull to behold', with piles of bodies of those who had died still lying unburied. 'At the time of my being there,' he wrote, 'I could have bought many goodly Tartars Children, if I would have had a thousand, of their owne Fathers and Mothers, to say, a Boy or a Wench for a Loafe of bread worth six pence in England, but we had more need of victuals at that time then of any such Merchandise.' (But it seems that, probably on his way home, he did in fact purchase one – a girl named 'Aura Soltana', whom he presented to Queen Elizabeth on his return to England.) It would, he reflected, have been 'an easie thing to have converted that wicked Nation to the Christian Faith, if the Russes themselves had been good Christians'.

[1] Now Gorki.

Unlike the elder Polos and Ibn Battuta, Jenkinson chose to continue his journey from the Volga by sea, but in its latter stages he followed approximately in the footsteps of the former to Bukhara. 'Having bought and provided a Boate in company with certayne Tartars and Persians, wee laded our goods and imbarked our selves, and the same day [6 August] departed I, with the said two Johnsons, having the whole charge of the Navigation downe the said River Volga, being very crooked, and full of flats toward the mouth thereof', where they entered the Caspian Sea. Hugging its northern coast they came to the mouth of the River Ural and dropped anchor. Here most of the crew and passengers went ashore, leaving Jenkinson, 'who lay sore sicke', and five Tartars – one of them 'reputed a holy man, because hee came from Mecca' – to guard the ship. Suddenly an armed band of thirty Turkomans appeared and boarded the vessel, demanding the handing over of any 'Russes, or other Christians' and their merchandise. It would have been an easy matter, and doubtless a pious act, for this Meccan Moslem to have complied; instead he denied, with the most solemn oaths, that any infidel was on board, and the brigands believed him and went on their way. Thus once again Jenkinson showed his remarkable talent for winning the confidence and respect of a Moslem.

The intention had been to follow the coast as far as the port of Mangyshlak (Fort Novo-Alexandrovsk), but a storm drove the ship ashore on the opposite side of the bay. Here the local inhabitants – 'brute field people, where never Barke nor Boat had before arrived' – were aggressive and obstructive; but a deputation who went to reconnoitre discovered the local governor and brought back 'comfortable words and faire promises of all things'. This prince did in fact 'gently entertayne' them and was prepared to arrange for the hire of camels and purchase of provisions; but over the transactions that followed the Turkomans showed themselves in their true colours, demanding double the fair price for everything, begging and stealing, and even charging for drinking water. Payment, incidentally, was in kind, chiefly in skins and wooden dishes.

On 14 September the caravan of one thousand camels and a number of horses set out eastwards, and on the fifth day entered the territory of 'Prince Timor Sultan', another of the innumerable petty rulers who fought for survival in territory which under Jenghiz Khan had once been united. Here it was set upon by a band of Turkomans, who opened everything and helped themselves to gifts allegedly for their Sultan. Jenkinson visited the Prince and found him 'in a little round house made of reeds covered without with Felt, and within with Carpets. There was with him the great Metropolitan of that wilde Countrey, esteemed of the people, as the Bishop of Rome is in most parts of Europe, with divers others of his chiefe men'; this Metropolitan would be the local Shaikh ul-Islam, or Moslem spiritual leader. Jenkinson was 'well feasted with flesh and mares milke', much cross-questioned about western Europe and the object of his journey, and finally given a letter of recommendation and a horse which was worth about a half of the wares that had been seized.

'Twentie dayes in the Wildernesse', during which the party were obliged to kill camels and horses for food, brought them to what Jenkinson believed to be another gulf of the Caspian but which must have been Lake Sari-Kamish. Here certain 'Customers of the King of Turkeman' appeared and appropriated presents for their King, Azim [Hajjim] Khan, to whom Jenkinson also paid his respects. The Khan lived in the castle of 'Sellizure' [Vezir], which was at that time the capital of Khorazmia. Jenkinson describes his castle as 'built of earth very basely, and not strong'; but the surrounding country was fertile and well cultivated, and famous for the large variety of fruit and vegetables that grew there.

After spending a week at Sellizure the caravan continued on its way to Urganj, where it arrived two days later and was immediately subjected to further extortions. The petty Princes of Transcaspia, most of whom were closely related, were perpetually at war with one another, and Urganj had been won and lost four times during the past seven years; thus great poverty prevailed, and Jenkinson was able to dispose of only a small quantity of his cloth. Ali Sultan, ruler of Urganj, was a half-brother of Azim Khan, and like all the local Princes 'lived viciously' with innumerable concubines and catamites to supplement the services of his legal wives. Hawking was the great pastime of the local inhabitants; 'Arte or Science they have none, but live most idlely, sitting round in great companies in the fields, devising, and talking most vainely.'

From Urganj they followed the course of the Oxus, past the castle of the Sultan of Kait (who intended to rob them, but was bought off). One night the watch captured and disarmed four spies, who told them that they had come across the tracks of a large number of horses and that a band of brigands was abroad. An appeal was immediately sent to the Sultan, who arrived on the scene with a force of three hundred men and by rougher methods extracted the truth from the spies. 'A banished Prince with fortie men' were lying in wait 'three dayes journey forward' to attack the caravan, and they themselves were members of this robber band.

The Sultan left an escort of eighty well-armed men to accompany the travellers, and returned to his castle. During the next two days the escort made serious inroads into the limited food supplies of the caravan, and on the third day, when the enemy were sighted, declared that they would not fight unless they were given a preposterously large reward. On this being refused they returned to their Sultan 'who (as we conjectured) was privie to the conspiracie'. Auguries were now taken, using the blade-bones of sheep sacrificed for the purpose, and a happy outcome of the encounter predicted. Though Jenkinson set no store by these omens, they gave courage to the Moslems of the party.

There were some forty combatants on each side, but the enemy were in general better armed; the Englishmen, however, had 'hand-guns' (arquebuses), and in a long day's fighting, with many casualties on both sides, these proved decisive. When night fell, 'we encamped ourselves upon a hill, and made the fashion of a Castle, walling it about with packes of wares, and layde our horses and camels within the same to save them from the shotte of arrowes: and the theeves also incamped within an arrowe shotte also of us, but they were betwixt us and the water, which was to our great discomfort, because neither we nor our camels had drunke in 2 days before.'

At midnight the Prince sent an emissary to parley, and a Moslem went out from the caravan, under a flag of truce, to meet him. Jenkinson could hear all that was said. The Prince demanded the handing over of the Christians and their goods; if this was done he would leave the caravan in peace. It was an anxious moment until Jenkinson heard a stout denial that there were any Christians in the caravan – only 'two Turkes which were of their Law'; and even had there been, he added bravely, he would rather have died than surrender them.

In spite of their sworn word the brigands seized the man and, 'crying with a lowde voyce in token of victorie, *Ollo, ollo* [Allah! Allah!]', dragged him back to their camp where, though 'cruelly handled and much examined', he stubbornly refused to betray his Christian companions. But both sides had had enough of fighting, and next morning the caravan agreed to pay a small tribute for the return of the envoy and permission to go on their way without further molestation. That evening the caravan again reached the Oxus, 'where we refreshed ourselves . . . and tarried there all the next day, making merry with our slaine horses and camels'. On 23 December, after not a few further scares and adventures, they arrived at 'the Citie of Boghar [Bukhara], in the land of Bactria'. It was five months since they had set out from Astrakhan.

Bukhara, though no longer the great cultural centre it had formerly been, was an important mart. 'There is yeerely great resort of Merchants to this Citie of Boghar', wrote Jenkinson, 'which travell in great Caravans from the Countries thereabout adjoyning, as India, Persia, Balgh [Balkh], Russia, with divers others, and in times past from Cathay, when there was passage.' From India, even as far as Bengal, came cotton goods of all kinds, which were exchanged for Persian silks, horses, Russian hides, and slaves; Bukhara had the greatest slave market in central Asia. The Russians also brought cloth, bridles and saddles, and wooden vessels to barter for cottons and silks; but the disturbed state of the country to the east had put a stop to the caravans of 'Muske, Rubarbe, Satten, Damaske, with divers other things' which had formerly come from China.

Jenkinson was, however, frankly disappointed with the prospects for trading. Though caravans from Russia, India and Persia arrived while he was at Bukhara, the quantity of goods they brought was small; and, worse, none of the merchants showed the slightest interest in his woollens, which could be bought more cheaply from the Persians. In fact, his only purchaser was the King, Abdullah Khan, who showed himself a 'very Tartar' by slipping off to attack Samarkand without paying for the nineteen pieces of kersey he had taken. In general, however, Jenkinson soon established excellent relations with Abdullah Khan, who much enjoyed firing his guest's English arquebus and who 'devised with me familiarly in his secret chamber, as well of the power of the Emperour, and the great Turke, as also of our Countries, Lawes, and Religion'. Moreover, when he heard of the attack that had been made upon the caravan, he sent a hundred armed men in pursuit of the bandits. The Englishmen lent their arquebuses, which once again proved very effective; a number of the bandits were killed in the skirmish which ensued, and four who were taken prisoner were duly hanged at the palace gates.

Jenkinson describes Bukhara as 'walled about with a high wall of earth, with divers gates into the same: it is divided into three partitions, whereof two parts are the Kings, and the third part is for Merchants and Markets, and every Science hath their dwelling and market by themselves. The Citie is very great, and the houses for the most part of Earth, but there are also many Houses, Temples and Monuments of stone sumptuously builded, and gilt, and specially Bath-stoves so artificially built, that the like thereof is not in the world: the manner where of is too long to rehearse.' The language spoken was Persian, though at the time of Jenkinson's visit the Bukhariots were constantly involved in petty wars with the Persians. Any pretext, preferably a religious one, was it seems good enough to start a scrap, one breaking out because the Persians, who were Shia Moslems 'will not cut the hayre of their upper lips, as the Bogharians and all other Tartars doe, which they account a great sinne.' The Bukhariots were Sunnis, members of the other great Moslem sect, who to this day shave the upper lip immediately below the nose.

The water of the little river Zarafshan that flowed through Bukhara produced worms 'an ell long' in the legs of those who drank it, and Jenkinson explains how these had to be coaxed out at the ankle and rolled up, an inch a day, without breaking them; if they broke, the patient died. This was the well-known *rishta* or Guinea worm, mentioned by all who visited Bukhara. Since the water was tainted and wine forbidden, there was nothing to drink except mares' milk. The regulation about wine-drinking was strictly enforced by the religious authorities; these appointed special officers to enter the houses and smell the breaths of suspected offenders who, if found guilty, were 'whipped and beaten most cruelly through the open markets'. It was the Shaikh ul-Islam, 'more obeyed than the King', who was all-powerful, who could make or break a monarch and who did not stop short of murder when the need arose. The King had little power and little money; when he was short of the latter he was obliged either to rob the shop-keepers or (like Governments today) to devalue the currency.

There is not much doubt that Jenkinson had hoped to travel beyond Bukhara, perhaps to Cathay itself; but no caravan had come out of China for the past three years, and such a journey was not even to be contemplated. He also discovered that China was a great deal further off than he had imagined – it took nine months to get there, people said. So he had to be content with picking up such titbits of information and gossip as he could about the inaccessible further Orient: about the 'very beautiful' inhabitants of Comoron (Comari, in southern India) who 'use Knives and Forks of gold and silver to eate their meate, not touching it with their hands'; about the 'Musk-beast, as big as a Hound'; about the fire-worshippers of Teray; and about the later stages of the road to Cathay, where women in plenty were available 'at too easie rate'.

Since Cathay was ruled out, Jenkinson considered the possibility of returning to the Caspian by way of Persia, but at that moment 'great Warres did newly begin betwixt the Sophie [Shah] and the Kings of Tartaria, whereby the wayes were destroyed'. Also the Shaikh ul-Islam had taken possession of the Tsar's letter to

Bukhara: the Chashma Ayub ('Job's Well') Mausoleum, which has four types of cupola

Abdullah Khan, without which Jenkinson would certainly have been seized and sold into slavery. When news came that the King, who had marched on Samarkand, had fled the field, and that Bukhara was about to be attacked, the Englishmen attached themselves to a caravan of six hundred camels which very opportunely was about to leave for the Caspian. With them travelled two ambassadors, one from Bukhara and the other from Balkh, on their way to Moscow. It was 8 March 1559, and ten days later the King of Samarkand appeared in strength outside the walls of Bukhara.

At Urganj four more local ambassadors were added to the party, which six weeks after Jenkinson's departure from Bukhara reached the point on the Caspian where he had disembarked on the outward journey. Here he must have been agreeably surprised to find his boat still beached on the shore, though all its fittings had been stolen. But he was a handy and resourceful man; before long, with his companions working under his direction, he had spun a new cable of hemp and a sail of 'cloath of Cotton-wooll', and improvised an anchor out of an old cart-wheel. Fortunately he was soon able to buy a proper anchor from a vessel from Astrakhan which carried a spare one. 'Thus being in a readinesse, wee set sayle and departed, I, and the two Johnsons, being Master and Mariners our selves, having in our Barke the said six Ambassadours, and twentie five Russes, which had beene Slaves a long time in Tartaria, nor ever had before my comming, libertie, or means to get home, and these slaves served to row when need was.'

Of course there were storms in the Caspian, during one of which the homespun cable broke and the anchor was lost, and they hourly awaited 'present death'. But God brought them into 'a creeke full of Oze' where they sheltered until the gale had blown itself out. The Tartars were deeply impressed by the navigational skill of the Englishmen, and still more so when Jenkinson succeeded in recovering the lost anchor. 'Note', he added, 'that during the time of our Navigation, we set up the red Crosse of Saint George in our flagges, for honour of the Christians, which I supposed was never seene in the Caspian sea before.'

Astrakhan was reached on 28 May. Here Jenkinson made a gallant attempt to dispose of what remained of his kerseys, asking six roubles apiece for them, but there were no bidders; it seemed that Persian wool was as good as English, and everywhere cheaper. His journey beyond Moscow had, so far as business was concerned, been a failure, because it had shown him that there was no present possibility of trading with India or China direct through Central Asia; it did, however, lead to the establishment of diplomatic contact between Russia and Turkestan. A fortnight later Jenkinson left Astrakhan with a company of a hundred gunners provided by the Tsar as escort for the six ambassadors; these men, together with the twenty-five rescued slaves, he delivered in September personally to the Tsar, when he 'kissed his hand, and presented him a white Cowes [i.e. yak's] tale of Cathay, and a Drum of Tartaria, which he well accepted'.

At Kholmogory, where he arrived in May of the following year, Jenkinson drew up for the Directors of the Muscovy Company his account of his journey, which, he told a friend, had been 'so miserable, dangerous and chargeable with losses, charges and expenses as my penne is not able to expresse the same'. He concludes his report, 'And heere I cease for this time, intreating you to beare with this my large discourse, which by reason of the varietie of matter, I could make no shorter, and I beseech God to prosper all your attempts.'

Though Jenkinson was never again to reach Central Asia, he was still only at the beginning of a distinguished and adventurous career. On his next visit to Russia, in 1561, he went on behalf of Queen Elizabeth to the Tsar, and at last succeeded in continuing his journey into Persia. There the King of Shirvan befriended him;

OPPOSITE *A map of Central Asia made by Ortelius in 1570 from one by Jenkinson that no longer exists*

OVERLEAF *Meshed: the Mosque of Gawhar Shad and the golden dome surmounting the tomb of the Imam Reza*

*Oil paintings by the Russian
V. V. Vereshchagin:
TOP Apotheosis of War;
and BOTTOM Celebration,
where Moslem warriors in
Samarkand give thanks to
Allah for a victory over the
Russians*

but at Qazvin, then the Persian capital, Shah Tahmasp proved a good deal less than amiable to this 'unbeleever', and Jenkinson, as he hurriedly left the palace after a hostile reception from the Sophy, observed that he was 'followed by a man with a Basanet of sand, sifting all the way that I had gone'. He was, he realized, lucky to have escaped with his life.

Jenkinson was in Russia on several further occasions and was often called upon to handle highly delicate situations, including, it seems probable, a proposal of marriage made by the Tsar to Queen Elizabeth. His last visit was in 1571, shortly after much of Moscow had been burned by the Tartars; though only in his early forties he was now 'weary and growing old'. In 1578 he went briefly to Denmark on behalf of the Queen, but the last years of his life were for the most part spent in peaceful retirement in the country. He died in 1611, at the age of about eighty.

CHAPTER TWELVE

Dr Joseph Wolff, the 'Grand Derveesh of Englistaun'

One could probably count on the fingers of one hand the number of country parsons in Victorian England who had been bastinadoed by the Kurds in Iraq, horsewhipped 'tremendously' by the Wahabites in Abyssinia and, after being robbed and stripped by Afghans, reduced to wandering 'naked, like Adam and Eve, without even an apron of leaves' some two hundred miles[1] across the snowbound Hindu Kush. Yet these things, and much else as unpleasant and as unlikely, had happened to Dr Joseph Wolff when in 1838, at the age of forty-three, he accepted the incumbency of the tiny parish of Linthwaite in Yorkshire. Stranger still, the greatest adventure of his life was yet to come.

Wolff, the son of a German-Jewish rabbi, was born near Bamberg, in Franconia, in the year 1795. A pious upbringing in the Jewish faith was early undermined by contact with Christians, and when asked, at the age of seven, what he wanted to be when he grew up, the boy disconcertingly replied, 'The Pope'; he was never one to underrate his potentials. Rejected by his family when barely in his teens, he began *wanderjahren* which led to his baptism in 1812 by the abbot of the Benedictines of Emaus, near Prague. Determined now to become a missionary, and having a great flair for languages, he added to the Latin, Greek and Hebrew with which he was already familiar, a good working knowledge of Arabic, Syrian, Chaldaean and Persian; nor was theology neglected.

We next find him in Vienna, Switzerland, Germany and Italy – everywhere making distinguished friends; 'everybody delighted in the charming young man.... To see and to embrace him were almost the same thing', as was, of course, to support him financially. In Turin he met Madame de Staël; at Weimar the great Goethe patted his head and told him always to follow the dictates of his conscience. He was for some months the guest of 'that beautiful poet and grand nobleman, Count Stolberg', and his family of eleven 'sons like thunder' and seven 'daughters like lightning', and seems to have submitted without protest to the Count's curious practice of 'kissing and tickling him in a droll, good-natured way'. Clearly he was irresistible.

In the autumn of 1816 he was accorded a private audience by Pope Pius VII, who received him 'not as a King his subject, but as a father receives his son'; as for

---

[1] Wolff estimates the distance at *six* hundred miles – a gross exaggeration.

Wolff, he expressed his appreciation 'by gently and caressingly patting him on the shoulder and saying, "I love your Holiness. Give me your blessing".' On the recommendation of the Pope Wolff now entered the Collegio Romano and subsequently the Collegio di Propaganda, where he remained for two years. Among the books given to the students of the Propaganda to read was a Latin translation of Father März's *Method of Confuting a Protestant in Arguments*. According to Wolff the Roman Catholic was instructed

> to take the whole matter very easy; but should it happen that the Protestant produced a powerful argument, the Roman Catholic was not to attempt to answer it, but, laughing, 'Ha! ha! ha! ha!' he should look into the face of the other, folding his arms, and say, 'Sir, look into my face, and see whether, with open countenance, and without blushing, you can dare to produce such a silly argument.' . . . This will discourage the Protestant. . . .

But Wolff considered these institutions to be in many ways very civilized, later comparing them favourably with their Protestant counterparts in England where students were 'sent to a paltry lodging-house in Holborn and submitted from time to time to the humiliation of being lectured by some long-nosed, snuff-taking lady of the Evangelical party, whose only care is to bid them beware of Puseyism, over-formalism, or whatever happens to be the religious bugbear of the day'.

At this date Papal Infallibility was not yet a dogma, but it was dangerous to attack it. Wolff, in spite of his personal affection for the current Pope, did so – and provocatively, at a public lecture; it was the first of a number of unfortunate incidents, the result for the most part of his arrogance and impetuosity, which were finally to lead to his dismissal. The evidence necessary to effect this was easily obtained by tapping Wolff's correspondence. The Holy Office examined his letters, in one of which he had written, 'I will go to the East and preach the Gospel, but I will always be the enemy of the Anti-Christian tyranny of Rome.' The following day there arrived in Wolff's room in swift succession the College tailor, shoe-maker and hatter, all requesting permission to take his measurements; they offered no explanation, but Wolff understood: he was to be fitted out with the clothes of a layman. In other words, he had been sacked.

Next came Vienna again, and then a spell at the monastery of the Redemptionists at Val Sainte, in Switzerland. Here Wolff was soon found to be undermining the discipline by showing his fellow neophytes how to cheat at the Friday auto-flagellation sessions, which were held in the dark, by flogging their leather breeches instead of their bare backs. He was always getting into trouble. He openly declared that it was wrong for the Church to burn heretics, and when the Rector pointed out that thirty-eight popes had done this, Wolff replied, 'Then thirty-eight popes were wrong.' Finally, after Wolff had been caught biting the toes of some monks whose feet he had been ordered to kiss, the Rector felt that the time had come to tell him that he appeared to be temperamentally unsuited to monastic life.

So Wolff went to England, where he was hospitably received by the wealthy banker, politician and religious enthusiast, Henry Drummond, whom he had met at Rome and who became his lifelong friend and supporter. After toying briefly with the Baptists, the Quakers and the Methodists, Wolff finally decided to join the

Joseph Wolff in old age   Church of England. Money was immediately produced by the London Society for Promoting Christianity among the Jews, to enable him to go to Cambridge, where he spent two years working fourteen hours a day at Oriental languages and studying theology. He was now twenty-six, and ready to set out on his first missionary journey.

In the opening pages of his *Narrative of a Visit to Bokhara* Wolff has summed up in a single paragraph the first thirteen years of his missionary work:

> I began in 1821, and accomplished in 1826, my missionary labours among the dispersed of my people in Palestine, Egypt, Mesopotamia, Persia, Krimea, Georgia and the Ottoman Empire. My next labours among my brethren were in England, Scotland, Ireland, Holland and the Mediterranean, from 1826 to 1830. I then proceeded to Turkey, Persia, Tūrkistaun, Bokhara, Affghanistaun, Cashmeer, Hindūstan, and the Red Sea, from 1831 to 1834. Bokhara and Balkh . . . occupied especially my attention, on the ground that I expected to find in them the traces of the lost Ten Tribes of the Dispersion. . . .

Wherever Wolff went he made friends – and enemies; wherever he went he argued. He argued, wrote Sir Fitzroy Maclean, 'with Christians and Jews, with Hindus and Mohammedans, with Catholics and Protestants, with Sunnis and Shiahs. He argued about almost everything: about the Pope, and the Millenium, and Mohammed, and the Lost Tribes, and the Second Coming, and the End of the World, and about what would happen to all the fishes when the sea dried up.[1] He argued good-humouredly, tirelessly and without any regard whatever for the consequences.'

Indeed, wherever he went he exposed himself fearlessly to dangers of every kind. He had much in common with St Paul, who was 'beaten with rods . . . In journeying often, in perils of waters, in perils of robbers, in perils by mine own countrymen, in perils by the heathen, in perils in the city, in perils in the wilderness, in perils in the sea . . . In weariness and painfulness, in watchings often, in hunger and thirst, in fastings often, in cold and nakedness . . .' But there was this difference: whereas Paul followed up his proselytizing by the establishment of churches, Wolff rushed in a wild *wanderlust* from place to place, preaching here (in a dozen different languages), debating there, scattering Bibles everywhere; here today and gone tomorrow, often with a hostile mob at his heels.

It was during his first missionary journey that Wolff was savagely bastinadoed near Mardin and left for many weeks unable to walk. He was rescued by the local inhabitants and carried to the house of the Bishop of the Jacobite Christians. Mardin was apparently well-stocked with bishops of various denominations, and when Wolff was well enough he found himself invited to a dinner party at which two Armenian Catholic Bishops were present. During the meal he got into a 'terrible scrape':

> In the heat of discussion and argument, he got hold, accidentally, of a small paper picture of our Lord, which, in accordance with a bad habit he had when excited, he put into his mouth, and bit at and chewed, till he had, by degrees, swallowed it altogether. Of course, he was quite unconscious of what he was doing; but he could not persuade the bishops and company that it was an accident, and they were greatly scandalised. . . .[2]

From Mardin Wolff went to Baghdad, where a surgeon of the East India Company's forces, Dr Lamb, treated his feet till he was once again able to walk. Wolff was often to be indebted to the kindness of British officers who, though considering him crazy, admired his incredible pluck. He, for his part, was duly grateful to the British Army and his last and greatest adventure was to be undertaken to give expression to this gratitude.

Wolff's second journey was preluded by his marriage, in February 1827, to Lady Georgiana Walpole, sixth daughter of the second Earl of Orford (of the second creation), and five months later he sailed with his 'glorified angel' for the Levant. Lady Georgiana, when not ill or parturient, travelled around with him; but she had of course to be left behind (at Alexandria) when in January 1831 her husband headed for Central Asia. Wolff reached Tehran safely, where he was entertained at the British Embassy and warned on every hand that in proceeding to Bukhara – then under the rule of the bloodthirsty Amir Nasrullah, the Nero of

Amir Nasrullah of Bukhara

[1] When questioned about this, Wolff replied, 'You may pickle them!'

[2] Joseph Wolff, *Travels and Adventures . . .*, 1860 – a dictated autobiography written in the third person.

Central Asia – he was courting almost certain death. 'God will protect me,' he replied, and, hiring a handful of camels (four of which he loaded with bibles) he set out with two Persian servants, 'both tremendous rogues', to win glory or the martyr's crown.

Even before reaching Meshed he ran into trouble, being captured by Turkoman bandits, stripped, robbed and tied to a horse's tail, while 'one with a whip came behind and flogged him'.

'Wolff prayed! In such hours one learns to pray.'

The chief of the gang, a 'horrid-looking fellow, of black complexion with a blue diseased tongue', began to price the prisoners (there were some fifty other men in the caravan with which Wolff travelled); Wolff's value in the slave market was variously estimated at from twenty-five to fifty shillings, that of his servants at £5 apiece. They were then chained together and cast naked into a dungeon. From this fate the whole party was ultimately rescued by the timely intervention of Abbas Mirza, Governor of Khurasan and heir apparent to the Persian throne. After kindly treatment in Meshed, where he received a new wardrobe and money from England, Wolff continued on his way in bitter weather to Merv and Bukhara.

Contrary to every expectation, Wolff found himself most amiably received in Bukhara by the Amir's secretary, a man known as the 'ear of the King'. He remained there for more than two months, meeting the best people and baptizing no fewer than twenty Jews. He describes Bukhara as being fifteen miles in circumference, and having a population of a hundred and eighty thousand (of whom fifteen thousand were Jews), eleven gates, three hundred and sixty mosques, and a hundred *madrasas*. When he came to leave he was provided with a passport for Kabul. Three servants accompanied him.

But at Doab, beyond Balkh, his troubles began all over again when he fell into the hands of a band of religious fanatics who told him, 'You must either say: "There is God and nothing but God and Mahomet is the Prophet of God", or we will sew you up in a dead donkey, burn you alive and make sausages of you.' Wolff immediately answered, 'There is God and nothing but God and Jesus is the Son of God.' His fate now seemed certain; but when by crafty argument he persuaded his captors that his death might incur unpleasant reprisals, they decided instead to strip him naked and abandon him. Wolff expressed himself more than satisfied with their decision: 'I am a dervish,' he said, 'and do not mind either money, clothing, or anything.'

Though it was April, snow still lay thick in the Hindu Kush. But eventually Wolff and his servants – presumably naked also – reached Bamiyan, whose Governor gave him a letter to the Governor of Ghazni in which he described Wolff as an ambassador; he was, however, 'too poor to provide him with clothes'. The Governor of Ghazni took a poor view of the 'naked ambassador' when he arrived. 'What!' he cried, 'a ragamuffin like you, without clothing! Do you want me to believe that you are an ambassador?' and threw him out. So, protected from the cold by (it would seem) still no more than a passport, Wolff continued on his way through the mountains towards Kabul, befriended at times, though grudgingly, by Afghan peasants who 'permitted him to sleep among them', brought him milk, and pulled him out of the snowdrifts into which he repeatedly fell. Then at last his way lay downhill into the warm and smiling valley in which Kabul lay.

Wolff spent the night in a village a few miles short of Kabul, sending one of his servants ahead to announce to the authorities his impending arrival and the depleted state of his wardrobe. The man returned next morning with three horses, some splendid clothes and a friendly greeting from the brother of the *de facto* Amir, Dost Muhammad; he also brought a warmly welcoming letter from Lieutenant (later Sir Alexander) Burnes, who had just arrived in Kabul on his way to Bukhara on a sponsored mission.

During the month that he remained in Kabul, Wolff was treated *en prince*. He had long talks with Burnes, who particularly warned him against a 'horrible scoundrel' at Peshawar – Abd as-Samut Khan. 'Should he call on you,' Burnes added, 'take hold of his shoulder and kick him out of the room.' Wolff did briefly encounter and thus deal with this murderous brute when he reached Peshawar; he had cause to regret having done so when, a dozen years later, he was unlucky enough to fall into his clutches in Bukhara, by which time he had become the *Nayeb* (Prime Minister) and evil genius of the Amir.

Dervishes, of the kind that Joseph Wolff claimed to be

With each stage of his journey across northern India, Wolff, whose fame had preceded him, found himself more enthusiastically fêted and acclaimed. At Attock a twenty-one-gun salute was fired in his honour, while officers of Ranjit Singh, the Maharajah of the Punjab, showered him with rupees and pots of sweetmeats, and enough linen for twenty shirts. At Lahore, the Maharajah's capital, he was tactless enough to plaster the walls with Christian tracts, and the Maharajah was liberal-minded enough to forgive his indiscretion and to ply him with further gifts. At Ludhiana he was the guest of Sir Jeremiah and Lady Bryant, relations of his wife; at Simla he stayed with the Governor-General of India, Lord William Bentinck, and his wife – a 'most holy lady'. While visiting Kashmir, Shir Singh, the Prince Governor, patted his knee, gave him French liqueurs and sent his dancing-girls to entertain him in his lodging, where 'rose-leaves were strewed upon the ground, and they danced so as to form the petals into roses again'; he was prepared to be shocked, but in the event found the girls 'rather modest-looking than otherwise'. At Delhi he met the Grand Moghul, who remarked that his cap made him look 'more like a captain in the navy than a padre', and at Agra he was duly overwhelmed by the majesty of the Taj Mahal.

Between Agra and Cawnpore Wolff's palanquin broke down, and he was rescued and given a bed by a young lieutenant in the 6th Bengal Native Light Cavalry, Arthur Conolly, who had also made an adventurous journey through Central Asia. The two men formed a sudden friendship which was later to have for Wolff important consequences unforeseen at the time. At Cawnpore Wolff met another of Georgiana's cousins, Sir John Bryant, whose wife's heart 'leaped like an antelope' at the sight of this remarkable man; indeed the 'ladies of Cawnpore' were (Wolff assures us) so captivated by his charm that when he came to leave 'many wept and cut off pieces of his hair'. Success was going dangerously to his head, and his pleasure in the company of people of title is each day more naïvely recorded.

And so the royal progress continued. But it must not be imagined that Wolff

A mulla at prayer

passed all his time in idleness or the social round; he was interminably preaching – sometimes for twelve hours a day – or disputing with learned *mullas* whom, apparently, he always routed. At Nellore, north of Madras, he was struck down by cholera, and his life saved by brandy, laudanum, and the unattractive native remedy of branding the stomach with red-hot irons. On 4 April 1834, after innumerable further adventures in southern India, Abyssinia and Arabia, he rejoined his long-suffering wife and four-year-old son Henry[1] in Malta.

Back in England he found himself sometimes lionized, sometimes snubbed. When the clergy of Gloucester refused to meet him because they considered that he had 'run wild', he replied that he hoped to see them in heaven though they did not wish to see him on earth. But soon he was off again – to Sinai, and to Abyssinia, where he was mistaken for the newly appointed Abuna (Primate) and wildly acclaimed, then seized by Wahabites and horsewhipped. After a severe attack of typhus he was carried, still a very sick man, in a British warship to Bombay and thence, on medical advice, in a Swedish ship to try the restorative effects of the balmy air of the United States. In New York he met the Bishop of New Jersey, who, after examining him rather whimsically – he asked him, among other things, to explain the workings of the common pump – ordained him deacon. For a month he acted as curate at Salem, then returned to England. While on a visit to Dublin he was ordained priest by the Bishop of Dromore and given an honorary LL.D. at Trinity College.

He was now forty-three, and when he accepted the living of Linthwaite, and subsequently the curacy of High Hoyland, also in Yorkshire, it was generally believed that the Wandering Jew had at last found rest. Yet, five years later, he was to set out on the 'most gallant and quixotic of all his enterprises'.

*   *   *

To understand the circumstances which led to Wolff's last great expedition into Central Asia, we must look at the political situation at the time.

Afghanistan, during the nineteenth century, found herself in a position of extreme peril. Over the years the might of Russia had been advancing southwards, wave upon wave, particularly since the middle of the previous century; the explorer Nansen calculated in 1914 that during the last four hundred years her territories had been expanding at the rate of fifty-five square miles a day, making a grand total of some eight million square miles. Between Russia in Central Asia and the British Raj in India, now mutually hostile and suspicious, there was before long to remain a single buffer: Afghanistan. To complicate the situation still further, Persia was attempting – and very reasonably – to recover Herat, an ancient Persian province which had become an independent principality. Persia's intervention and her pro-Russian leanings were the ultimate causes of the first Afghan War (1838–42).

It was inevitable that a handful of adventurous Englishmen and Russians besides Wolff should find their way, semi-officially or freelance, to Bukhara and Khiva in the 1820s and 1830s. A William Moorcroft, who added so much to our knowledge of Kangra painting, was in Bukhara in 1825, where he 'met with as much kindness

[1] Later Sir Henry Drummond Wolff (1830–1908); an older child had died in infancy.

Colonel Charles Stoddart

from the king as could be expected from a selfish, narrow-minded bigot'; he died on his way back to India. Burnes was there in 1832, soon after Wolff, and got away safely – but only to be killed by a mob of Afghans in 1841; and a few years after Burnes a Lieutenant Wyburd met his death in Bukhara on his refusal to embrace Islam. In 1838 the British Government, daily more alarmed by the growing Russian threat to India, felt that the time had come to send an official emissary to the Amir of Bukhara, promising him British assistance in the event of a Russian attack. The man chosen for this delicate mission was Colonel Charles Stoddart, at that time on the staff of the British Embassy in Tehran.

The choice was unfortunate: Stoddart was one of those brash Englishmen who believe that they know how to deal with Asiatic potentates; he was soon to learn that the Amir of Bukhara and his Nayeb also knew how to deal with the Stoddarts of this world. After Stoddart had refused to dismount on reaching the Registan,[1] and had even lashed out at an official who had attempted to remonstrate with him, it was hardly surprising that he found himself arrested and imprisoned. But what most irked the Amir was that the letter which Stoddart had brought had been signed by the Governor-General of India, not by Queen Victoria in person; a letter from the Queen, written as monarch to monarch, repeatedly asked for and as often refused, would almost certainly have saved Stoddart's life.

The prison into which the unfortunate young Englishman was thrown was the

The Registan and the Arg, at Bukhara, where Stoddart and Conolly were imprisoned: a photograph taken in the 1880s

notorious *Siah Chah,* or Black Well – a noisome twenty-foot pit stocked with specially bred sheep-ticks and reptiles which were fed on offal when no victim was in residence. But after a time Stoddart was released and allowed a modicum of freedom; indeed, when news came through of a British victory at Herat he was for a time treated well. It was, however, all part of a game of cat-and-mouse played by the Amir and his unspeakable Nayeb, and in due course Stoddart found himself once again persecuted. Now he was offered the choice between becoming a Moslem and being burnt alive. When, in July 1838, his grave was dug before his very eyes his resistance finally broke, and after making the declaration of faith he was publicly circumcised and restored to favour. News of his apostasy (which he later revoked) reached the Government of India and caused some embarrassment – enough to make it decide, though against the advice of Burnes, to organize a rescue operation.

[1] The square in front of the Arg (or citadel) within which was the royal palace.

Captain Arthur Conolly

The officer chosen for the purpose was Captain Arthur Conolly – a man of a very different stamp from Stoddart: romantic, adventurous, pious, a dreamer. Having just been jilted, he was in a mood to take any risk. His instructions were to try to persuade the three Khanates of Khiva, Kokand, and Bukhara to stop squabbling among themselves and with the promise of British support present a united front should Russia attempt to attack them; he was then to bring Stoddart back to India. After visiting Khiva and Kokand he reached Bukhara in November 1841, but unluckily just at the moment when news was coming through of the successful uprising against the British at Kabul – a disaster which was soon to lead to the retreat of a considerable British force of whom all but one man were massacred before reaching India. It was evident to the Amir that for the moment he had nothing to fear from the English, and in December he threw Stoddart and Conolly into a filthy, verminous, unheated cell of the Nayeb's private gaol in the Arg, where they languished throughout the winter. On 11 March 1842 Conolly, who like Stoddart was now struck down by fever, wrote a pathetic 'last note' to his brother John in England – a letter which somehow or other finally reached its destination:

> This is the eighty-third day that we have been denied the means of getting a change of linen from the rags and vermin that cover us; and yesterday, when we begged for an amendment in this respect, the Topshee-Bashee [the Nayeb], who had before come occasionally as our host to speak encouragingly, set his face like a flint to our request. . . .

He had, continued Conolly, at first believed that the Amir's conduct was 'dictated by a mad caprice'; now he realized that it was simply the 'deliberate malice of a demon' who took a sadistic pleasure in watching their spirits slowly break:

> I did not think to shed one warm tear among such cold-blooded men; but yesterday evening, as I looked upon Stoddart's half-naked and nail-lacerated body . . . I wept on entreating one of our keepers . . . to have conveyed to the chief my humble request that he would direct his anger upon me, and not further destroy by it my poor brother Stoddart, who has suffered so much and so meekly here for three years. My earnest words were answered by a 'Don't cry and distress yourself'; he also could do nothing. So we turned and kissed each other, and prayed together.

Yet the two prisoners recovered from their fever, and with the coming of warmer weather were able to discard the filthiest of their garments. Then came the news that they were soon to be given robes of honour by the Amir and set free; but they knew by now what credence to attach to such promises. There was at this time a small Russian mission in Bukhara, led by a Colonel Butenyov, and there can be no doubt that this rival emissary, who had received preferential treatment from the Amir, generously tried to get the Englishmen released; but he failed, and in April the Russians left Bukhara. At the same time the Amir marched out to attack the Khan of Kokand, whom he contrived to murder in cold blood, together with other members of his family. 'No change has taken place in our treatment,' wrote Stoddart on 28 May, adding that the return of the Amir was expected hourly; it was the last letter that he wrote, and it was subsequently learned that on 17 June the two Englishmen were led out from their prison and publicly executed behind the Arg.

Meanwhile in England Wolff, having discovered that he could not make ends meet on his stipend as a Yorkshire curate, had resigned and was filling in time at Richmond, in Surrey, while awaiting news of his application for a chaplaincy abroad. When rumours reached London that Stoddart and Conolly were dead he refused to credit them, and on 2 July 1843 he put the following letter, addressed 'to all the Officers of the British Army', in the *Morning Herald*:

> Gentlemen,
>
> Though a missionary and a clergyman myself, and not an officer, I do not take up my pen in order to excite your sympathy in behalf of a clergyman or missionary, but in behalf of two of your fellow officers, Captain Conolly and Colonel Stoddart, who are at present captives in the great city of Bokhara; but having been myself two

months at Bokhara, and knowing, as I do, the character of the inhabitants of Bokhara, I am fully convinced that the report of their having been put to death is exceedingly doubtful. . . .

If, therefore, one of you, gentlemen, would be inclined to accompany me to Bokhara, or merely pay the expenses of my journey, I am ready to go there and I am fully confident that I shall be able, with God's help, to liberate them from captivity. . . . I would undertake the journey without making myself responsible to the British Government, and entirely on my own responsibility. I merely want the expense of my journey, and *not one single farthing as a compensation*, even in the case of complete success.

I shall be ten days more at Richmond, Surrey; if, therefore, one of you brave officers is now ready to accompany me, or to assist me in making the journey, let him come to me, and we may talk over the matter more fully.

I am, Gentlemen, your humble servant,

Joseph Wolff,

Late Curate of High Hoyland, Yorkshire, formerly Missionary in Persia, Bokhara, and Affghanistaun.

A Captain John Grover accepted the challenge; but when Lord Aberdeen, the Secretary of State for Foreign Affairs, refused official recognition of his mission he drew back, deciding that it was safer – though that was not how he put it – to demonstrate his concern by forming a 'Stoddart and Conolly Committee' to raise the £500 that Wolff considered he would need if he went alone. The money was soon collected, and on 14 October the intrepid curate sailed from Southampton for Constantinople. In his luggage were his clergyman's gown, cassock, hood and shovel-hat; a quantity of Hebrew bibles, testaments and prayer-books; several dozen silver watches for mullas and khans (but 'the Ameer of Bokhara shall not get one single thing, in case he was the cause of their death'); a number of maps 'in the Arabic characters'; and finally 'three dozens of *Robinson Crusoe,* translated into Arabic by Mr Schlienz at Malta' – a book which Wolff had earlier distributed with tremendous success among the Moslems in Arabia.

Wolff was in fighting form during the voyage, lecturing and preaching incessantly to the seasick passengers (for it was very rough) and proudly conversing with a lady of title until her ladyship, pleading queasiness, escaped to her cabin. At Athens he was accorded an hour's audience with King Otto of Greece – a 'tall, meagre-looking gentleman, dressed in Greek costume' – and his amiable wife. At Constantinople he received a warm welcome from the English ambassador, Sir Stratford Canning, and was provided with letters from the Sultan to the Amirs of Bukhara and Khiva together with other high-powered documents which Lady Canning personally sewed up in the lining of his coat.

On 24 November he sailed in an Austrian ship for Trebizond, from where he began his overland journey of nearly two thousand miles to Bukhara. It was a bitter winter, and the state of the mountain roads such that in places he had to crawl forward on hands and knees. On reaching Erzerum a tremendous snowstorm delayed his departure until after Christmas, when, fitted out by Colonel

Williams, one of her Majesty's commissioners there, with voluminous clothes lined with wolf's fur (which rendered him, he wrote, 'a Wolff in wolf's clothing'), he continued on his way to Tehran.

Here he was housed, entertained, and provided with further potent credentials by Colonel Sheil, the British ambassador, who assured him that Stoddart and Conolly were certainly dead; many years later Wolff admitted that he now realized this to be true, but that he would have cut a ridiculous figure on his return to England had he not pursued his investigations to the bitter end. In March he reached Meshed and in April Merv, where the Jews implored him to turn back: 'Joseph Wolff, Joseph Wolff, Joseph Wolff! you are a son of death as soon as you enter Bokhara. For God's sake do not enter. . . .' But Wolff, though admitting that he was now rather frightened, ignored their warning. Realizing that his safety depended upon his widely advertising his presence and his position as a *mulla,* he set out on the last lap of his journey 'dressed in full canonicals' and with an open bible in his hand.

He had been warned that as he approached Bukhara he would be met by horsemen carrying baskets containing chains to fetter him and knives for his execution. A few miles short of the city just such a posse of horsemen duly appeared; but their baskets proved to be luscious picnic hampers, and the chief 'assassin' no less a person than the Amir's Grand Chamberlain, bearing friendly greetings from his master.

The entire population of Bukhara had turned out to witness the arrival of this extraordinary visitor from another world:

> Shouts of 'Selaam Aleikoom' from thousands rang upon my ear. It was a most astonishing sight; people from the roofs of the houses, the Nogay Tatars of Russia, the Cassacks and Girghese from the deserts, the Tatar from Yarkand or Chinese Tartary, the merchant from Cashmeer, the Serkerdeha or grandees of the king on horseback, the Affghauns, the numerous water-carriers, stopped still and looked at me; Jews with their little caps, the distinguishing badge of the Jews of Bokhara, the inhabitants of Khokand, politely smiling at me; and the mullahs from Chekarpoor and Sinde looking at me and saying, 'Inglese Saheb'; veiled women screaming to each other, 'Englees Eljee', 'English ambassador'; others coming by them and saying, 'He is not an Eljee, but the Grand Derveesh, Derveesh Kelaun, of Englistaun'.

Wolff as he acknowledged this amazing reception scanned the crowd for a sight of Stoddart or Conolly, but in vain.

Though weary and dusty after his journey, he was taken straight to the palace, at whose gates everyone dismounted. Here he was met by an official who asked him whether he was prepared to submit to the 'Salaam' as practised at the Bukharan court. Wolff enquired what was involved; he was told that the Minister of Foreign Affairs, holding him by the shoulders, would lead him before the King, where he would have to stroke his beard three times and bow three times saying '*Allahu Akbar*' – 'God is the Greatest'. It was by his refusal to comply with this harmless ceremony that Conolly had given great offence; Wolff replied that he would gladly do it thirty times if it were necessary.

Wolff was left waiting on a stone bench while his credentials were sent up and examined; then he was brought before the Amir. Having performed the three prescribed salaams, he continued bowing and chanting 'Peace to the King!' until the monarch 'burst into a fit of laughter' and begged him to desist. So ended the first audience. Wolff described the Amir as:

> about five feet six inches high, rather stout, black eyes and small, of dark complexion, with a convulsive twitching of the muscles of his face; his voice not remarkably powerful, but rapid in intonation; his smile appears forced. He has the whole appearance of a *bon-vivant*. His clothes are quite those of a common mullah, without any pomp or decoration. . . . On his accession to the throne he killed five of his brothers. . . .

Wolff was then conducted to an office in the palace where he was interrogated by the Minister of Foreign Affairs, whom he informed that 'thousands in England', on hearing the report that Stoddart and Conolly had been put to death, were crying, 'War with Bukhara!' The Minister neither confirmed nor denied the report, and it was from the Nayeb, to whose country house he was now taken, that Wolff finally learned of their fate. The Nayeb, whose duplicity (in spite of Burnes's warning) he still did not suspect, posed as the friend and protector of Stoddart and Conolly, and was even able to produce a flattering testimonial from the no less gullible Stoddart. 'He pressed me to his heart,' wrote Wolff, 'kissed me for about ten minutes, pinched my hands and my fingers, as I suppose (for I am no Free-mason) the Freemasons do', and over a sumptuous breakfast explained that the murders, which he had tried to prevent, were ordered by the wicked Amir. He added, 'I intend, if the British government gives me twenty thousand tillahs, to invite the king, place him upon a seat undermined, and the moment he sits down I will blow him up.'

All that now remained for Wolff to do was to get away from Bukhara as soon and as safely as possible; and to ensure his safety he proposed to the Nayeb that he should be accompanied by an ambassador sent by the Amir 'to apologise for his conduct'. At this moment a most surprising event interrupted their conversation: a band of soldiers who had formerly been in the service of Ranjit Singh struck up 'God save the Queen'.

As a guest of the Nayeb Wolff was at first well treated, allowed to ride freely about the town and to visit his fellow Jews; he soon realized, however, the elaborate system of espionage that existed everywhere in Bukhara, and trod warily. Each day the Amir sent one of his ministers to ask him various questions – for example, 'Are you able to awake the dead?'; 'When is the Day of Resurrection?' The latter question was embarrassing; Wolff, when in Bukhara twelve years earlier, had publicly predicted the year 1847 for this important event, and it was drawing dangerously close. He now announced that the passage in the Book of Daniel, on which he had based his calculations, admitted of 'a two-fold interpretation', but he was none the less convinced that the time was 'at hand'. Many years later, when asked why he had ever made his rash prediction, he very sensibly replied, 'Because I was a great ass.'

Other questions put to him (and sometimes by the Amir in person) included: Why does not the Queen of England's husband rule?[1] Can she kill anyone she

[1] The same question was put to the author by an Afghan villager in 1956.

pleases? Why do the English like old coins? Who are the richest Jews in England? Are there witches in England? How many *farsakhs* an hour does a steamship go? How do the English govern India? Why do you dress in black and red? To the last, Wolff replied, 'The black colour indicates that I mourn over my dead friends; and the red colour indicates that *I am ready to give my blood for my faith.*' Once he nearly got himself into trouble:

> The Ameer wished another day to have the names of the four grand Viziers, the twelve little Viziers of England, and the forty-two Elders. I gave to his Majesty a list of the names of the present Ministry, when the Makhram returned in a fury, and said that his Majesty had found me out to be a *liar*; for the four grand Viziers, according to Colonel Stoddart's account, were Laard Maleburne, Laard Jaan Rawsall, Laard Malegraave, Seere Jaane Habehaase.[1] I was brought in to the King, and then had to give a complete idea of the Constitution of England. . . .

Stoddart, when similarly subjected to an impertinent interrogation of the kind only too common in England today, put a stop to it by replying 'Eat dung!' No doubt Wolff's survival was in part due to his greater tact.

As the days passed, Wolff began to see the situation more clearly. He realized at last that the Nayeb was the villain of the piece, and that the Amir, who was afraid of him (but retained his services because his knowledge of gunnery was indispensible), had an uneasy conscience – he was known to have said as much – for having ordered, or at all events acquiesced in, the murder of Stoddart and Conolly. Moreover the Amir was also frightened of England and utterly at a loss to understand what had induced her to send this strange emissary – this 'Star with the tail', as he obscurely called Wolff – to his court. 'How extraordinary!' he was reported to have said. 'I have two hundred thousand Persian slaves here – and nobody cares for them; and on account of two Englishmen a person comes from England, and single-handed demands their release.'

It is also evident that the Amir had no real intention of letting his 'guest' go. Again and again Wolff was told that he was about to be allowed to leave Bukhara, dressed in robes of honour and in the company of an ambassador; but each time excuses were found for postponements, the most reasonable following upon the Amir's discovery that his ambassador in Meshed was being detained as a hostage until Wolff returned there safely. This news left Wolff 'in a great stew', and he wrote at once to Sheil to beg him to get the Shah to release the Bukharan ambassador immediately. Gradually, too, the Nayeb showed himself in his true colours, first by demanding promissory notes and finally, after Wolff had lost his temper and called him to his face, 'a *liar, a traitor,* and a *rascal*', by making a full confession: 'Yes, I have killed them. . . . I know how to treat you Franks as you ought to be treated.' It was utterly impossible, Wolff wrote, to describe the countenance of this 'bloodhound' as he said this: 'His whole face became convulsed, distorted and crooked, and pale with anger and rage; grinning, laughing, raging, just like an apparition from hell.'

It was a declaration of war, and not long afterwards Wolff was shown a letter from the Nayeb to one of his officers, which read, 'Hasrat (his majesty) has at last decided to put to death the Englishman, and nothing will save the man. Let him

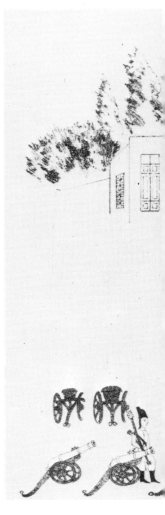

The Garden of the Nayeb, Bukhara

[1] Lord Melbourne, Lord John Russell, Lord Mulgrave and Sir John Hobhouse – four leaders of the Whig government which had fallen in September 1841.

go to the devil!' Wolff looked at the seal, saw that it was indeed the Nayeb's, and gave himself up for lost.

He was now moved from the Nayeb's house to the one which Stoddart and Conolly had occupied immediately before their execution, and put under house arrest. Living in the same building he found the newly-arrived Persian ambassador, Abbas Kouli Khan, who had been sent by the Shah with orders to try to effect his release; this admirable man proved a tower of strength to Wolff in the difficult and anxious days that followed.

One morning a *mulla* came with a message from the Amir asking whether Wolff was prepared to become a Moslem. 'Tell the king, NEVER – NEVER – NEVER !' he replied. Next arrived the executioner who had put Stoddart and Conolly to death, and said, 'Joseph Wolff, to thee it shall happen as it did to Stoddart and Conolly.' As he said this he 'made a sign at my throat with his hand. I prepared for death, and carried opium about with me, that, in case my throat should be cut, I might not feel the pain. However, at last I cast away the opium and prayed, and wrote in my Bible these words:

> My dearest Georgiana and Henry,
> I have loved both of you unto death.
> Your affectionate husband and father,
> J. Wolff.'

But it proved to be darkest just before the dawn. At this moment the Persian ambassador received a letter from his master to the Amir, which he showed to Wolff before delivering it at the palace. It read: 'The greatest friendship subsists between England and Persia. If you do not send back Joseph Wolff with Abbas Kouli Khan, I shall become enraged with you.' The Amir, now thoroughly frightened, saw at last that the time had come to capitulate. 'Well,' he said, 'I make a present to you of Joseph Wolff; he may go with you.' So the miracle finally happened, and on 3 August, after he had been more than three months in Bukhara, Wolff, laden with royal gifts, passed for the last time through cheering crowds and out of the city gates.

The Bukharan ambassador, who also travelled with him, got no further than Tehran, where, denounced as the representative of a murderer, he was sent back to Bukhara and duly executed by his master for the failure of his mission. The Nayeb fared no better, for in 1847 the Amir 'did at last take an axe and actually cut him in two with his own hands'. The Amir lived on until 1860, the last recorded command of this unpleasant man being to a servant to stab to death one of his wives before his eyes as he lay dying. For Wolff there were to be no more adventures after his return to England, and he passed the remainder of his days as the beloved but eccentric Vicar of Ile Brewers, in Somerset, where he died in 1862.

During the second half of the nineteenth century the Russians continued to extend their influence southwards; in 1868 the kingdom of Bukhara became a vassal state, and in the same year they captured Samarkand. The growing threat to Afghanistan, and so to British India, that this advance created, led to the Second Afghan War of 1878–80. In 1920 Bukhara became the Bukharan Peoples Soviet Republic, and four years later her territory was divided up between the newly-formed Turkmen and Uzbek Soviet Socialist Republics.

CHAPTER THIRTEEN

Aurel Stein and the Caves of the Thousand Buddhas

The greatest of all Central Asian explorers of modern times was the Russian Nicolai Przhevalsky (1839–88) – geographer, zoologist and botanist, best remembered for the early type of horse which he discovered and which bears his name – and among his numerous successors perhaps the most widely known is the Swedish geographer Sven Hedin (1865–1952). English pioneers include R. B. Shaw (1839–79) and his nephew Sir Francis Younghusband (1863–1942). Serious scientific investigation of ancient remains may be said to date from the closing years of the last century, and the archaeologists principally associated with it are the wealthy German amateur Albert von Le Coq (1860–1930), the Frenchman Paul Pelliot (1878–1945), and the Hungarian-born Mark Aurel Stein (1862–1943) who became a British subject in 1904.

If we are to single out one man, one place and one moment from this crowded story of exploration and discovery it should surely be that May afternoon of the year 1907 when Aurel Stein first entered the rock-hewn chamber at Ch'ien Fo-Tung, the Caves of the Thousand Buddhas, near Tun-huang – a room which had remained sealed for nearly a thousand years – and saw by the dim light of a Buddhist priest's little lamp what was to prove the greatest single find in the whole history of Central Asian archaeology.

Marc Aurel Stein

Marc Aurel Stein was born in Budapest and after studying at Austrian and German universities came to England in 1884. Here he continued his education at Oxford and at the British Museum, and in 1888 went out to India as Principal of the Oriental College at Lahore. In 1899 he joined the Indian Education Service and became Principal of the Calcutta Madrasa; but his thoughts had long been turning towards Central Asia, and the following year he was able to start on the first of his four great expeditions there, the last being in 1930. But these were only a part of his labours in the field of archaeology, which continued unabated until his death, at the age of over eighty, in Kabul, just after he had at long last succeeded in obtaining permission to explore Afghanistan. He was appointed a K.C.I.E. in 1912, and received honours from learned societies all over the world.

We have called Stein an archaeologist, but the description needs qualification; he was not an archaeologist in the same sense as was Layard or Flinders Petrie. He

Stein with Chiang and other members of the expedition

was rather an archaeological surveyor: a gifted observer and assessor of evidence, an intrepid traveller, and above all a great literary scholar eager to find and to rescue manuscripts of historical importance. He viewed his work as a salvage operation. He must have long known of the existence of the Caves of the Thousand Buddhas, but in 1902 he received a first-hand account of them from Professor L. de Loćzy, a Hungarian archaeologist who had seen them in 1879.

Tun-huang, which lies in the westernmost corner of the Chinese province of Kansu near the border of Chinese Turkestan, had had a chequered history since the time of Hsuan-tsang's visit in the year 645. In 787 it fell to the Tibetans, who retained it until the middle of the following century. From 919 it was for more than a hundred years virtually independent, but recognized the Chinese court. In 1035 it passed to the Tanguts, in 1227 to the Mongols, and in 1524 to the Mongol Khan of Turfan. In 1725 the Manchus established a military post there, and thirty-five years later it was reoccupied by the Chinese.

Stein first set eyes on the Caves one bitterly cold March day in 1907, when he also learned through his faithful Chinese assistant and friend, Chiang-ssu-yeh, of a report that a great deposit of manuscripts and paintings had been discovered not long before in a sealed chamber leading off one of the chapels. The finder, it was

said, was Wang Tao-shih, the priest-in-charge of the Caves, when after clearing ten feet of drifted sand from one of the ground-floor chapels he had noticed a crack in a wall and had investigated it.

Wang was at the moment away on a begging tour with his two acolytes; but Stein was able to see one manuscript said to have been extracted from the hoard, and to be shown the locked door, about four feet above the level of the floor, behind which the treasure reputedly lay hidden. He spent a crowded day getting a tourist's-eye view of the mural paintings and sculptures, then went off to investigate other remains in the neighbourhood.

By the middle of May he was back at Tun-huang and eager to begin the delicate negotiations he knew would be necessary before he could hope to gain access to the treasure-house. Spring had now come, and he pitched his tents in an orchard among blossoming peaches and pears; the elms were in leaf, and in the fields 'the blue of wild irises mingled with the bright green of young corn'. But it was the season of the annual pilgrimage, which brought ten thousand of the faithful to the Caves, and Wang was far too busy to attend to him; so Stein went off for a few days to a famous beauty-spot, the Lake of the Crescent Moon, a sapphire-blue little stretch of water hidden among the sand-dunes on the southern fringe of the Tun-

The court of the temple at the Lake of the Crescent Moon on the border of the Tun-huang oasis

huang oasis. Here in the hospitable lakeside temple he wrote up his notes, while Chiang amused himself by verifying the truth of the story of the 'singing sands', mentioned by Marco Polo and other travellers; then they set out for the Caves, which lie about ten miles to the south of the town.

To visit the Caves today is of course virtually impossible, and Mr Basil Gray was exceptionally fortunate to have found his way to Tun-huang in 1957. So to gain any impression of this astonishing agglomeration of rock-hewn chapels and monastic cells – five hundred or so of them in all – and of the mural paintings and sculptures to be found in many of them, the reader must turn to the illustrated works listed in the bibliography at the end of this book. But grateful though we must be for pictures of any kind, it is only too plain that these photographs were taken under difficulties and with apparatus that was little better than amateur; however, the Tun-huang Institute is now working in more favourable conditions to provide a complete pictorial record, and one day we may be able to study this great Asiatic picture and sculpture gallery in our armchairs at all events as satisfactorily as we can now study the frescoes of Piero della Francesca at Arezzo or of Michelangelo in the Sistine Chapel.

In lands where wood is scarce and the rock of a conglomerate unsuited to quarrying, an artificially constructed cave is the obvious way in which to create a permanent receptacle for the apparatus of religious worship; there are many such caves in India and no doubt the idea travelled to Central Asia when Buddhism was carried to China. An inscription in one of the Thousand Buddha Caves tells us that in A.D. 366 a monk named Lo Tsun, while in the neighbourhood of Tun-huang, had a vision of a thousand Buddhas in a cloud of glory; this divine revelation led to the construction of some of the first shrines, and soon the Caves of the Thousand Buddhas, for being situated near the last Chinese outpost on the caravan routes to the West, became an important centre of pilgrimage. Here travellers setting out on the long and perilous journey prayed for a safe arrival at their destination, while those returning offered thanks for delivery from danger.

The Caves – some no bigger than a boxroom in which a man can scarcely stand upright, others almost as large as a small country parish church – rapidly increased in number. Many of them are more or less square, with ceilings which, in imitation of those made of wood, are in the form of truncated pyramids. Opposite the entrance there is usually a rectangular platform upon which stand the principal image and its attendant figures, while walls and ceilings are elaborately painted in tempera on two coatings of plaster applied to the rough surface of the conglomerate. The earliest sculptures and paintings date from the late fifth century (Wei period), and the embellishment of the Caves continued energetically until the fourteenth century and thereafter more spasmodically.

One can picture something at any rate of Stein's excitement as he began to take a closer look at the sculptures and, more especially, the murals in the Caves – for the most part miraculously preserved from deterioration or desecration by the dryness of the climate and the piety of the pilgrim visitors, though well-intentioned restoration had sometimes had unfortunate results. Here were scenes from Buddhist

OPPOSITE A bodhisattva dancing, from a wall-painting in the Caves of the Thousand Buddhas, Tun-huang, Wei dynasty, c. A.D. 500 (It is interesting to compare this painting with the works of Rouault.)

and Taoist mythology, graphically portrayed because the artists had seen them enacted in morality plays. There were the paradise paintings, with music and the dance; religious processions and scenes of the chase; mountain landscapes and fortified castles; skies like marbled paper, teeming with thunder-demons and monsters. A proud benefactress, a Princess of Khotan, stands in the centre of a line of ladies-in-waiting, just as the Empress Theodora stands with her suite in San Vitale at Ravenna. In another and surprisingly modern painting men are seen rushing a great vermilion fireman's ladder to the rescue of Raudraksha, caught in the toils of the hurricane raised by his enemy Sariputra. Sometimes the groups of figures are composed with all the skill of a Mantegna; elsewhere the artist's only intention seems to have been the covering of a given area with incident, though in fact the impulse was the earning of merit, and perhaps of payment, not the abhorrence of a vacuum. Some of the walls and ceilings have abstract decoration of miraculous beauty; others are monotonously wallpapered with row upon row of little stencilled Buddhas – the Thousand Buddhas that give the caves their name.

But Stein was an acquisitive archaeologist, and even as he looked with wonder he knew well enough that nothing that he saw was potentially acquirable. Even the most corrupt custodian, though bribed to the hilt, could never risk selling sculptures well known to countless pilgrims, while the murals enjoyed the additional security of being irremovable by any means that he had at his disposal. In the sealed chamber, however, there would be portable objects – books, and perhaps paintings on silk also – whose disappearance would not be noticed. Already in his mind's eye he saw the great packing-cases of what other people might call loot, reaching India and thence passing to the safe keeping of the Indian Government or the British Museum.

The immediate problem was how best to win the confidence of Wang, the self-appointed custodian of the caves – a discharged soldier who had settled there in the guise of a priest and dedicated his life to the care of the site. He had protected the giant statue of Buddha from exposure to the weather, had deflected a stream to form a little oasis which he planted with poplars, and had built a small guest-house for pilgrims. He supported his charities by the begging-bowl and himself by the sale of Taoist spells to Chinese pilgrims. 'He looked a very queer person, extremely shy and nervous, with an occasional expression of cunning which was far from encouraging'; it was obvious that he was not going to be easy to handle, and Stein mentally prepared himself for a long and arduous siege. His campaign began by a day of casual photographing, during which he observed with dismay that in his absence the door leading to the secret chamber had been plastered up. Meanwhile his secretary, Chiang, paid a call on Wang in his cell, and began to sound him 'in confidential fashion' about the possibility of admittance to the chamber:

> Backed up by the promise of a liberal donation for the main shrine, Chiang's tactful diplomacy seemed at first to make better headway than I had ventured to hope for. The saintly guardian of the reputed treasure explained that the walling up of the door was intended for a precaution against the curiosity of the pilgrims. . . . But evidently wary and of a suspicious mind, he would not yet allow himself to be coaxed into any promise about showing the collection to us as a whole. All that he would agree to,

OPPOSITE *Vaisravana with attendants, a painting on silk; and* OVERLEAF *a scroll that shows two kings of Stell ruling the lower regions: found by Stein in the Caves of the Thousand Buddhas*

An embroidery found by Stein in the Caves of the Thousand Buddhas, depicting the Buddha with bodhisattvas and disciples on the Vulture Peak

with various meticulous reservations, was to let me see eventually such specimens as he might conveniently lay his hands on. When Chiang, in his zeal momentarily forgetting the dictates of diplomatic reticence, was cautiously hinting at the possibility of my wishing, perhaps, to acquire for future study one or other of those specimens, Wang showed such perturbation, prompted equally, it seemed, by scruples of a religious sort and fear of popular resentment, that my sharp-witted secretary thought it best to drop the subject for a time.

During the course of this conversation Wang also mentioned that the find had been reported to the Viceroy of Kansu, adding that he believed that orders had been given for everything to be removed to a place of greater safety. Fortunately this proved untrue: one or two scrolls of Buddhist texts had indeed been sent to Lan-chou, but they had not apparently aroused much interest there. Feeling that money alone would not overcome religious scruples where any question of acquisition was concerned, Stein decided that his best plan would be to get to know Wang better, to 'study his case in personal contact'.

Now, Wang's pride and joy was a chapel for the pious restoration of which he himself had laboriously collected the necessary money; it was in fact the very chapel which gave access to the walled-up chamber. Stein asked to be shown it, and as he tactfully admired the hideous modern sculptures which filled it he could not help feeling 'something akin to respect for this quaint little priest, with his curious mixture of pious zeal, naïve ignorance, and astute tenacity of purpose'; but he wisely decided to make no reference at the moment to the treasures which lay concealed only a few feet from where he stood.

Stein had always been deeply attached to the memory of Hsuan-tsang, and on more than one occasion his devotion to his 'Chinese patron saint', as he called him, had stood him in good stead. Feeling sure that Wang, uneducated though he was, would have heard of him, he decided to tell him, as well as his limited colloquial Chinese permitted, of his affection for the saintly traveller in whose footsteps he had followed 'from India for over ten thousand Li[1] across inhospitable mountains and deserts; how in the course of this pilgrimage I had traced to its present ruins, however inaccessible, many a sanctuary he had piously visited and described.' It never, he wrote, cost him any effort to grow eloquent on this theme.

The effect of his speech was instantaneous. Bursting with pride, Wang at once conducted him to a newly built loggia where he had commissioned a local artist to paint the legendary exploits of the 'saintly Munchausen'. 'Here the holy pilgrim was seen snatched up to the clouds by a wicked demon and then restored again to his pious companions through the force of his prayer or magic. Two queer-looking figures – one horse-, one bull-headed – were represented as his constant attendants. Elsewhere he was shown forcing a ferocious dragon which had swallowed his horse to restore it again, and so on.'

But there was one picture which struck Stein as particularly applicable to the present situation. It showed Hsuan-tsang standing on the bank of a formidable river, and beside him his horse laden with a big bundle of manuscripts. As the pilgrim hesitates to risk his treasures to the swirling waters, an enormous turtle swims towards the shore to lend a helping hand. 'Here was clearly a reference to

[1] A Li is about one-third of an English mile.

the twenty pony-loads of sacred books and relics which the historical traveller managed to carry away safely from India. But would the pious guardian read this obvious lesson aright, and be willing to acquire spiritual merit by letting me take back to the old home of Buddhism some of the ancient manuscripts which chance had placed in his keeping?' The reasoning seems somewhat disingenuous: certainly India was the 'old home of Buddhism'; but the British Museum – even its oriental department – could hardly qualify as such, and it was for the British Museum that a half of the spoil was intended. Stein decided to postpone any attempt to point the moral to Wang, but he came away with the feeling that he had definitely made progress.

ABOVE *Chiang, Stein's secretary, at his desk*

OPPOSITE *Wang Tao-shih, the self-appointed guardian of the Caves*

Stein had left Chiang behind with Wang in the hope that he might be able to take advantage of the improved atmosphere; but Wang again became nervous when the loan – now referred to as the *promised* loan – was mentioned, and spoke vaguely of delivery later. So Stein was as surprised as he was delighted when, towards midnight, 'Chiang groped his way to my tent in silent elation with a bundle of Chinese rolls which Wang had just brought him in secret, carefully hidden under his flowing black robe, as the first of the promised "specimens".' Since the chamber was still walled up, these must have come from manuscripts put on one side before it had been re-sealed.

Chiang, enthusiastic as always, sat up for the rest of the night examining the rolls. He appeared next morning at daybreak with the exciting news that they were translations of certain Buddhist *sutras* which, so the colophons declared, had been brought from India and translated *by Hsuan-tsang himself!* Stein felt sure that this strange coincidence – for Wang in his ignorance could not possibly have known the contents of what he had chosen at random – was bound to have a most favourable effect on the credulous little priest, who was immediately informed of the discovery. It did: an hour or two later Chiang brought news to Stein, who had discreetly kept out of the way, that the plaster blocking the entrance to the chamber had been removed.

It was past noon of a hot and cloudless day, and the soldiers who followed Stein everywhere while he took his photographs had settled down to the opium-induced sleep of their daily siesta. Accompanied only by Chiang, he hurried to the

A bundle of manuscripts from the sealed chamber at Tun-huang

Caves, where he found Wang still nervously combating his scruples; but Stein saw at once that the first battle of his campaign had been won, and a moment later the key grated in the lock and the door was open:

> The sight of the small room disclosed was one to make my eyes open wide. Heaped up in layers, but without any order, there appeared in the dim light of the priest's little lamp a solid mass of manuscript bundles rising to a height of nearly ten feet, and filling, as subsequent measurement showed, close on 500 cubic feet. The area left clear within the room was just sufficient for two people to stand in.

It was obviously going to be impossible to examine the manuscripts in this black hole, but it was equally obvious that Wang was not yet ready to agree to their being taken in any quantity to a more convenient place. The man was, and not unreasonably, afraid that the news would get around and that he would be ejected. So for the moment Stein had to be satisfied with taking out a bundle or two at a time and carrying them to a little nearby room with paper-covered windows which made a convenient reading-room safe from prying eyes.

The date at which the chamber had been sealed was naturally a matter of great importance. Part of a mural painting had been hacked away when Wang opened up the chamber, and from what remained of it Stein felt fairly sure that it was not of a later period than the Sung dynasty, which immediately preceded the Mongol invasion. It was subsequently found that the dated manuscripts ranged from A.D. 406 to A.D. 996, which seemed to suggest that the library had been immured early in the eleventh century, perhaps shortly before the Tanguts invaded the country in 1035. 'So there was evidence from the first', he wrote, 'to encourage my hopes that a search through this big hoard would reveal manuscripts of importance and interest:

> But the very hugeness of the deposit was bound to give rise to misgivings. Should we have time to eat our way through this mountain of ancient paper with any thoroughness? Would not the timorous priest, swayed by his worldly fears and possible spiritual scruples, be moved to close down his shell before I had been able to extract any of the pearls? There were reasons urging us to work with all possible energy and speed, and others rendering it advisable to display studied *insouciance* and calm assurance. Somehow we managed to meet the conflicting requirements of the situation. But, I confess, the strain and anxieties of the busy days which followed were great.

The real trouble was that Stein was totally ignorant of literary Chinese, while Chiang knew nothing of Buddhist literature. But certain facts were soon apparent. The titles of the first batch of scrolls which they examined were all different, so that Stein's fear that he might find 'that inane repetition of a few identical texts in which modern Buddhism in Tibet and elsewhere revels', was gradually stilled. Further, it was evident that there was not the slightest damage from damp, as was only to be expected in a place where rain may not fall once in twenty years. Stein now set Chiang to make a rough list of titles; but as Wang, growing bolder, began to drag load after load of bundles from the chamber, Stein realized that it would have required 'a whole staff of learned scribes' to cope with this deluge of documents and had to abandon all thoughts of a catalogue.

To the general public, ignorant of oriental languages and indifferent to the niceties of Buddhist exegesis, the importance of the discovery of a hoard of Buddhist texts has to be taken on trust. But soon Stein came upon a large packet containing paintings on silk, *ex-votos* in silk and brocade, and miscellaneous fragments of painted paper and cloth – lovely things, many of which have now come to rest in the British Museum. A number of these paintings had triangular tops and streamers and were clearly temple banners; they were brilliantly painted with figures of Buddhas and Bodhisattvas, and most of them were in excellent condition. Later he found much larger silk paintings, carelessly folded and so brittle that all examination of them was for the time being impossible, but which ultimately yielded to the expertise of specialists at the British Museum.

It was now that Stein made the encouraging discovery that Wang was little interested in the paintings; so he began to put on one side 'for further inspection' (a euphemism for intended appropriation) as many as he felt he dared. Wang for his part, delighted to see Stein's enthusiasm for what he considered little better than rubbish, began to ply him with bundles of paintings, in the hope that he would forget about the, to him, far more precious rolls of Chinese canonical texts.

But Stein too was even more interested in the books than in the paintings, and he had already found treasures of every kind, including manuscripts in Sanskrit, Brahmi, and certain 'unknown' languages used in Turkestan Buddhism. By the end of the day he was completely exhausted; but he summoned up the energy to tell Wang yet again of his deep devotion to Buddhist lore in general and to the memory of his patron saint in particular. 'What better proof of his guidance and favour could I claim', he said, 'than that I should have been allowed to behold such a wonderful hidden store of sacred relics belonging to his own times and partly derived, perhaps, from his Indian wanderings, within a cave-temple which so ardent an admirer of Hsuan-tsang had restored and was now guarding?' He even ventured to refer to the painting of Hsuan-tsang crossing the river and to point the moral which had so forcibly struck him.

Wang had already as good as admitted that the great scholar-saint, in revealing to his disciple the hiding-place of those precious remains, must have had a purpose, and that this purpose could only be that the world should be allowed to see them and study them. And Wang, who was barely literate, could himself do nothing but hand them over to the right person. Now Chiang joined in, pleading 'with all the force of his soft reasoning that by allowing me, a faithful disciple of Hsuan-tsang, to render accessible to Western students the literary and other relics which a providential discovery had placed so abundantly in his keeping, he would do an act of real religious merit.' Then for the first time there came the vaguest, half-whispered hint of a possible transaction – of purchase in exchange for a substantial donation for the benefit of the shrine that Wang had so meritoriously and so hideously restored.

Late that night Stein heard cautious footsteps; they were those of Chiang, making sure that the coast was clear. Soon afterwards he returned with a large bundle over his shoulders containing everything that Stein had put aside that day 'for further inspection':

> For seven nights more he thus came to my tent, when everybody had gone to sleep, with the same precautions, his slight figure panting under loads which each time grew heavier, and ultimately required carriage by instalments. For hands accustomed only to wield pen and paper it was a trying task, and never shall I forget the good-natured ease and cheerful devotion with which it was performed by that most willing of helpmates.

As Stein struggled to sort and classify the ever-growing pile of manuscripts he began to curse his total lack of Sinological training. 'How gladly', he wrote, 'would I then have exchanged one-half of my Indian knowledge for a tenth of its value in Chinese!' For though Wang still stubbornly refused to let any Chinese sacred texts out of his sight, there was a quantity of Chinese records – letters, monastic certificates and accounts – to which he attached no importance but which were probably of great interest. Each day brought its new and exciting discoveries.

Kwan-yin, a painting on silk from the Caves of the Thousand Buddhas

There were manuscripts in Uighur, Sogdian and Runic Turki, and a bilingual text which later led to the interpretation of a known but hitherto untranslatable Central Asian language. Some of the Uighur manuscripts were in book form, not scrolls – quarto size and sewn like a modern book. A Chinese scroll, dated A.D. 868, with a fine block-printed picture, established that the art of printing from wooden blocks was far older than had previously been believed. Among the silk paintings Stein found a superb embroidered picture showing an almost life-sized Buddha between four Bodhisattvas; above them is an '*art nouveau*' canopy, below two groups of donors in adoration.

A new stage had by this time been reached in the negotiations, for Wang had been brought so far as to accept 'judiciously administered doses of silver'. Though still at times refractory, he had gradually been led from one concession to another, 'and we took care not to leave him much time for reflection'. He had agreed to two of Stein's most trustworthy servants lending a hand with the laborious task of clearing the chamber, and had himself produced 'a sort of famulus whose discretion could be relied on' to assist them. On 28 May, after the outer temple gates had been locked, more than a thousand bundles of Chinese rolls and a quantity of Tibetan texts were carried out and laid in neat rows on the floor of the spacious main cella of the temple.

Then Wang took the initiative and made a business proposition. In return for a substantial donation to his temple he was, he said, prepared to surrender a certain number of manuscripts and paintings for removal to a 'temple of learning in Ta-Ying-Kuo', or England; these could not, however, include any Chinese religious texts. But Stein was still determined to get everything – to 'rescue' everything, as he put it – and he enjoined Chiang to use to the utmost his powers of persuasion. Chiang did. He spoke of the piety of such an act, which would meet with the warmest approval of the Buddha and his Arhats, and let slip the mention of a sum such as 'forty silver horse-shoes' (about Rs. 5,000) – though Stein was in fact prepared to give double that amount if necessary. This money would enable Wang to 'beautify' his temple beyond his wildest dreams or, if he could overcome his scruples, to retire and live in style in his distant native province of Shan-hsi.

But Chiang pleaded in vain: the Chinese religious scrolls, said Wang, must stay, and two days of intensive persuasion failed to budge him. Then one morning Stein arrived at the caves to find that Wang had spent the night shifting all the disputed scrolls back into their gloomy prison. But Stein held two trump cards in his hand: he had in his tent a considerable number of manuscripts and paintings; and Wang, sullen though he had now become, could not conceal the fact that he coveted the money. Finally he agreed to let Stein have fifty bundles of Chinese scrolls and five of Tibetan, as well as all that had been carried night after night to Stein's tent 'for further inspection'; for these he was to receive four silver horse-shoes – only one tenth of the sum suggested for the whole collection.

Wang's seasonal begging tour in the Tun-huang oasis was now due, and he vanished for a week. He returned in a still more cooperative mood, having assured himself that his secret had not been discovered in Tun-huang and prepared now to sell another twenty bundles of scrolls. Stein and Chiang spent many

凡於讀經先念淨口業真言□通
　　唵
　　唵
　　唵
　　唵
　　摩訶唵唎
　　補唵唎　　娑婆訶
補唵唎　　唵唎
奉請八大金剛
奉請青除災金剛
奉請辟毒金剛
奉請黃隨求金剛
奉請白淨水金剛
奉請赤聲金剛
奉請定除災金剛
奉請紫賢金剛
奉請大神金剛
奉請陀尼金剛
金剛般若波羅蜜經
如是我聞一時佛在舍衛國祇樹給孤獨園與大
北在眾十二百五十人其食時著□□□城乞□□

The earliest known example of printing from a wooden block, A.D. *868*

hours carefully packing all these in twelve cases, some of which had to be brought from Tun-huang without arousing suspicion. 'When I finally said goodbye to the "Thousand Buddhas", [Wang's] jovial sharp-cut face had resumed once more its look of shy but self-contented serenity. We parted in fullest amity.'

Four months later Stein was back again at the Caves, to find that in the interval the secret had not leaked and that Wang's spiritual influence, such as it was, had suffered no diminution; he therefore had little difficulty in persuading him to part with two hundred more bundles of manuscripts. Stein congratulated himself upon the successful issue of his negotiations; 'but', he added, 'my time for feeling true relief came when all the twenty-four cases, heavy with manuscript treasures rescued from that strange place of hiding, and the five more filled with paintings and other art relics from the same cave, had been deposited safely in the British Museum.'

Arthur Waley, in an 'Afterword' to his *Ballads and Stories from Tun-huang,* and Mrs Vincent in her *The Sacred Oasis,* have described the subsequent fate of the caves and their treasures. A year after Stein had made his great haul, Professor Paul Pelliot, who could read Chinese, brought to Paris a smaller but more discriminatingly chosen selection of scrolls, and in 1910 the Chinese Government secured ten thousand manuscripts – the residue of a still larger number from which many had been pilfered on their way to Peking. The following year the Japanese obtained six hundred scrolls that Wang had cunningly hidden in the stucco images he had dedicated at the caves. In 1920 a band of White Russians, fleeing from the Communists, found asylum in several of the caves, where they lit fires whose smoke damaged the murals, and defaced the walls with drawings 'of that type which shows a man with a cigar in his mouth', scratched in the soft plaster. Wang died in harness in 1931.

In the late thirties, during the Sino-Japanese war, the ancient road passing near Tun-huang was put into a state of repair just sufficient to allow the passage of trucks carrying war materials from Russia, thus rendering the shrine 'accessible to a horde of casual sight-seers and, bluntly expressed, vandals'. To combat this, in 1943 the Chinese Government officially declared the Caves a site of archaeological and historical importance and set up the National Art Institute of Tun-Huang to safeguard the sculptures and murals. This task it has worthily fulfilled, and the present régime has continued the good work.

Stein's booty, though half of it was ultimately destined for India, was sent to the British Museum for the laborious and highly-skilled work of restoration. Among those who played a part in this was F. W. Andrews, Stein's 'devoted friend and helpmate' and the brother of Augustus George Andrews – better known as the actor George Arliss.

One further point, already touched upon, remains to be considered: the ethics of Stein and Pelliot in cajoling and bribing the custodian of the shrine to sell – and to foreigners at that – the manuscripts and paintings under his charge. 'The Chinese', wrote Waley, 'regard Stein and Pelliot as robbers'; and he suggests that, to understand their feelings on the subject, we should try to imagine how we should react 'if a Chinese archaeologist were to come to England, discover a *cache* of medieval MSS at a ruined monastery, bribe the custodian to part with them, and carry them off to Peking.' The Elgin marbles and the Linnaean collections were at least purchased openly.

Stein's attitude was of course that of all European archaeologists in the nineteenth century: he regarded it as a rescue operation. And he did at least *rescue* what he found, whereas another well-known Central Asian archaeologist, who though also now dead had better remain unnamed, did untold damage by the crude methods he employed to cut paintings from walls. However, though there might be some justification for behaviour such as Stein's in Moslem countries, where all appreciation of pre-Muhammadan culture had disappeared, in China – even in this remote backwater – it had no comparable excuse. Moreover the contents of, for example, Tutankhamen's tomb have come to rest in the land of their origin; the finest of the spoils of the Caves of the Thousand Buddhas are today in London, Paris and Delhi.

Epilogue: Samarkand Today

Today you can fly to Samarkand.

But then, of course, no doubt you always could: there has always been air transport in the Orient – the instant, silent flight of the magic carpet, the more leisurely but no less silent progress of the dove-drawn car. Mahomet ascended to heaven on the back of a mythical, composite animal and Elijah in a whirlwind-propelled chariot of fire, while Alexander the Great, as we have already seen, explored the stratosphere in a glass cage drawn by hungry griffins. These were the great pioneer days of Asian aviation.

Yet the aeroplane, almost compulsory transport for the long-distance traveller in this feverish age in which we live, lacks all romance, and I am glad that once, forty-five years ago, I crossed on camel-back a part of the northern Sahara; for now I know something at any rate of the feel of golden journeying: the great unbroken silence and the great unmolested landscape; the blistering heat of the day, and the blessed moment when the sun drops, a ball of fire, below the horizon; the succulent smell from the camp fires on which the rice and *kebab* are being pre-pared; the sharp cold of the desert night; the songs of the cameleers and their prayers as they turn towards Mecca; God's priceless gift of water (for no man needs wine in the desert, where water tastes like wine), and his yet greater gift of perfect sleep without the crude aid of a sleeping-pill. This was what those merchants knew who, century after century, crossed the heart of Asia bearing silks, spices and jewels from India and Cathay, hides and cloth from the West. I am glad, too, that I visited Afghanistan in the 'fifties in the proper discomfort of broken-down and constantly breaking down peasant and pilgrim buses (thus seeing Herat when there were still only two resident Europeans in a population of a hundred thou-sand, one of whom was murdered soon after I left); for travel only stops being tourism when you have the front half of your neighbour's sheep on your knees and her hens picking at your shoe-strings, and even then it is a long way short of exploration.

You can still find the East of the *Arabian Nights* if you are prepared to travel rough; if you are young and fit and bold enough, and if you know where to go. But in the spring of 1971 I flew to Russian Central Asia, accepting the disagreeable fact that a septuagenarian must travel 'smooth' and that as Intourist so unroman-

An early 20th-century saph (13 ft 4 in. by 3 ft 7 in.), a type of rug made in western Turkestan and marketed in Samarkand

tically puts it, 'The Golden Road to Samarkand begins at the London Offices of Intourist at 292 Regent Street, London W1, or at any of its 50 or so accredited agencies', and continues in comfortable planes by way of Moscow to what it is still an effort to call 'the Soviet Central Asian Republic of Uzbekistan'.

A part of what I now write, a fortnight after my return from Samarkand, will probably be out of date almost before the ink is dry on the paper, because each day 'progress' is cutting out more and more of the picturesque but insanitary canker of the old city and replacing it by Western-style buildings: housing-blocks for the workers, shops and offices and cinemas, schools and museums and a modern university. The Samarkand – a twenty-storey Intourist hotel, towering and characterless and of a kind that has become only too familiar all the world over – has mushroomed almost overnight, and for all I know its lifts may already be working. Trolley-buses and cars roar past the Registan, the heart of the old city, where the gardens are municipally bright with cannas, floribunda roses and summer bedding, and where a cafeteria such as one might find on the front at Blackpool sells very welcome ice-creams. Undeniably all this is a fantastic achievement, and no one, whatever his political views, can visit Russia today without marvelling at the Soviet economic miracle – something almost incredible to one who, like myself, had not been back there since 1935. So I suppose that one is selfish in wishing that Samarkand had been treated more tenderly, that the new town had not been allowed to burst its banks and overwhelm the picturesque, unpractical, unsalubrious capital of Tamerlane.

Lord Curzon, who visited Samarkand and Bukhara in 1888 by the newly opened Transcaspian railway, admired modern Samarkand (then still a separate town) and wrote of Bukhara that he was glad to have seen it in 'the twilight epoch of its glory. Were I to go in later years it might be to find electric light in the highways.' He deplored the invasion of cheap and hideous Russian fabrics, and of vodka and champagne although the sale of these was still illegal in Bukhara. 'Westward civilisation in its Eastward march', he lamented, 'suggests no sadder reflection than that it cannot convey its virtues alone, but must come with Harpies in its train, and smirch with their foul contact the immemorial simplicity of Oriental life.' What would he have written of Samarkand could he have revisited it in 1971?

But in one respect Curzon would have found cause for satisfaction. In his day no attempt was being made to arrest the decay of Samarkand's historic ancient buildings. 'What with the depredations of vandals, the shock of earthquakes and the lapse of time,' he wrote, 'the visitor in the twentieth century may find cause to enquire with resentful surprise what has become of the fabled grandeurs of the old Samarkand. . . . A Society for the Preservation of Ancient Monuments should at once be formed in Russian Central Asia, and a custodian appointed to each of the more important ruins.' But he saw little hope of this happening, it being 'a step which can hardly be expected from a Government which has never, outside of Russia, shown the faintest interest in antiquarian preservation or research, and which would sit still till the crack of doom upon a site that was known to contain the great bronze Athene of Pheidias, or the lost works of Livy.' (Did the future Viceroy of India know, one may ask, when he wrote so scathingly of the Russians, that a former Viceroy had once proposed the sale of the Taj Mahal to serve as a quarry for marble?)

Thus it was in Russia, under the Tsars. But today all is changed, and skilful and loving restoration is now being carried out wherever damage is not irreparable. Tottering buildings are being propped up, leaning minarets straightened, and fallen tiles replaced. For the great advantage which tile-mosaic has over carved stone, carved wood or painting is that new tiles are, at even a short distance, indistinguishable from old. One has only to look at photographs of Samarkand taken by Count Morra[1] in the 1890s, or those reproduced in Lord Curzon's *Russia in Central Asia,* to appreciate how much restoration has taken place and how successfully it has been done.

Nonetheless, the visitor who goes to Samarkand with his Flecker in his pocket, with his mind stored with dreams of Omar Khayyam and the *Arabian Nights,* must be prepared to sustain an initial shock. Shadows still pass gigantic on the sand (or, more probably, the tarmac); but they are those of articulated lorries, not of a camel caravan. That jam at breakfast has been meticulously jarred in a Samarkand canning factory, and may not be such as God's own Prophet eats in Paradise. Those broideries of intricate design, those printed hangings in enormous bales, have been mass-produced in the Tashkent textile *kombinat,* and true native dress will soon be extinct. Yet the visit to Samarkand is enormously worth while; for its 'fabled grandeurs' have not disappeared: they have merely been crudely incorporated, like the Colosseum in Rome or the Duomo in Florence, in a thriving modern city whose name even the Soviets have not dared to change to Gargarinobad or Kosygingrad.

There are four principal ancient buildings, or groups of buildings, in Samarkand: the Gur-i-Mir mausoleum, the mosque and *madrasa* of Bibi Khanum, the three great madrasas that command three of the four sides of the Registan, and, just outside the old boundaries of the city, the string of mausolea known as the Shah-Zinda.

If the tourist stays, as presumably he will if he visits Samarkand in the near future, at the Samarkand Hotel (where *café-au-lait*-coloured doves fly in and out of the bedroom windows), he is strongly advised to visit first, and unescorted by even the most sympathetic of guides, the Gur-i-Mir – the great mausoleum built by Tamerlane to receive the body of his favourite grandson, Muhammad Sultan. A pleasant, informal avenue, shaded by white mulberry trees whose dropping fruits taste like muscatel grapes, leads in a few minutes from the hotel to the mausoleum. And there, suddenly, one is in a different world, where something of the calm of an English cathedral close prevails. For the avenue leads no further, except to humble alleys no doubt destined soon to be swept away. There, as the sun drops low and the last busload of sightseers vanishes, or in the cool of early morning before the first arrives, one can almost dream oneself back into the days of Tamerlane.

The immense cantaloup-shaped dome, turquoise and ultramarine, dominates the building which also contains the tomb of Tamerlane and those of other

[1] See Derek Hill and Otto Grabar's *Islamic Architecture and its Decoration.*

Timurid princes, among them that of his astronomer grandson, Ulugh Beg. The actual tombs lie in the crypt, the tombstones being in the main chamber whose roof is decorated in almost Moorish style. 'Only a stone, and my name upon it,' Tamerlane is said to have whispered as he lay dying at Otrar; it is, however, and very properly, no ordinary stone which marks the last resting-place of this extraordinary man, but a monolith (now broken in two: some say by Nadir Shah) of dark green jade, or nephrite – the largest in the world – brought by Ulugh Beg to Samarkand from the mountains of Chinese Turkestan. Accustomed as one is to the pompous tombs and fulsome epitaphs so often to be seen in Christian churches, it comes as a pleasant surprise to find this modesty; yet possibly the greatest butcher the world has ever known could have been more fittingly commemorated by the ingenuous inscription on an anonymous tomb in an anteroom of the Gur-i-Mir: 'If I were alive, people would not be glad.'

At the time of Curzon's visit one minaret of the Gur-i-Mir was still standing; now no more than a stump of it remains, and little more than an arch and some foundations of the madrasa and other buildings of which the mausoleum once formed a part. In the court, to the right of the entrance, may be seen the so-called *kok-tash*, a large and beautifully carved slab of whitish stone on which, according to tradition, Tamerlane and his successors were enthroned, and beside it a kind of well-head which our very intelligent guide alleged to have been the Amir's bath.

The hub of Samarkand is the Registan, which Curzon declared to be, even in its ruin, the noblest public square in the world. 'I know of nothing in the East approaching it in massive simplicity and grandeur,' he wrote, 'and nothing in Europe,

In the courtyard of the Gur-i-Mir, Samarkand: the stone on which Tamerlane is said to have been enthroned

save perhaps on a humbler scale the Piazza di San Marco in Venice, which can even aspire to enter the competition. No European spectacle indeed can adequately be compared with it, in our inability to point to an open space in any Western city that is commanded on three of its four sides by Gothic cathedrals of the finest order.'

In Tamerlane's day the Registan was a market-place, none of its three madrasas having been erected in his lifetime (though one or more of them may have replaced earlier buildings). The oldest of the existing colleges is that of Ulugh Beg, built about 1420, in which the royal astronomer is said to have lectured. Opposite, and clearly in imitation of it, is the Shir Dar or 'Lion-bearing', erected between 1619 and 1636 and so named from the crude representations of the Lion and Sun of Persia above the great central *ivan*; though inferior to its model, it has been treated more kindly by time, and its two turquoise ribbed domes still stand. On the north side of the square rises the Tila Kari (or 'Gilded') *madrasa*, built about the middle of the seventeenth century.

Splendid though the Registan undoubtedly is, I would rate the Maidan at Isfahan, which Curzon allows to be 'one of the most imposing piazzas in the world', as even finer. What, in my opinion, makes the Registan less effective than its counterpart in Isfahan is the colour of much of the tilework, both on the façades of the *madrasas* and in their courts. Admittedly the domes of the Shir Dar are a dazzling turquoise; but elsewhere the brilliance is often diminished by the too liberal use of alternating unglazed buff tiles which reduces the overall colour to a washy glaucous. In Isfahan the dome of the Lutfullah mosque is frankly buff; but so rich is the blue of the tiles on the façade that a blue dome would have been too overpowering. The blue of the Royal mosque is for the most part softer, and thus one can accept the vast acres of it.

The tremendous ruins of the *madrasa* and the mosque – once the largest in Central Asia – of Bibi Khanum tower like the skeleton of a great whale over a busy market which is now enclosed, but which a generation or two ago sprawled to the very portal of the buildings and even within their crumbling walls. Legend associates the mosque with Bibi Khanum, reputedly the favourite wife of Tamerlane and the daughter of the Emperor of China, and further asserts that she fell in love with the young architect who designed it and who, to avoid the Amir's wrath, took off – air transport again – from the top of one of the minarets and was never more heard of. The sober facts are that the mosque was simply a Friday (or Congregational) mosque, ordered by Tamerlane to replace an older one on the same site, and built with the loot from his Indian campaigns. It was begun on 11 May 1399 – a day chosen as astrologically favourable – and craftsmen from all over the Timurid world, aided by 'ninety-five mountainous elephants' to drag materials to the site, were responsible for it.

The Bibi Khanum is noble even in its decay, for which too hurried construction, frequent earthquakes, and Russian neglect in the nineteenth century, are principally responsible. The dome is tremendous, the entrance portal sixty feet wide and higher than that of Peterborough cathedral – prompting a chronicler to write of the Bibi Khanum, 'Its dome would have been unique had it not been for the heavens, and unique would have been its portal had it not been for the Milky Way.' Within the sanctuary, but moved now to the court to prevent damage from falling masonry, once stood a white marble *rahla,* or lectern, made to support a Koran whose pages were more than six feet high and which was intended to be read from a gallery.[1] Crawling under the lectern is said to be a remedy for lumbago, but this difficult performance would seem more calculated to induce than to alleviate it.

The finest tile-mosaics in Samarkand are to be found in the Shah-Zinda, a chain of buildings ascending a flowery, now tomb-strewn hillside about three-quarters of a mile to the east of the Bibi Khanum. Here, too, a blessed peace still reigns in the early and late hours of the day. Qasim ibn Abbas, known as the Shah-Zinda or 'Living King', was a cousin of the Prophet who came to Samarkand in the early days of the Hegira to convert its fire-worshipping inhabitants to Islam, and was duly beheaded for his pains. Legend has it that the martyr, following the example of St Denis, picked up his severed head and plunged with it into a well from which he will one day re-emerge. A prophecy, believed to date from the fourteenth century, foretold that he would arise and save Samarkand if the Russians attacked the city; but 1868 came and Qasim did not stir a finger to help, thus permanently damaging his reputation.

The Shah-Zinda, which is entered through a gate-house built by Ulugh Beg, consists of a steep flight of steps bordered on either side by a series of exquisite mortuary chapels, mostly Timurid and dating from the late fourteenth or early fifteenth centuries. Tamerlane's niece, Shad-i-Mulk, lies here, his wife Tuman Aka and other members and friends of the royal family who died too soon to find a place beside the Amir in the Gur-i-Mir, or who were considered unworthy to join such distinguished company. Another tomb is that of Qasi Zadeh Rumi, one of Ulugh Beg's two principal scientific collaborators. Qasim himself sleeps – putting in time, as it were – in an elaborate four-tiered richly-tiled tomb which has been described as the most splendid of its kind in Asia.

On rising ground to the north of the Shah-Zinda once stood the Marakanda of Alexander the Great, and its successor the medieval Samarkand that was sacked and looted by Jenghiz Khan and his Mongol hordes in 1221. The extensive site, which is now being excavated, is of interest chiefly to the archaeologist; but the finds are displayed in a handsome new museum, erected on the spot and soon to be opened. Here will be seen a copy of a magnificent though much damaged mural, representing processional scenes and dating from about the seventh century, which decorated the four walls of a large hall in a house or palace on the hillside above the museum; the original is in the Hermitage.

Still further from the town, on high ground above the River Zarafshan, once stood Ulugh Beg's observatory – in its day among the most important in the world, but destroyed by fanatics some years after his death. The site, long forgotten, was rediscovered in 1908 by a Russian archaeologist named Viatkin, and excavation has brought to light the lower part of the enormous quadrant – somewhat resembling a 'subway escalator', says the Intourist leaflet – by means of which Ulugh Beg and his colleagues calculated, without the aid of a telescope, the positions of more than a thousand stars. They also observed the sun, moon and

[1] Leaves from a giant koran may be seen in Tehran and in Meshed.

planets, and determined the inclination of the ecliptic, the precession of the equi-
noxes and the length of the year. A small but interesting museum, perhaps an
attempted reconstruction of Ulugh Beg's three-storeyed[1] observatory, has been
erected nearby; but here, as almost everywhere in Russia, the visitor must regret
that nothing has been labelled in any western European language.

Two expeditions may be made in a day by car from Samarkand: to Shahr-i-Sabz,
and to Panjikent; Bukhara can be visited in a day by air, but those who are prepared to face the mild discomfort of the Hotel Bukhara should certainly stay for
several nights. Khiva is also said to be very rewarding; but it is four hundred miles
from Samarkand, and Intourist is not over-eager for one to go there – presumably
because it blushes for the accommodation available to tourists.

An old man of Samarkand

Clavijo's account of Shahr-i-Sabz, the birthplace of Tamerlane and at one time
his intended capital, has already been given.[2] The town lies fifty miles to the south
of Samarkand, across a five-thousand-foot pass in the Hissar range. Of the Akserai,
Tamerlane's great palace, only two gigantic fragments of the piers of the entrance
portal still stand; but the tilework, even in its decay, is magnificent, and with the
eyes of faith one can picture something at all events of the splendours that once
existed. There are also at Shahr-i-Sabz the remains of three Timurid mausolea.

I did not get to Panjikent. This ancient city, which had its heyday in the seventh
and eighth centuries A.D., lies about forty-five miles to the east of Samarkand, and
a visit to it is rewarding to archaeologists; but the fine though damaged mural
paintings and the wooden figures found there may now be seen in the Hermitage
in Leningrad. There are reproductions, some in colour, of a number of them in
Aleksandr Belenitsky's *The Ancient Civilisation of Central Asia*.

Bukhara I saw in a temperature of 105°F and all too hurriedly, for there still
remains a great wealth of mosques and *madrasas* which require leisure to track
down. Devout Bukhariots used to boast that they could worship Allah in a different
mosque on each day of the year; and though this was probably always an exaggeration, Bukhara, ever since the coming of Islam, was, and remained until relatively recently, a great religious centre. Today only one is functional. Moreover,
modernization has not yet totally extinguished the old way of life, and as in Curzon's day one can still occasionally see in some back alley a pauper who 'walks
abroad with the dignity of a patriarch and in the garb of a prince'. But since the
time of Curzon's visit much of the magic has vanished. No longer do the muezzins
call from a hundred mosques; and if a part at least of the town is still a 'wilderness
of crooked alleys, winding irregularly between the blind walls of clay-built
houses', these alleys are now crossed by pipes conveying natural gas. No longer,
alas, is Bukhara the 'most interesting city in the world'.

The most conspicuous monument in Bukhara is the lovely Kalayan minaret.
Built in 1127 of honey-coloured bricks so disposed as to produce a texture like
that of an 'Aran' knitted sweater, it rises above a complex of religious buildings to
a height of nearly one hundred and fifty feet. From its summit, which is crowned
by a stork's nest, the muezzin once summoned the faithful to prayer, and in times
of war – which meant most of the time – watchmen scanned the horizon for the

---

[1] So described by Babur.
[2] See page 146.

approach of an enemy army. It was also a convenient place from which to hurl down malefactors to their death – a practice far from extinct when Curzon was there. He himself witnessed a public flogging, and heard gruesome accounts of tortures recently enacted with official approval.

The Arg or citadel, both palace and prison in the time of the Amirs, is still much as it was on the day when Conolly rode insolently through its gates. Inside there is now a little historical museum, and in a square behind the Arg stands the Zindan prison in which Stoddart and Conolly were at one time incarcerated. Though a recent guidebook describes as a tourist attraction the Amir's snake-pit, furnished with 'two dummy prisoners and a dummy gaoler looking down on them from above', our guide – a formidable woman – denied all knowledge of it; presumably taste in Soviet propaganda has changed (Russification is undoubtedly slowing down), and only a gigantic rhinoceros-hide whip in the citadel museum now remains as visible evidence of the brutality of the Amirs before the kindly Russians came to the rescue.

In the Kirov Park of Rest and Culture, and not to be missed by even the most hurried visitor, is the recently restored mausoleum of the Samanids – a cubical, domed brick building erected in the first half of the tenth century as a tomb for several princes of the ruling Samanid dynasty, under whom Bukhara, the capital of an empire which included such famous and widely separated towns as Samarkand, Merv (now Mary), Nishapur, Rayy, Amul, Herat and Balkh, fully deserved its title of *Sherif,* 'the Noble'.

Such today are Samarkand and Bukhara – cities for so long virtually inaccessible to all but the daring few, but now, in a sense, as open to tourism as any of the historic towns of Western Europe. In a sense – for there is this difference: the visitor to Russian Central Asia, unless he speaks fairly fluent Russian and is prepared to pay three times the proper price, is still virtually obliged to go there in a guided packaged party. Intourist can of course keep a more watchful eye, a more controlling hand, on a herd of sheep than on an independent-minded and inquisitive goat, and the unresisting sheep, even before he leaves Moscow, may well have had his fill of Lenin and the constant parroting of 'our glorious October Revolution'. The Russians ought by this time to feel themselves secure enough to stop behaving like the child who goes on pestering his father to admire his new clockwork toy.

So it would be an excellent thing if Intourist, which has already been persuaded to tolerate cultural tours to Moscow and Leningrad by members of the National Art-Collections Fund, could bring itself to accept that there are also a large number of people who, while in no way wishing to belittle or decry the Soviet achievement, go to Russian Central Asia primarily to see its *pre*-Soviet heritage. Further, there must be many who would like a Central Asian tour (so advertised) to *be* a Central Asian tour, and not one which devotes to Moscow (and thus to Lenin-worship) almost a half of its brief fortnight.

Therefore at least one such tour might be designed for the art-lover and the archaeologist, and be given over entirely to Samarkand, Bukhara and Khiva, with no more than the necessary night in Moscow on the inward and outward journeys. Alma Ata, or 'Father of Apples' – a handsome and well-designed new town which has acquired in less than half a century a population of more than half a million – could well be omitted from its itinerary, though admittedly there is excitement in seeing the distant peaks of the T'ien Shan (or Celestial) Mountains which constitute the frontier with China. Tashkent too, the million-inhabitant capital of Uzbekistan, is since the great earthquake of 1966 a purely modern city, and of interest only for its museums.

The visitor to Isfahan – the Persian equivalent of Samarkand – is free to go there when and as he likes, to stay as long as he likes, and indeed to travel everywhere in Iran without Nannie holding his hand, guiding his steps and his thoughts and, an eye always on her watch, for ever urging him onwards. Could not the Russians give similar facilities to politically uncommitted students of Islamic architecture who simply wish to see at their own pace, in their own way, and for a fair price, what still remains of the wonders of the fabled cities of Russian Turkestan?

W.J.W.B.

A flying carpet borne by doves

OVERLEAF *General Map*

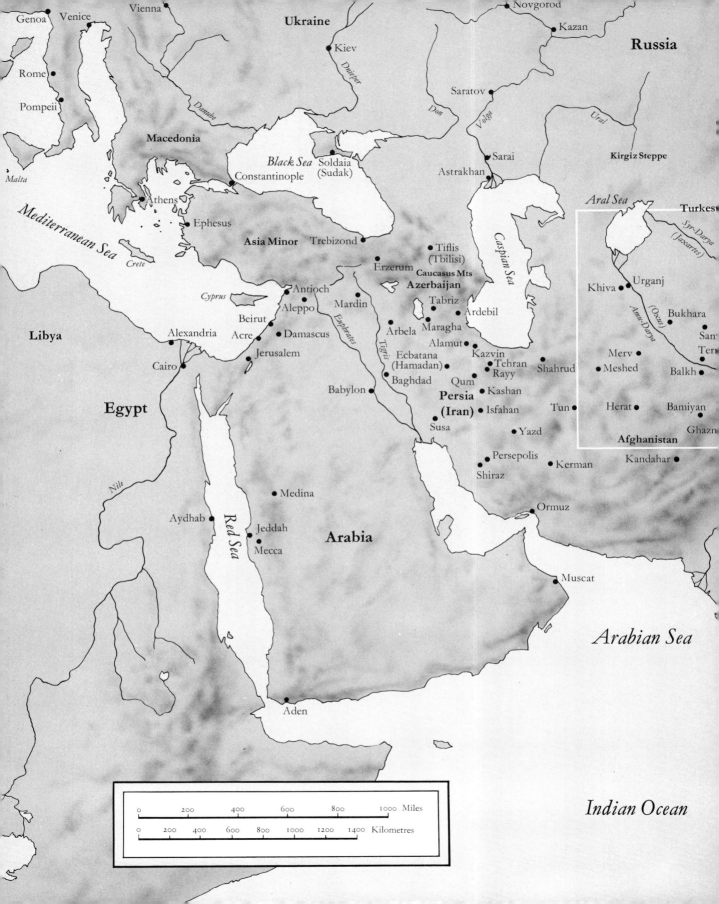

Genoa
Venice
Vienna
Rome
Pompeii
Macedonia
Malta
Mediterranean Sea
Athens
Crete
Ephesus
Asia Minor
Ukraine
Danube
Dnieper
Kiev
Black Sea
Constantinople
Soldaia (Sudak)
Trebizond
Erzerum
Tiflis ('Tbilisi')
Caucasus Mts
Azerbaijan
Tabriz
Ardebil
Caspian Sea
Novgorod
Kazan
Russia
Saratov
Don
Volga
Ural
Sarai
Astrakhan
Kirgiz Steppe
Aral Sea
Turkes
Syr-Darya (Jaxartes)
Khiva
Urganj
Bukhara
Sam
Amu-Darya (Oxus)
Ter
Merv
Balkh
Meshed
Libya
Cyprus
Antioch
Aleppo
Mardin
Beirut
Euphrates
Acre
Damascus
Arbela
Maragha
Alamut
Kazvin
Tehran
Rayy
Shahrud
Tun
Herat
Bamiyan
Ghazn
Afghanistan
Alexandria
Cairo
Jerusalem
Babylon
Ecbatana (Hamadan)
Baghdad
Qum
Kashan
Isfahan
Persia (Iran)
Susa
Yazd
Kerman
Kandahar
Egypt
Nile
Medina
Aydhab
Red Sea
Jeddah
Mecca
Arabia
Persepolis
Shiraz
Ormuz
Muscat
Aden
Arabian Sea
Tigris

Indian Ocean

| 0 | 200 | 400 | 600 | 800 | 1000 Miles |
| 0 | 200 | 400 | 600 | 800 | 1000 | 1200 | 1400 Kilometres |

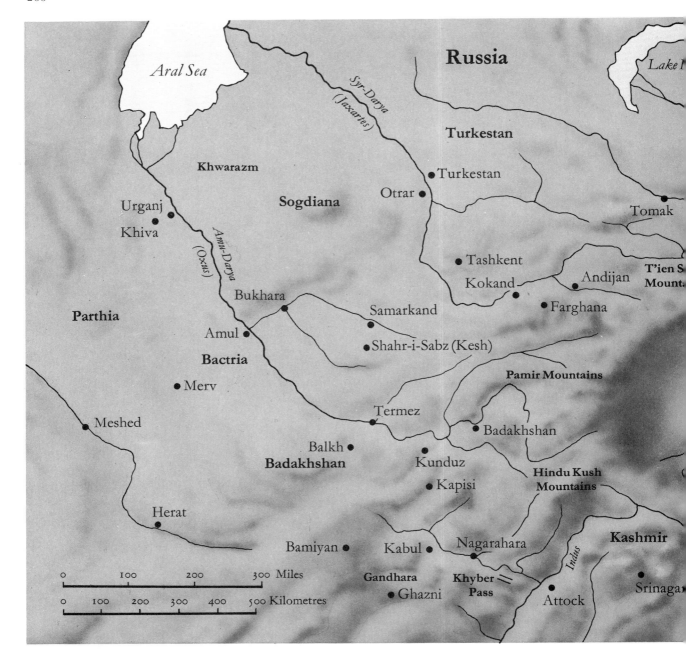

Aral Sea

Syr-Darya
(Jaxartes)

Russia

Lake I

Khwarazm

Turkestan

Sogdiana

● Turkestan

Otrar ●

Tomak ●

Urganj ●
● Khiva

Amu-Darya
(Oxus)

● Tashkent

Kokand

● Andijan

T'ien S
Mount

Parthia

Bukhara ●

Samarkand ●

● Farghana

Amul ●

Shahr-i-Sabz (Kesh) ●

Bactria

Pamir Mountains

● Merv

Termez ●

● Badakhshan

Meshed ●

Balkh ●

Badakhshan

Kunduz ●

**Hindu Kush
Mountains**

● Kapisi

Herat ●

Bamiyan ●

Kabul ●

Nagarahara ●

Indus

Kashmir

Gandhara

**Khyber
Pass**

Srinagar ●

● Ghazni

Attock ●

0   100   200   300 Miles

0   100   200   300   400   500 Kilometres

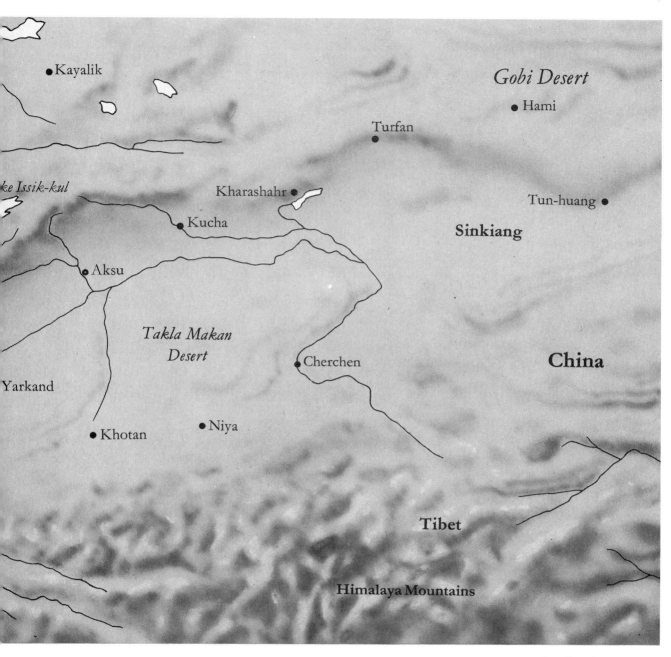

Gobi Desert

● Hami

Turfan

Tun-huang ●

Sinkiang

● Kayalik

ke Issik-kul

Kharashahr ●

● Kucha

● Aksu

*Takla Makan
Desert*

● Cherchen

China

Yarkand

● Khotan

● Niya

Tibet

Himalaya Mountains

*An enlarged section of the
general map*

Bibliography

The field covered is so large that it is possible to list only a few of the books that I have read or consulted.

Arrian. *Campaigns of Alexander the Great*. Translated by Aubrey de Selincourt. Harmondsworth, Penguin, 1958, 1962, 1972.

Babur. *The Babur-nama in English*. Translated by Annette S. Beveridge. London, Luzac, in parts 1912–22.

Bamm, Peter. *Alexander the Great*. London, Thames & Hudson, 1968.

Belenitsky, A. *The Ancient Civilisations of Central Asia*. Translated by J. Hogarth. London, Barrie & Jenkins, 1969.

Bitsch, Jørgen. *Mongolia: Unknown Land*. Translated by Reginald Spink. London, Allen & Unwin, 1963.

Borodin, George. *Cradle of Splendour*. London, Staples Press, 1945.

Boulnois, L. *The Silk Road*. Translated by D. Chamberlain. London, Allen & Unwin, 1966.

Burn, Andrew Robert. *Alexander the Great and the Hellenistic Empire*. London, Hodder & Stoughton for the English University Press, 1947.

Burnes, Sir Alexander. *Travels into Bokhara*. London, John Murray, 1834.

Byron, Robert. *The Road to Oxiana*. London, Macmillan, 1937. London, John Lehmann, 1950.

Cable, Alice M., and French, F. *The Gobi Desert*. London, Hodder & Stoughton, 1942, 1946.

Caldecott, R. M., editor. *The Life of Baber*. Abridgment of the translation by J. Leyden and W. Erskine. London, James Darling, 1844. Edinburgh, John Chisholm, 1844.

Carpine, Jean Piande. *Histoire des Mongols*. Translated by P. Clément Schmitt. Paris, 1961.

Cary, George. *The Medieval Alexander*. Edited by D. J. A. Ross. Cambridge, University Press, 1956.

Christie, Ella R. *Through Khiva to Golden Samarkand*. London, Seely Service, 1925.

Curzon, Lord. *Russia in Central Asia*. London, Longman's, Green, 1889.

Dulles, F. R. *Eastward Ho!*. London, John Lane, 1931.

Edwardes, S. M. *Babur: Diarist and Despot*. London, A. M. Philpot, 1926.

Fa(Hsien). *Travels of Fah-hian and Sung-yun*. Translated by S. Beal. London, Trubner, 1869.

Gascoigne, Bamber. *The Great Moghuls*. London, Cape, 1971.

Gerasimov, M. M. *The Face Finder*. London, Hutchinson, 1971.

Gibbon, Edward. *The Decline and Fall of the Roman Empire*. First published 1776–81. Numerous editions.

Glubb, Sir John Bagot. *The life and Times of Muhammad*. London, Hodder & Stoughton, 1970.

Gonzales de Clavijo, Ruy. *Embassy to the Court of Tamerlane*. London, Hakluyt Society, 1859. London, Broadway Travellers, Routledge, 1928.

Gray, Basil. *Buddhist Cave Paintings at Tun-Huang*. London, Faber, 1959.

Green, Peter. *Alexander the Great*. London, Weidenfeld & Nicolson, 1970.

Grousset, René. *Sur les Traces du Bouddha*. Paris, 1929.

Hambly, G., and others. *Central Asia*. London, Weidenfeld & Nicolson, 1969.

Hamilton, Angus. *Afghanistan*. London, Heinemann, 1906.

Hill, Derek, and Grabar, Otto. *Islamic Architecture and its Decoration*. London, Faber, 1964.

Hiouen Thsang. *Mémoires dur les Contrées Occidentales*. Translated by Shamans Hui-Li and Yen-tsung. Paris 1857–8.

Hui-Li, *The Life of Heuen-Tsang*. Translated by S. Beal. London, Kegan Paul, 1911.

Ibn Arabshah. *Tamerlane*. Translated by J. H. Sanders. London, Luzac, 1936.

Ibn Battuta. *Travels in Asia and Africa*. London, Broadway Travellers, Routledge, 1929. London, Hakluyt Society, 1958, 1962, 1971.

Irving, Washington. *The Life of Mahomet and His Successors*. London, George Routledge, 1851.

Jenkinson, Anthony, *see* Morgan, E. O., and Coote, C. H.

Lamb, Harold Albert. *Genghis Khan: The Emperor of All Men*. London, Thornton Butterworth, 1928.

Lamb, Harold Albert. *Tamerlane the Earth Shaker*. London, Thornton Butterworth, 1929.

Lane-Poole, Stanley, editor. *Babur*. London, 1899.

Le Coq, Albert von. *Die Buddische Spatantiken in Mittelasien*. Edited by E. Waldschmidt. 1922–33.

Le Coq, Albert von. *Buried Treasures of Chinese Turkestan*. Translated by Anna Barwell. London, Allen & Unwin, 1928.

Le Strange, Guy. *The Lands of the Eastern Caliphate*. Cambridge, University Press, 1896, 1905, 1930.

Lunt, James. *Bokhara Burnes*. London, Faber, 1969.

MacColl, Réné. *The Land of Ghenghis Khan*. London, Oldbourne, 1963.

Maclean, Sir Fitzroy. *A Person from England*. London, Cape, 1958.

Maclean, Sir Fitzroy. *Back to Bokhara*. London, Cape, 1959.

Malcolm, Sir John. *History of Persia*. London, 1815.

Mandel, Gabriele. *The Life and Times of Genghis Khan*. Translated by M. Cunningham. London, Hamlyn, 1970.

Mannin, Ethel. *South to Samarkand*. London, Jarrolds, 1936.

Milns, R. D. *Alexander the Great*. London, Robert Hale, 1968.

Morgan, E. D., and Coote, C. H. *Early Voyages and Travels to Russia* (including Jenkinson's voyages). London, Hakluyt Society, 1886.

O'Donovan, Edmond. *The Merv Oasis*. London, Smith, Elder & Co., 1882.

Olschiki. *Marco Polo's Asia*. Translated by John A. Scott. Berkeley and Los Angeles, University of California Press, 1960.

Palmer, H. P. *Joseph Wolff*. London, Heath Cranton, 1935.

Pelliot, Paul. *Mission Pelliot en Asie Centrale: les Grottes de Touen Houang*. Paris, 1914–24.

Pétis de la Croix, F. (the Elder). *The History of Genghizcan the Great*. 1722.

Phillips, E. D. *The Mongols*. London, Thames & Hudson, 1969.

Pigoulevskaya. *Sculpture and Frescoes of Ancient Penjakent* (text in Russian). 1959.

Plutarch. *Lives*. Numerous translations.

Polo, Marco. *The Travels of Marco Polo*. Numerous translations.

Polovtsoff, Aleksander. *The Land of Timur*. London, Methuen, 1932.

Prawdin, Michael (pseudonym). *The Builders of the Mongol Empire*. London, Allen & Unwin, 1963.

Rachewiltz, I. de. *Papal Envoys to the Great Khans*. Stanford, University Press, 1971.

Rice, Tamara Talbot. *Ancient Arts of Central Asia*. London, Thames & Hudson, 1965.

Rubruck, William of. *The Journey of William of Rubruck to the Eastern Parts of the World*. Translated by

W. W. Rockhill. London, Hakluyt Society, 1900.

Runciman, Sir Steven. *A History of the Crusades*. Cambridge, University Press, 1951–4.

Schafer, Edward H. *The Golden Peaches of Samarkand*. Berkeley and Los Angeles, University of California Press, 1963.

Schafer, Edward H. *The Vermilion Bird*. Berkeley and Los Angeles, University of California Press, 1967.

Schuyler, E. *Turkistan*. London, 1876.

Sharaf ad-Din, Ali. *Histoire de Tamerlane*. 1723.

Skrine, F., and Ross, E. D. *The Heart of Asia*. London, Methuen, 1899.

Stein, Sir Marc Aurel. *Ruins of Desert Cathay*. London, Macmillan, 1912. And other works.

Sykes, Sir Percy. *A History of Persia*. London, Macmillan, 1921.

Sykes, Sir Percy, editor. *The Story of Exploration and Adventure*. London, George Newnes, 1938–9.

Sykes, Sir Percy. *A History of Afghanistan*. London, Macmillan, 1940.

Tarn, William Woodthorpe. *Alexander the Great*. Cambridge, University Press, 1948.

Vambéry, Armin. *Travels in Central Asia*. London, 1864.

Vambéry, Armin. *History of Bokhara*. London, 1873.

Vambéry, Armin. *A. Vembéry: His Life and Adventures*. London, T. Fisher Unwin, 1884.

Wolff, Joseph. *Travels and Adventures*. London, 1860.

Notes on the Illustrations

Where the following abbreviations appear in the notes, they are intended to indicate the locations of pictures, and to acknowledge permission to reproduce photographs that the museums, art galleries and other institutions (or specifically their governing bodies) have granted in cases where they hold the copyright.

BM: The Trustees of the British Museum, London. BN: Bibliothèque Nationale, Paris. Bodleian: The Curators of the Bodleian Library, Oxford. Mansell: The Mansell Collection, London. NPG: National Portrait Gallery, London. RAS: Royal Asiatic Society, London. RGS: Royal Geographical Society, London. SMB: State Museums of Berlin: Museum of Indian Art. V & A: The Trustees of the Victoria and Albert Museum, London.

*Of the two hundred and fifty items in the Stein Collection only eighteen have been positively dated.

Gerasimov. Photos: John Massey Stewart.

166 Drawings from *Nauchnyi Podvig Samarkandskikh Astronomov* by N. I. Leonov, 1960. Gosudarstvennoe izdatelstvo fiziko-matematicheskoĭ literatury, Moscow. Photos: John Freeman.

166–7 Engraving by Carolus de la Haye from *Johannis Hevelii Prodromus Astronomiæ,* 1690. Bodleian.

168 Sketch by E. Durand, 1885. Photo: Peter Jennings.

169 Photo: Josephine Powell.

171–2 Miniatures from the Shah-nama of Firdausi, 1486. On loan to the BM by the RAS.

175 Copy of a 14th-century miniature, reproduced from *History of Persian Literature* by Edward G. Brown. Photo: John Freeman.

176 Woodcut by Marina Myunts from *Alisher Navoi,* Tashkent, 1968. Photo: Peter Jennings.

177 Medal struck at Tashkent, 1968. Photo: Peter Jennings.

180 Sculpture, Han Dynasty, 266 B.C.–A.D. 220. V & A (Crown Copyright).

182 Miniature by Mohammed Moumin of Herat, early 16th century. MS. Arabe 6075, f. 9. BN.

185 Indian miniature, Moghul period. BM.

186–7 Moghul painting, *c.* 1590. Drawing and colour by Bishan Das, faces by Nanha. V & A (Crown Copyright).

188 Photo: Christina Gascoigne.

191 Miniature, *c.* 1605. Raza Library, Rampur. Photo: Christina Gascoigne.

192–3 Photo: Josephine Powell.

195 Photo: Josephine Powell.

200 Drawings from *Sketches in Afghanistan* by James Atkinson, 1842. India Office Library. Photo: R. J. Fleming.

201 Photo: Josephine Powell.

203 Oil painting by B. M. Vasnetsov, 19th century. Tretyakov Gallery, Moscow. Photo: Novosti Press Agency.

204 Turkish miniature, 16th century. Topkapi Museum, Istanbul. Photo: Giraudon.

205 Engraving from *Travels into Muscovy, Persia, etc,* by Cornelius de Bruin, 18th

century. Photo: Peter Jennings.

206 Photo: Wilfrid Blunt.

211 Photo: John Massey Stewart.

213 Map from *Theatrum Orbis Terrarum* by Ortelius, 1570. Owned and photographed by John Massey Stewart.

214–15 Photo: Robert Harding.

216 Oil paintings by V. V. Vereshchagin (1842–1904). Tretyakov Gallery, Moscow. Photos: Novosti Press Agency.

220 Illustration from *Travels and Adventures* by Joseph Wolff, 1860. BM.

221 Illustration from *Bokhara: Its Amir and its People,* trs. by G. A. de Bode, 1845. Photo: J. Freeman.

223 Engraving from *Turkistan* by Eugene Schuyler, 1876. Photo: Peter Jennings.

224 Engraving from *Campaigning on the Oxus* by J. A. MacGahan, 1874. Photo: John Freeman.

225 Drawing by William Brockedon, 1835. NPG.

226 Photograph from *Russia in Central Asia* by George Nathaniel, Lord Curzon, 1889. Photo: Peter Jennings.

227 Drawing by J. Atkinson, *c.* 1840. NPG.

233 Engraving from *Narrative of a Mission* by Joseph Wolff, 1845. BM.

235–7 RGS.

239 Fresco from Cave 272, Tun-huang, *c.* 400. Photographed from a Japanese calendar. Photo: John Freeman.

241 Painting on silk from Tun-huang. Stein Collection,* BM.

242–3 Scroll from Tun-huang. Stein Collection,* BM.

244 Embroidery from Tun-huang. Stein Collection,* BM.

246–8 RGS

251 Painting on fabric found at Tun-huang. Stein Collection,* BM.

253 Woodcut found at Tun-huang, A.D. 868. Stein Collection, BM.

256 Perez (London) Ltd.

258 Photo: Josephine Powell.

261 Photo: Wilfrid Blunt.

263 Illumination from *Tarikh-i-shamshir khani,* Indian MS. Photo: Peter Jennings.

264–5 Cartographer: Tom Stalker Miller.

266–7 Cartographer: Tom Stalker Miller.

Index

Page numbers in *italics* refer to illustrations.

LIBRARY
WITHDRAWN